Easy Computing for Seniors

By the Editors of FC&A

Publisher's Note

The editors of FC&A have taken careful measures to ensure the accuracy and usefulness of the information in this book. While every attempt was made to assure accuracy, some Web sites, addresses, and telephone numbers may have changed since printing.

This book is intended for general information only. It does not constitute medical, legal, or financial advice or practice. We cannot guarantee the safety or effectiveness of any treatment or advice mentioned. Readers are urged to consult with their personal financial advisors, lawyers, and health care professionals.

The publisher and editors disclaim all liability (including any injuries, damages, or losses) resulting from the use of the information in this book.

FC&A
103 Clover Green
Peachtree City, GA 30269

Produced by the staff of FC&A

Fifth printing October 2003

ISBN 1-890957-68-2

Table of contents

Hardware how-to's

Getting to know your computer

Welcome to the wonderful world of computers. It's an exciting world, where you'll experience the magic of the Internet, e-mail, and much, much more. But it can also be a scary world if you enter it alone.

As you make your way through this new world, let *Computers for Seniors* be your guide. It's the easiest computer book for seniors you'll ever read — or your money back.

For best results, read the book in order, as each section builds on the previous one. This book will occasionally refer to Macs, but its main focus is personal computers (PCs).

In this section, you'll learn the computer's basic parts, or hardware. You'll discover how to shop for a PC, how to set it up, and how to deal with any problems.

You'll also conquer your fear of computers. Just remember this secret — you are in control and are smarter than your machine. A computer is simply a tool, like a toaster or a car, you use to make your life easier. If you can operate a car, you can operate a computer, too. Don't let confusing computer jargon stop you.

Don't let your age stop you, either. Thousands of folks over 50 now use a computer — and they never thought they could.

Ready to join them? Then take the first step and learn about these basic parts of a desktop computer.

CPU. Think of the central processing unit, or CPU, as the "brain" of the computer. This amazing little chip can perform complex calculations in a fraction of a second.

A CPU's speed is measured in megahertz (MHz) or even gigahertz (GHz). The higher the number, the faster the chip can process information. Companies like Intel and AMD are always striving to make faster CPUs. Right now, the fastest is 3 GHz, but that's bound to change soon.

Some programs work better with a faster CPU, but for basic computing tasks, such as word processing and Web surfing, you really don't need that much speed. Most new computers have at least a 2.2 GHz CPU, which is more than enough for beginning computer users.

Here are some common brands of processors. Celeron and Duron are cheaper chips, and Motorola's chips are for Macintosh computers.

Intel CPUs	AMD CPUs	Motorola CPUs
Pentium 4 or II	Athlon	PowerPC G4
Celeron	Duron	PowerPC G3

RAM. Random access memory (RAM) also affects how quickly a computer can process tasks. If the CPU is the computer's brain, RAM is the short-term memory. It's where the computer stores information currently in use. When it's done using this information, the computer "forgets" it — like when you look up a number in the phone book and remember it just long enough to dial it. Most new computers come with at least 128 megabytes (MB) of RAM, and that's probably the minimum you'd want.

Hard drive. Sort of like your basement or attic, the hard drive acts as a permanent storage area. It holds your computer's operating system, programs, and whatever files you save. The more gigabytes (GB) your hard drive has, the more information it can store. On new computers, hard drives are usually 40 GB or more. The bare minimum you'd want is 20 GB, and you can find some as big as 120 GB.

If some of these terms seem confusing to you, check out the following handy chart that helps explain them.

Term	Explanation
Bit	Smallest unit of computer information, consisting of a 0 or 1
Byte	Unit of storage made up of 8 bits. Equivalent to one character, such as a letter or number
Kilobyte	Roughly 1,000 bytes
Megabyte	Roughly 1,000 kilobytes, or 1 million bytes
Gigabyte	Roughly 1,000 megabytes, or 1 billion bytes

CD-ROM drive. A compact disk-read only memory drive lets you listen to compact discs on your computer. It's also used for installing software or playing games. Once you locate your CD drive, using it is a breeze. Simply push the button, and a tray will pop out. Lay the compact disc in the tray, and gently push it back in.

Lately, computers feature a CD-RW (rewritable) drive instead. With a CD-RW drive, you can record music and back up large files onto a blank CD. Some computers now also come with a DVD-ROM drive, so you can view DVD movies on your computer. If you can't afford a computer with both drives, choose the CD-RW drive because, for now at least, it offers more versatility than a DVD-ROM drive.

Floppy drive. A floppy drive accommodates a 3 1/2-inch floppy disk. These disks don't hold as much information as CDs, but they are ideal for storing small amounts of information, such as text documents. Macintosh computers no longer come with floppy drives, but most PCs still have them.

Modem. This device allows computers to communicate over telephone lines. Most computers now come with a built-in 56k modem. This means it can receive data at a rate of 56 kilobits (56,000 bits) per second.

While dialing up via a modem was once the only way to connect to the Internet, today there are other options. You may decide to use a cable modem or a digital subscriber line (DSL), which provide much faster connections than conventional modems but are only available in certain areas.

Quick tip ▶ If you plan on getting a DSL Internet connection, make sure your computer comes with an Ethernet card.

Sound card. Along with speakers or headphones, the sound card lets you hear music, newscasts, or sound effects. Your computer will come with a sound card and a set of speakers, and most likely this sound system will be fine. But if you're not satisfied — say you're a music lover — you might want to invest in a better set of speakers or even hook up your computer to your stereo system.

Tower. All of the previously mentioned components are located in the tower. This sleek container can sit on your desk or on the floor to save space.

Monitor. Most computers come with a 17-inch monitor, or screen. Like a television, it's measured diagonally and can be adjusted for contrast and brightness.

You can opt for the standard cathode ray tube (CRT) or the flat-panel liquid crystal display (LCD) model. You can also find 19-inch or even 21-inch screens. The monitor works with the computer's video card, found inside the tower.

Keyboard. If you can use a typewriter, you can use a computer keyboard. It's set up like a typewriter, with a few additions — like a number keypad to the right and some extra keys, such as the CONTROL, ALT, and WINDOWS keys.

Quick tip ▶ Keep your keyboard clean with a can of compressed air.

Mouse. Eek! This little device moves the pointer around on your monitor. It comes with two buttons, one on the left and one on the right, which you use to click on certain items on your screen. The mouse is attached to your keyboard by its cord, or "tail," and rests on a mousepad. If you prefer, you can invest in a wireless mouse.

Now that you're familiar with all the hardware, are you ready to buy a computer? Not so fast. There are some things to think about first.

All desktop computers come with these basic parts. But not all desktop computers are alike.

Unfortunately, there's not one perfect system for everyone. It all depends on how you plan to use your computer.

For example, your teenage grandson might want a computer so he can download the latest music and play the most advanced games, while you might want one so you can e-mail your grandkids and surf the Web for shopping bargains.

In that case, his computer would require a faster CPU, more RAM, a bigger hard drive, and better sound and video cards than yours would. That means it would also cost more.

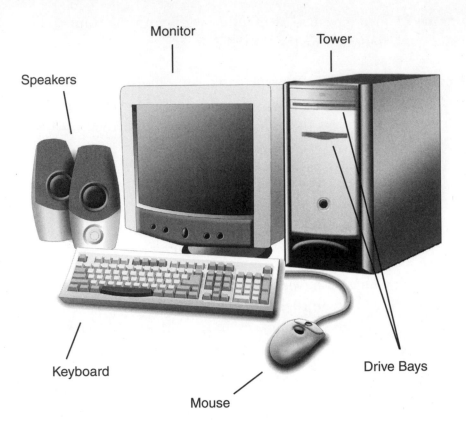

Monitor

Tower

Speakers

Keyboard

Mouse

Drive Bays

Typical computer system

Knowing your needs will help you find the best system for you. It might even help you save money.

That's why the most important question to ask the salesman before you buy your computer is "Will this computer meet my needs?"

Quick tip ▶ Make sure the CPU, memory, hard drive, and sound and video cards can be easily removed and replaced. That way, you can upgrade your system later and get more mileage out of it.

Pick a PC substitute

Knowing your needs will not only help you find the ideal desktop PC, it might lead you to choose one of the following alternatives instead.

Macs. Once upon a time, there were just IBM and Apple computers. While several companies now make IBM-style PCs, only Apple makes Macintosh computers. These machines are generally easier to set up and use than a PC. However, fewer software programs and peripherals are available for Macs.

Laptops. Also known as notebooks, these portable machines can do pretty much everything a desktop computer can. If you travel a lot, this might be the option for you. Just remember, you pay more for slimmer and lighter models. Another drawback — it's very difficult to upgrade a laptop.

PDAs. A Personal Digital Assistant, or handheld device, is a high-tech address book and appointment calendar. Perfect for on-the-go types, these gadgets keep changing as technology improves.

Internet appliances. These machines were designed to introduce people to the Internet without the complications of a PC. While they sound useful, high prices and poor design kept them from catching on. But keep your eyes open for new, cheaper, redesigned models.

Overseas overview

Most of the advice in this book will help computer users in Canada, the United Kingdom, and Australia as well as those in the United States. But you need to keep several important issues in mind when living or traveling overseas.

Verify voltage. Not all electricity is the same. Some countries, like the U.S. and Canada, use a voltage of 120 volts, while other areas, such as the U.K. and Australia, use a higher voltage of 230 or 240 volts.

Luckily, most modern computers are dual voltage. That means they can work at either the lower or higher voltage. Some systems will detect the difference automatically, while others might require you to turn a switch. Make sure your computer is capable of accepting the local voltage — and switched to the right setting — before plugging it in.

A good way to tell is to check your manual or back of the computer for a message reading 110-220 V, 50-60 Hz. Ask if a computer is dual voltage before buying it. If your computer only accepts one voltage, you can buy a transformer to get it to work with a higher or lower one.

"Adapt" to your surroundings. You might have trouble plugging in your computer without the proper adapter. Plugs differ around the world. Some have flat blades, while others are rectangular or slanted.

Telephone jacks also vary. The common RJ-11 jack is used in several countries, including the U.S., Canada, and parts of Australia, but you will often need an adapter if you plan on connecting to the Internet overseas.

Tackle telephone troubles. Besides needing an adapter, you may encounter the following obstacles when trying to use a phone line to connect to the Internet.

- **Digital phone lines.** Some hotel rooms feature digital phone lines, which will fry your modem because the voltage is so high. Before hooking up your computer, make sure the line is analog. You can buy equipment to test the line or work around the problem.

- **Dial-up woes.** Your modem may not recognize a foreign dial tone or pulse dialing. You might have to reset it or dial it manually.

- **Steep fees.** You might encounter expensive surcharges for connecting through your usual Internet Service Provider.

A good way to avoid these headaches is to go to a cybercafe, a public place where you can rent a computer and an Internet connection by the hour. They're fairly common and relatively cheap.

While using foreign computers, you may also notice slight differences in the keyboard. You can easily remedy this by changing the KEYBOARD layout in the CONTROL PANEL to that of your own country.

Learn more online. There are numerous Web sites dedicated to the international traveler and computer user. You can find useful information, cybercafes, and essential products, like adapters or transformers, to help you safely use your computer — wherever you go. Here are just a few of them.

Steve Kropla's Help for World Travelers	www.kropla.com
Road News	www.roadnews.com
Walkabout Travel Gear	www.walkabouttravelgear.com
Laptop Travel	www.laptoptravel.com
Cyber Café Search Engine	www.cybercaptive.com
Cybercafes.com	www.cybercafes.com

Computer shopping secrets

You're ready to take the plunge and buy a computer. But there are so many options you don't know where to begin. All you know is that

9

you want a good PC without spending a fortune. Read on to discover top stores, brands, buying strategies, and ways to save.

Should you buy a "top brand" computer, or will one of the less expensive models do? You've probably heard of the major computer brands — Compaq, Dell, Gateway, Hewlett-Packard, IBM, and Sony.

You can find cheaper computers that work just as well, but the bigger companies probably offer better technical support if something goes wrong.

No matter what the brand, computers can be roughly divided into budget, mid-range, or cutting-edge models. Budget models have fewer features, slower processors, and little room for upgrades, but they're fine for everyday tasks.

Cutting-edge models have the fastest processors, largest hard drives, most RAM, and most room for upgrades. Mid-range models are somewhere in the middle.

Prices are always changing, but here is a general estimate of how much a computer will cost.

Model	Price range
Budget	$600 to $1,100
Mid-range	$1,200 to $1,800
Cutting-edge	$2,000 to $3,000

You can buy a computer almost anywhere — electronics stores, department stores, computer stores, or online stores. Some of the more popular places include manufacturers like Dell or Gateway, retail stores like CompUSA or Best Buy, and mail order companies like PC Connection.

Before you run out and spend your nest egg, find out how you can save $1,000 or more on a computer. Here are five ways you can get more bang for your buck.

Do your homework. Buying a computer is like buying any major item. You want to do some research first. Read reviews of products, ask computer-savvy friends and family members for recommendations, and comparison shop. Some good magazines to look at include *Consumer Reports*, *PC World*, and *Computer Shopper*.

But you can't research forever. At some point, you have to pull the trigger and buy. There's never a perfect time, and you'll never find the perfect deal.

That's because a faster, better, and cheaper computer will hit the market as soon as you plunk down money for your machine. Don't be discouraged. That's just the nature of rapidly changing technology. Don't worry, either. The computer you bought will still work just fine.

Play it safe ▶ Read the fine print. An ad might show a full computer system, but the listed price might not include the monitor.

Configure your own system. Forget about clever ads talking about computer speed and power — get what you really need without spending money for what you don't need.

Some stores or manufacturers let you configure your own system. It's a good way to save money on some areas and improve your computer in others. If you don't need your computer to do the latest, high-tech tasks, don't get a state-of-the-art system.

For example, pass on the DVD drive if you have no interest in movies or the CD-RW drive if you don't plan on burning your own compact discs. You can also opt for a slower processor, smaller hard drive, and less RAM than the top-of-the-line models. As long as the computer meets your needs, it's OK to downgrade.

Save a "bundle." Take advantage of free software bundles that might come with your system. It will save you from buying expensive software later. Common free software includes Microsoft Works, Microsoft Office, Corel WordPerfect Office, and Lotus Smart Suite. These programs will let you do word processing, spreadsheets, and other common tasks. Make sure your system also comes with some anti-virus software, such as Norton or McAfee.

Hunt for bargains. Some of the best prices are available through mail order or on the Internet. Here are just a few places to save money. Ask for free catalogs or check out their Web sites at the library or on a friend's computer.

> Computer Discount Warehouse
> CDW Computer Centers, Inc.
> 200 North Milwaukee Avenue
> Vernon Hills, IL 60061
> 800-840-4239
> **www.cdw.com**
>
> Dartek Computer Supply Corporation
> 175 Ambassador Drive
> Naperville, IL 60540
> 888-432-7835
> **www.dartek.com**
>
> MicroWarehouse
> P.O. Box 3013
> 1720 Oak Street
> Lakewood, NJ 08701
> 800-397-8508
> **www.warehouse.com**

- My Simon. This Internet site checks all the major retail stores on the Web, then tells you which sites to go to for the cheapest prices. Check it out at **www.mysimon.com**.

- Outpost. Like many retail sites, this site offers free delivery and a guarantee on its products. So if your computer is damaged in the mail, you can easily return it. Look for computer specials on their Web site, **www.outpost.com**.

Be creative. Buy your computer from the post office. Computers, televisions, radios, silverware — anything people mail can be snatched up at a bargain.

The U.S. Postal Service occasionally conducts auctions of damaged and unclaimed items. It's a great way to stamp out high prices. Contact one of the following recovery centers for more information.

Atlanta Mail Recovery Center
P.O. Box 44161
Atlanta, GA 30336-9590

St. Paul Mail Recovery Center
443 Fillmore Ave. E
St. Paul, MN 55107-9607

San Francisco Mail Recovery Center
P.O. Box 7872
San Francisco, CA 94120-7872

You can also find great deals on recycled or refurbished computers. Some companies specialize in fixing up old computers — and then sell them dirt-cheap.

RE-PC
206-575-8737
www.repc.com

Outlet Computer
800-588-9468
www.outletcomputer.com

Back Thru the Future Micro Computers
888-622-7278
www.backthruthefuture.com

Used Computer Mall
www.usedcomputer.com

Play it safe ▶ Used computers might seem like a deal, but they're often more trouble than they're worth. A used computer could actually prove costly when you factor in repairs and upgrades to get it to work with the latest software and equipment. Unless you're getting a used computer for free, you might be better off buying a cheap new system — especially for your first computer.

Perhaps you've seen ads for what sounds like a great deal — a free computer. You might jump at these offers without thinking. But, just as there's no such thing as a free lunch, there's no such thing as a free computer.

Most of them work in one or more of these ways. You're either locked into an expensive, long-term contract with an Internet service provider or bombarded with annoying ads while you surf the Web. You might even surrender your privacy, meaning companies can track what sites you look at so they can better target you with more ads. For many people, it's just not worth it. But if you don't mind the drawbacks, it's another creative way to save money on a computer.

Besides a good price, you should also consider the following when shopping for a computer.

- Technical support. If you have problems — and you probably will at some point — you need to know how to get help. Can you get help 24 hours a day? Do the experts respond quickly to your questions? Is there an 800 number you can call? Get all the information in writing.

- Warranty. Aim for a three-year warranty, and never settle for less than a one-year warranty.

- Return policy. Make sure you can return the computer without any hassles or restocking fees. That means you don't pay the store to put the computer back on the shelf.

- Demonstrations. Ask the salesman to demonstrate anything he claims the computer can do. Sometimes salespeople might not know what they're talking about, make promises the computer can't keep, or lie just to clinch the sale.

Pointers for peripherals

No outfit is complete without some accessories. Same with a computer system — only they're called peripherals.

Peripherals, external devices that hook up to your computer, make your PC even more useful. And the most useful peripheral is the printer.

You can print letters, invitations, greeting cards, business cards — even photos. You'll learn how to use your printer to its best advantage. But first you need to pick out a printer.

Know your options. There are two major kinds of printers — ink jet and laser.

- Laser printers work like a photocopier, and use toner cartridges rather than ink. That's why you'll get more detailed images with a laser printer than from an ink jet printer. If you plan to print large quantities of documents, a laser printer may be your best choice.

- Ink jet printers work by squirting ink onto the paper. With a high-end ink jet printer, the black text quality is almost as good as a laser printer. Color ink jet printers are slightly more expensive, but just as affordable as a black-and-white laser printer.

Play it safe ▶ Before you buy an ink jet printer, check to see how much the ink cartridges cost. Sometimes the manufacturer will sell a printer for a low price, but make up the cost by charging more for the ink cartridges. It pays to compare before you buy.

Judge the quality. The quality of the image produced by a printer is measured in dots per inch, or dpi. In general, the higher the dpi, the better, or clearer, the image. But other factors may also affect print quality. Most stores have printers set up with sample printouts, so you can compare. Top brands include Epson and Hewlett-Packard.

Rank by speed. If you're just going to print a letter occasionally, you probably don't care about printer speed. However, if you plan to print large quantities of documents, you may want a faster printer. Sometimes you have to sacrifice speed for quality, so decide what is more important to you.

Fast fix ▶ Store paper in its packaging. Otherwise, it can dry out or absorb moisture from the air and cause a printer jam.

Adding a printer may not be as simple as plugging it in the right spot. You also have to install the software that comes with it, so your computer can recognize it. It's easy. Simply put the disk in the CD drive and follow the instructions. To avoid possible problems, close all other programs while installing the printer software.

Many printers come with extra software, and you can buy more separately. Choose programs that print business cards, greeting cards, labels, invitations, envelopes, or photographs. These packages make it quick and easy to get professional-looking results.

In fact, you can print photos from your computer that rival the quality of professional processors — at a fraction of the cost! For best results, seek out photo-quality paper and archival inks, which do not fade. A higher resolution (dpi) will give you a better picture, but it will also use more ink and take longer to print.

Printers aren't the only peripherals available. Technically, your mouse and keyboard are also peripherals, but because they come with your computer — and you need them to do anything with it — they were discussed with the basic parts.

You can jazz up your computer with any of the following accessories. Color laser printers start at around $1,200, so they are not included in this table.

Peripheral	What it does	Cost
Laser printer	Prints black-and-white documents	$250-$500
Ink jet printer	Prints black-and-white or color pages	$50-$500
Scanner	Turns hard copies into digital images you can view on your computer	$70-$200
Multifunction device	Serves as a printer, scanner, copier, and fax machine all in one	$200-$600
Web cam	Transmits photos or videos to the Web	$25-$250
Zip drive	Stores large backup files on a Zip disk	$80-$180

CD burner	Records music onto a compact disc	$100-$250
Microphone	Lets you record sound	$5-$50
Headphones	Allow you to listen privately	$3-$40

Whenever you buy a printer or other peripheral, make sure it's compatible with your computer's operating system. Also make sure your computer has the right port, or outlet, to accommodate your new addition.

Gizmos make computing easier

Let's face it — computers weren't designed with seniors in mind. If you find yourself squinting at the screen or aching when you type or use your mouse, computing can be a real pain.

Luckily, you can find a wide variety of gadgets and gizmos that help make computing easier for you. Here's a sampling of them.

Trackballs. Easier to use than a regular mouse, a trackball lets you scroll with your finger or thumb. Just move the wheel to navigate around the screen.

Touchpads. Another substitute for a mouse, a touchpad allows you to point or slide your finger over its surface to control the pointer on your screen.

Screen magnifiers. Not only do these special screens enlarge the icons and text on your monitor, they also reduce glare.

Large-print keyboards. Tired of hunting for the right key? Replace your standard keyboard with a large-print model. You can also find keyboard labels that fit over your keys and make each letter or symbol bigger and easier to read.

Comfort keyboards. Also known as ergonomic keyboards, they split into sections so you can separate, adjust, rotate, or tilt them until you find a setup that's comfortable for you.

These items will add to the cost of your computer, but they might be worth it. After all, you can't put a price on comfort.

Quick tip ▶ Even people with severely limited vision or movement can benefit from technology. Screen readers, Braille displays, speech recognition software, head-mounted pointing systems, and sip-and-puff switches for quadriplegics are just some of the available aids. For even more products, check out these Web sites: www.abilityhub.com or www.blvd.com/superstore or www.canaccess.org.

Save money with upgrades

Computer technology moves ahead at breakneck speed. Today's state-of-the-art computer system is tomorrow's ancient relic.

How long until your new computer is "obsolete?" Here's how to save money by extending the life of your computer.

Consider upgrading. This simply means you install new components to improve your computer's performance.

When you replace a software program with a newer version of that program, that's also called upgrading.

There are several ways to upgrade your computer. Adding peripherals is one. You can also replace your CPU or sound and video cards with faster and better models. But the most common hardware upgrades involve adding memory or disk space.

Quick tip ▶ Don't upgrade to a faster CPU unless you can double the speed of your current one.

Don't wait too long. It's time to upgrade if you have to wait a long time for a program to start or when you switch between programs. In that case, your first step should be to add more RAM. If you have less than 128 MB of RAM, boost it to 128 MB. Often this will solve your problems. If low disk space is your concern, you can add a second hard drive.

To find out what upgrades your computer might need, go to PC Pitstop at **www.pcpitstop.com**. Click on the FREE PC TUNE-UP icon, and it will analyze your computer and make recommendations for improving its performance. See the Internet essentials chapter for help navigating the Internet.

Unless you're really handy with electronics, you'll need to take your computer to a computer shop to be upgraded. Experts at the shop can add more memory or install a faster CPU or a bigger hard drive.

Play it safe ▶ If you have to spend more than $500 on upgrades, you're probably better off buying a new system instead.

Think ahead. It's never too early to start thinking about upgrading your computer. In fact, you should keep upgrades in mind when shopping for a PC.

Don't buy a computer that will be obsolete tomorrow. Here's what you need to keep it upgradeable. A computer that has a lot of extra ports, drive bays, and expansion slots inside will serve you well for years to come. These allow you to add memory, drives, and other gadgets so your computer stays up to speed as it ages.

Before you buy your next computer, find out how easy it is to upgrade. It could mean the difference between buying a new system next year or five years down the road.

Quick tip ▶ A bargain priced computer system isn't always a bargain. That's because these cheaper systems are often difficult to upgrade. They don't come with many free expansion slots or easily removable sound and video cards. You could be shelling out money for a new computer sooner than you'd like. It might be better to spend an extra $200 to $400 and get a system you can upgrade and use longer.

Simple steps to successful setup

You've picked out your computer. You know the speed of the CPU, the amount of RAM, and the size of the hard drive. Now what do you do with it? If you're not "wired" yet, don't worry. You don't have to be a technical wiz to use your computer. Follow these easy step-by-step instructions from setup to start-up and beyond.

Plan your workspace carefully. You're going to need several things to feel comfortable and be productive while using your computer. First look around your living space. Unless you have a laptop or portable computer, you'll want the best permanent home possible for your new hardware. While you may need to fine-tune some parts of the setup, you don't want to have to move everything later simply because you didn't take the time to plan.

Pick a place with room for a work surface, like a desk, and a comfortable chair. Plan space for your keyboard and a mouse. Depending on how you're going to use your computer, you may need room to spread out books and papers.

You'll need an electrical outlet for power, of course, and a phone jack or cable outlet nearby for Internet service. Check the distance from the phone or cable plug. You might need some extra cable.

Consider the lighting. Windows add natural daylight, but you'll also need a table or floor lamp. You'll learn how to position these so you don't get a reflective glare off your monitor.

FYI ▶ Computers generate some heat when they're turned on, so don't set up in a small, stuffy room. It's not only bad for the delicate electronics, but your body won't like it either.

Do you have a choice of work areas? Then decide if you'd rather be in a room by yourself for quiet and privacy, or if you want to interact with others while computing.

Unwrap and unpack. Give yourself plenty of time to sort things out. Plan to spend an hour setting everything up. Don't even open a box if you're tired or hungry, or if you're expecting company.

The best time to get to know your new computer is when you're setting up. And you'll feel more comfortable with it in the long run if you spend a few extra minutes now reading the manual and examining all the components.

So take your time. Unwrap things carefully. Save the packing and the boxes just in case things go wrong. Lay the parts out and really look them over.

If there are two of you on this computing adventure, take turns reading the manual or setup directions aloud. It will be more fun and, as the saying goes, two heads are better than one.

Quick tip ▶ Think about asking someone to help lift things and crawl around hooking up wires. It's not a hard job, but it would be perfect for a young neighbor or grandchild. You'd be surprised how technically savvy the younger generation is. Your back might appreciate the help, too.

Make the connections. This part is easier than you think. Computer manufacturers have finally learned that "simple sells." Many even color code the cables and connectors. Usually each one will only fit into one outlet, or port.

Don't ever try to force a connection because you think it looks right. For guidance, check for drawings or pictures, either in the manual or sometimes even on the computer itself.

Generally, here's how it works.

- The monitor is plugged into your tower. Sometimes it has a separate cable to plug into your power strip.

- The keyboard plugs into your tower.

- Your mouse may be plugged into your tower, or you might be able to plug it directly into the side of your keyboard.

- Your printer has a cable that connects to your tower and a plug that goes into your power strip.

- Most towers have a single plug you can insert into a power strip.

That's it. If your system did not come with color-coded cables, label them yourself. It's easy with a bit of masking tape or colored stickers.

Taking a few extra minutes now could save a headache if you ever have to move or rearrange your system.

Confused by all the slots and ports? Here's a quick rundown of some of the more common ports on a computer.

- Parallel and serial ports — traditional sites for printers and scanners.

- Universal Serial Bus (USB) — new, faster connection for a keyboard, mouse, scanner, or printer. Newer systems feature USB ports instead of parallel and serial ports.

- IEEE 1394 (FireWire) — high-speed connection for video devices.

- S-video output jack — lets you hook up your television to your computer, so you can use your DVD drive with your TV screen.

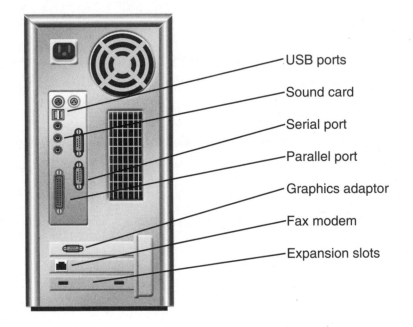

USB ports
Sound card
Serial port
Parallel port
Graphics adaptor
Fax modem
Expansion slots

Rear view of tower, with ports

If you really get stuck, don't hesitate to call the manufacturer's technical support line. You should have a toll-free number you can call 24 hours a day.

Play it safe ▶ Don't get "zapped" with high repair costs. It's easy to protect your computer from lightning bolts with an inexpensive device called a surge protector. It prevents your computer from getting fried if a large surge of electricity shoots through your electrical lines. This usually happens during a storm or in the summer when lots of people are running air conditioners. To be extra safe, unplug your computer during a lightning storm.

How to avoid strains and pains

There are many things more dangerous than sitting at a computer. Coal mining, skydiving, and bullfighting immediately spring to mind. But just because computers are relatively safe, that doesn't mean there aren't some risks involved.

Carpal tunnel syndrome, eyestrain, neck and shoulder pain, headaches, and fatigue are just some of the problems associated with computer use.

That's why it's important to set up and use your computer ergonomically. This simply means your working conditions and your body are not at odds.

Here are some ways to avoid strains, pains, and other discomforts while computing.

Position your monitor. While sitting at your computer, close your eyes and imagine you are looking straight ahead. Now open them and notice the first thing you see. This is your line of vision. The center of your screen should be 4 to 9 inches below this line.

Fast fix ▶ Generally, if you can see over your monitor, your screen is set too low. Prop it up on a wooden block or a heavy book.

Take care of your chair. Proper posture helps solve most computer-related problems — and your chair is the key to proper posture.

- Make sure your chair is high enough. Your knees should line up with your hips while your feet stay planted on the floor.

- Don't sit on the edge of your seat. Your back has no support and you'll start to slump.

- When your hips are against the back of your chair, you should be able to fit three fingers between the back of your knees and the edge of your seat. If you can't, try another chair.

- If your chair tilts, lean back slightly. If it doesn't, adjust your back support so you can sit at a slight backward angle.

Type right. The nerves running from your arm to your fingers pass through a narrow tunnel formed by the bones and ligaments in your wrist. Repetitive motion by your wrist and forearm can squeeze and irritate these nerves, causing pain to shoot up your arm. This is called carpal tunnel syndrome.

Keep your hands and elbows in a straight line, and you can avoid this pain. Place your keyboard even with your lap so you can reach it with your wrists as flat as possible. Tap the keys lightly when typing.

Manage your mouse. Grip your mouse loosely, keeping your upper arm and elbow as close to your body and as relaxed as possible. Never overreach for your mouse. Keep your wrist as straight as possible, using your elbow — not your wrist — as the pivot point.

Look after your eyes. Everybody gets tired eyes at the end of the day. But the burning, itching, and blurred vision you experience after using your computer too long is serious enough to have its own medical term — computer vision syndrome.

The muscles behind your eyeballs stretch and relax as you focus near and far. If they stay fixed in one position for too long, however, you feel the strain. In addition, when you stare at your screen, you forget to blink. This dries out your eyes, adding to your discomfort.

The simplest way to save your eyes while you work is to take mini-breaks. After every 20 minutes you spend in front of your computer, get up and walk around. Get a glass of water, talk on the phone, or focus on something far away.

You get double benefit from these breaks — your eyes will relax and your back will stretch.

Play it safe ▶ Opt for a liquid crystal display (LCD) monitor or a monitor with a high refresh rate. They flicker less than other monitors, so they're easier on the eyes.

Ease the tension. Poor posture puts stress on the muscles of your neck and shoulders. When they cramp, you can get a major tension headache. So don't twist your neck to look from a piece of paper on your desk to the screen.

Instead, set up a vertical document holder parallel to your monitor. And remember to breathe deeply every once in awhile. This will pull your shoulders back in line and relax the muscles in your neck.

Get a kick out of booting up

Everything is falling into place. You've bought your computer, you've set it up on a sturdy surface, and you've positioned the monitor, keyboard, and mouse so you don't injure yourself.

Now, like Dr. Frankenstein, all you need is electricity to bring your creature to life.

When you start your computer, it's called "booting up." It simply means you are turning on the power to your computer and waiting for it to automatically switch everything else on and load your operating system.

Fast fix ▶ Make sure you don't have a floppy disk, CD, or DVD in any of the drives when booting up. Take them out if you do. Otherwise, your computer will get confused and possibly try to boot from the disk.

Follow these simple instructions for booting up.

- Turn on your power strip with its surge protector. Now you have electricity to the system.

- You control the power to your computer with an on/off button or switch usually located on the front or side of your tower. Some systems have a power switch in other places, like on the keyboard. Look in your manual if you're not sure.

- When you turn the computer on, you'll probably see an indicator light go on and hear noises in the computer. This is normal.

- Your monitor also has a power button. Once you turn on your monitor, it's perfectly fine to leave this button alone.

- When you shut your computer down, the monitor will automatically go off. When you boot up, it will automatically turn on.

Now that you have power to your computer, watch your monitor. You'll probably see several startup screens flash by. It will look like a lot of gibberish, but you don't have to understand it — as long as your computer does. It's just your computer getting ready.

Eventually your desktop will appear. If your operating system is Windows 98, it will look something like this.

A typical desktop

From here you can begin using all your computer's wonderful tools.

Q **What if the computer asks for a password?**

A You can either press ENTER to bypass it or set a password. If you're the only person using the computer, you might not need a password. Otherwise, you might want one to protect your privacy. Choose one that's easy for you to remember but not easy for others to guess.

Q **What If I bought the computer from someone else?**

A Make sure the previous owner disabled the password — or shared it with you. Once you access Windows, you can change the password or eliminate it entirely. To learn how to do this, see *Sidestep pesky passwords* on page 77.

Best way to shut down your computer

In the following chapters, you'll learn how to do lots of things while your computer is on, but at some point you'll have to turn it off.

Here's how to shut down your computer properly.

1 Quit any applications you're using.

2 Move your mouse so the pointer arrow is on the START button at the bottom left of your screen. Click your mouse, and a menu will pop up.

3 Click on SHUT DOWN.

4 A box with a few options — SLEEP (or STANDBY), SHUT DOWN, RESTART — will appear. It's like a multiple-choice test. Click in the circle next to SHUT DOWN, then click OK.

5 Wait. Just as your computer takes some time to boot up, it might take some time to shut down. You might see a screen that reads, PLEASE WAIT WHILE YOUR COMPUTER SHUTS DOWN or WINDOWS IS SHUTTING DOWN. Eventually, your monitor will go black, your computer will quiet, and the light on your tower will wink off.

6 Your computer might not turn off by itself. Instead, after Windows shuts down, you'll see a screen that reads, IT'S NOW SAFE TO TURN OFF YOUR COMPUTER. Just push the same button you used to turn it on.

Your PC is now off until you reboot for your next computing adventure.

Fast fix ▶ Sometimes, with older computers, you'll get the message "Windows is shutting down," but it never does. If the screen doesn't change for a long time, just turn your computer off using the power switch.

Put your computer to sleep. You don't have to shut down your computer every time you step away from it. That would get tiresome. An alternative to shutting down is putting your computer in standby, or sleep, mode. When it's in sleep mode, your computer rests until you wake it up again. This saves energy for desktop computers and battery power for laptops.

To trigger sleep mode, you can go through the START menu, just as you would to shut down. Click on SHUT DOWN, then when the box pops up, click the option box next to SLEEP instead of SHUT DOWN.

Or you can simply walk away from your desk. After a certain amount of time, the computer will put itself to sleep. The monitor will go blank, but you won't lose what's on your screen. When you come back to your desk, press any key or jiggle your mouse, and your computer will wake up refreshed and ready to go.

Q **When should I turn off my computer and when should I just let it "sleep?"**

A Some people never turn off their computers. Others shut down every night. If you're not going to use your computer for a long time, it's probably a good idea to shut down. Otherwise, just let it sleep.

Q **What if I don't shut down the right way?**

A Maybe you accidentally unplugged your computer, experienced a power outage, or needed to restart your computer because it froze up. Or maybe you just forgot to shut down your computer before you turned off the power. In any case, your computer will run a program called Scan Disk the next time you boot up. It might take a while, so be patient. It's checking your computer to make sure no files were damaged. In fact, it's a good idea to run Scan Disk every once in a while, even if you're not having any problems with your computer.

Troubleshooting tactics

Computers are convenient, fast, and fun. But they're not perfect. Sooner or later, you'll have a problem.

To solve a glitch, you can contact technical support. Most computers, programs, and peripherals have a phone number or e-mail address for their company's tech support. Simply call or write, and someone familiar with the program or equipment will attempt to help you. Some tech support is free, but other companies charge for this service.

Tech support can be very helpful — but it can also be costly. Don't make expensive, time-consuming calls to technical support when you can solve many computer problems by yourself using these quick troubleshooting tips.

Eliminate the obvious. You'd be surprised how often people over-look the obvious. If you're staring at a blank screen, make sure your computer is still plugged in, turned on, and that all the cables are secure.

Think about what has changed. If your computer was working properly one day, and fouled up the next, think about what changed. Did you download a new program, or was there a light-ning storm? Some computers have a "go-back" feature that allows you to revert your hard drive to a previous time when you know it was working properly.

Pinpoint possible problems. Ask yourself a few questions. What is happening when your computer malfunctions? Does it freeze only when you're in a specific program? If so, that program could be the problem, and you may need to uninstall it and try installing it again. If there's no pattern to the crashes, bring your computer to a repair shop to check or replace the computer's power supply or its RAM.

Seek "HELP." You might be able to figure out what's wrong just by using the HELP menu on your computer. It's a simple thing to try before calling tech support. For more on the HELP feature, see *Good help is easy to find* on page 105.

Get answers online. Some Web sites offer free technical support. For instance, Microsoft Help at **http://support.microsoft.com** has a

Knowledge Base you can search for free or pay to submit a question.

Here are a few more sites that might help you solve your problems.

Blarp	www.blarp.com
Protonic	www.protonic.com
AskMe	www.askme.com
Tech Support Guy	www.helponthe.net
PC Mechanic	www.pcmech.com
CNET Help	www.help.com

Computers don't have to be frustrating — especially when you have problem-solving tips right at your fingertips.

Be prepared. If you do have to call technical support, be prepared so you can get your problem resolved quickly and efficiently. If the trouble is with a piece of hardware, have the model number and serial number handy.

If it's a software problem, make sure you know which version of the software you have. If you're getting error messages, write down exactly what the message says.

Take notes. When you're talking with tech support, always ask the name of the person you're talking with, and write down any advice they give you and what steps you took to correct the problem. That way, if you have the same problem again, you'll know what to do.

Mind your manners. Be polite and calm when dealing with a technician. You might be angry and frustrated with your computer, but taking it out on the person at the other end of the phone won't do any good.

Speak up. Don't be afraid to ask to speak with a manager or write a letter to the company if you're not satisfied with the service you received.

Computer problems can be frustrating. But every problem has a solution. Don't let problems — or the threat of problems — dampen your enthusiasm for computers. Remember, a computer is a great tool that can make your life easier, better, and more fun.

Beware of repairs

Sometimes you can't solve your computer problems through technical support or other do-it-yourself methods. You need to take your computer to a repair shop.

If your computer is still under warranty, you don't have much to worry about. But if the warranty has expired, it might be a pretty expensive trip.

Here are some guidelines to help you deal with computer repairs.

Seek authorization. Look for an authorized repair facility for your brand of computer. Companies don't let just anyone fix their components.

Find hidden fees. Ask about diagnostic fees up front. Some places charge a flat fee just to look at your computer. This might include labor — but it might not.

Do a checkup. Having doubts about a shop? Consult the Better Business Bureau to determine if the business in question is on the up-and-up.

Compare costs. Shop around. Be a smart consumer. You took the time to find a good deal when you bought the computer. It only makes sense to do the same when you get it fixed.

Get a second opinion. Some technicians jump to hasty conclusions — without even looking at your machine. Others try to sell you expensive new parts, whether you need them or not. If the diagnosis you get sounds fishy, don't hesitate to take your machine elsewhere.

Hear some friendly advice. Ask friends or relatives who use computers where they go for repairs. It's like finding a good auto mechanic — sometimes word of mouth is the best strategy.

Play it safe ▶ Having a strong manufacturer's warranty and knowing how to do your own troubleshooting are good ways to avoid the pitfalls of repair shops in the first place.

Start-up secrets

Wise up to Windows

Your computer is like a factory full of machinery. And like a factory, it needs a manager to run it. The operating system (OS) is a software program that does just that.

Like any good boss, the OS keeps all the parts running smoothly, helping the software and hardware work together. Best of all, it takes orders directly from you. With help from the OS, your computer can carry out your commands and make sure you have the tools you need.

You might not notice the operating system much since it tends to work behind the scenes. Your computer, however, couldn't do anything without it. That's why most manufacturers install the OS for you. All you have to do is turn on your computer. Once the machine boots up, the OS leaps into action, and you can get right to work.

Play it safe ▶ You probably received a copy of your operating system program on a compact disc (CD) when you bought your computer. It's a good idea to keep this CD in a safe place in case you ever need it.

Operating systems have names, too, just like printers and computers. You may have heard of UNIX, DOS, and Apple's Mac OS, but chances are your computer came with an OS called Windows made by Microsoft. Every few years, Microsoft updates their operating system and gives it a slightly different name. So your computer could be using Windows 98, Windows 2000, or Windows XP, among others.

This book talks about Windows 98 only. But even if you use a different version of Windows, you'll still find lots of help here. Some of the pictures may look a little different from what you see on your computer screen, but most tips and instructions should still apply.

FYI ▶ Aren't sure what version of Windows your computer uses? See *Get the specs on your PC* on page 88 to find out in a snap.

While programmers write long, confusing codes to tell a computer what to do, Microsoft Windows makes it easy for you to communicate with your computer. You'll use colorful pictures and step-by-step instructions.

One picture you'll see a lot is a rectangular box called a window. In fact, Windows uses so many windows that the OS is named after them. From now on, when you see the word Windows capitalized, it refers to the operating system. When it's spelled with a lowercase "w," as in windows, it means the boxes on your screen.

Tech term ▶ User friendly – computer software or hardware that's easy for beginners to learn and use, thanks to helpful pictures and simple instructions.

Windows tries to be user friendly by offering you lots of choices. You'll often find there are two or three different ways to do the same thing. It's like having several routes to get to one grocery store. Don't feel overwhelmed by all the choices. Just choose the method that's easiest for you, and stick with it.

This chapter shows you the basics of using your computer as well as all kinds of OS tricks — from working more easily in Windows to customizing your desktop.

Meet your virtual desktop

Your computer may replace your filing cabinets, but it will never replace your desk. After all, you still need a place to set your stapler, to stack books, and to shuffle papers. And without a desk, where would you put your new computer?

Desks are so useful that Windows has one of its own. After you turn on your computer and the operating system kicks in, a picture called the desktop fills your computer screen.

This electronic desktop works like a real desk surface, letting you set electronic papers, folders, and pictures on it. See a picture of a typical desktop in *Get a kick out of booting up* on page 29.

Your desktop should already have a few items on it — several small pictures called icons, and a gray strip along one side called the Taskbar. Take a minute now to learn about them so that later you'll know how to use them.

Picture the perfect icon. They may be small, but they have big jobs. Icons are electronic doors that open into your computer, giving you quick access to the information stored there.

An icon's picture and label tell you what door it opens. Look closely, and you'll notice that the icon labeled MY DOCUMENTS, for instance, looks like a folder. You would expect a real folder on your desk to hold papers or other documents, and that's what a folder icon does, too. In this case, the MY DOCUMENTS folder holds the files you create — such as letters or pictures.

All the icons in your computer fall into five main types: primary, program, folder, file, and shortcut icons. This table shows you some common icons, what kind they are, and what they do.

Icon	Type	Description
My Computer	Primary	MY COMPUTER is a primary icon — one that's already on your desktop when you first get your computer. Think of it as the main entrance to your machine. It lets you peek inside and poke around.
Recycle Bin	Primary	The RECYCLE BIN holds all the files and programs you delete from your computer, just as a real trash can holds all the garbage you throw away at home.
Internet Explorer	Program	Program icons start a program, and each icon tries to look like the program it starts. This one leads to the Internet browsing program called Internet Explorer.
My Documents	Folder	MY DOCUMENTS is a folder icon that generally houses the files and folders you create in your computer.
Word document	File	File icons lead to the files you create with your computer programs. Other file icons will look different from this one — a Word document icon — depending on what program you used to create them.
Outlook Express	Shortcut	You can create shortcuts to files, folders, and programs. Shortcut icons like this one for Outlook Express only appear on your desktop if you put them there. Desktop shortcuts have a small arrow in the bottom left corner that distinguishes them from regular icons.

You may not have all of these icons on your desktop, or you may have many more. No two desks — or desktops — are the same. Later, you'll learn how to use these icons. For now, take a look at the ones on your own desktop, and try to guess what doors they open.

Get on task with the Taskbar. This long, gray strip usually runs across the bottom of your screen, but you may also find it across the top or sides. You should always see the Taskbar on your screen, no matter what else you're doing.

This tool keeps you in control of your operating system at all times. If you can't find your Taskbar, or if it keeps disappearing, see *Add custom touches to your computer* on page 67.

A typical Taskbar

Start button   Quick Launch toolbar   System tray

Taskbars have three basic parts.

- **Start button.** True to its name, this button opens the START menu which provides instant access to many of the programs and files in your computer.

- **Quick Launch toolbar.** Like the START button, this piece of the Taskbar can offer you fast access to some often-used programs. It may not hold many icons now, but you can add more later.

- **System tray.** This section houses the clock and tiny icons for other parts of your computer system such as the printer, modem, and volume control.

No matter what work you're doing, the desktop always waits in the background, full of helpful tools that make your computer easier to use.

Get moving with your mouse

A mouse may be the last thing you want around the house, but keeping one by the computer can make your work a breeze.

In computer terms, a mouse is a pointing device — a piece of hardware that helps you move around on your computer screen. Think of it as an electronic hand you use to open, close, and move the objects on your desktop, the way you would use your hands to move items on a real desk.

There are different pointing devices to meet every need. You may prefer a touchpad or a trackball, especially if you have arthritis or difficulty holding a mouse. They all tend to work the same way, with buttons you can press and a part that lets you maneuver on the screen. Here you'll learn specifically how to use a mouse.

The computer mouse is small and has a tail, just like a real mouse. Most have a round ball on the bottom that lets it roll smoothly across a mousepad. If yours doesn't have a ball, you might not need a mousepad. Instead, it can slide across flat, hard surfaces like the top of your desk. Check your manual to see what kind of surface your mouse prefers.

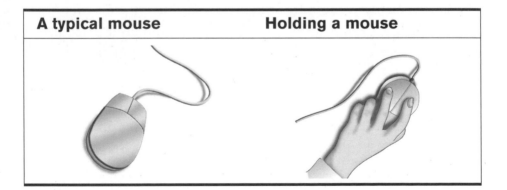

A typical mouse	Holding a mouse

You'll notice the top of your mouse is curved, and has buttons on one end you can press like piano keys. Take your right hand and rest your palm on the curved part. Place your index finger on the left button and your middle finger on the right button. This is how you hold the mouse.

Fast fix ▶ Mice are automatically set up for right-handed people. If you're a lefty, you'll have to change your computer's settings to use the mouse with your left hand. Check out *Turn on tools for special needs* on page 78 to make the switch.

Now let's get rolling. First, set the mouse on its mousepad or on your desk near the computer. If you have to stretch to reach it, it's too far away. Rest your hand lightly on its top, and gently push it across the surface. The mouse should glide around smoothly.

Moving your mouse is only half the fun. Turn on your computer, and look for a small arrow sitting on your desktop. This is your pointer. If the mouse is your electronic hand, then the pointer is your electronic finger. You can manipulate objects on your screen by pointing at them and clicking with your mouse buttons.

Give the mouse another light push, and watch the pointer. Each time your mouse moves, the arrow moves, too. They're connected. Now pick up your mouse and set it down again. This time, the arrow stayed put. It only moves when the bottom of your mouse touches a flat surface like the mousepad. Occasionally, your mouse may run off the edge of its pad before you get your pointer in place on screen. When that happens, just pick the mouse up, set it back on its pad, and finish moving your pointer.

Play it safe ▶ Using your mouse improperly could cause muscle strain and other serious problems such as carpal tunnel syndrome. See *How to avoid strains and pains* on page 25 for healthy tips on holding your mouse.

The pointer doesn't always look like an arrow. It changes shapes, depending on what you're doing. This chart shows some of the other shapes your pointer may take, and why.

Pointer shape	What it does
	This single arrow lets you point at an object on the screen. You then click with your pointing device to tell the computer to perform an action.
	The two-headed arrow gives you the power to shrink or enlarge certain objects. You can stretch the object in different directions — up and down, side to side, or diagonally — depending on which way the arrows point.
	The four-headed arrow allows you to move a whole object across your screen with your mouse.
	This cursor appears where you can type text on your screen. In fact, you can only type when you see this cursor.
	The hourglass asks you to wait patiently while the computer finishes whatever job you gave it. The computer may not let you do anything — even type — until the hourglass disappears.
	This hand points to words or pictures you can click on with your pointing device to get more information about them. You'll see this most when you begin using the Internet.

Take the time to practice with your mouse or whatever pointing device you choose. This tool is essential for using your computer, and knowing how to handle it can help you work with ease.

Master the art of clicking

Your mouse doesn't just scurry around on its pad. It has more tricks up its sleeve than the average magician — all aimed at making computing easy.

To convince the mouse to reveal its secrets, you have to get to know it. You've practiced moving the pointer around the screen. Now you'll learn to work with the buttons.

FYI ▶ The instructions here refer to the left and right buttons on a mouse, but other pointing devices often have buttons that do the same jobs. Check your manual if you need further help using your pointing device.

The mouse has five basic functions: point, click (left-click), double-click, right-click, and drag-and-drop. With these commands, you can tell your computer to do almost anything. So take a few minutes now to master these basic moves.

Learn to point perfectly. Pointing at people is rude, but it's the first step in communicating with your computer. Move your pointer until it's touching an object on your screen. This is pointing. Usually when you do this, your pointer is shaped like a single arrow or a hand.

Quick tip ▶ Point at the clock on your Taskbar. After a moment, a little box appears next to your pointer telling you the date. Letting your pointer rest on or hover over an object may give you more information about it.

Point at any of the tiny icon buttons in the Quick Launch section of your Taskbar. Notice how the icon changes slightly in appearance. Sometimes pointing at an object highlights it, puts a box around it, or otherwise alters the way it looks. This means you've selected the

45

item, and the computer knows you are about to use it.

Click once for action. Sometimes you have to click on an object — not just point — to select it. Clicking simply means you put your pointer on an object, press down the left mouse button — usually with your index finger — and then release it, like pressing a piano key and lifting your finger.

Click on a desktop icon to practice. First, place your pointer on it. Then, press the left mouse button down and release it. This icon should now look darker than the others because you have high-lighted — or selected — it. If you select another icon, the highlight moves, and the old icon becomes inactive, or unselected.

Quick tip ▶ Generally, clicking on a desktop icon selects it, while click-ing on a Taskbar item opens it.

Brush up on double-click. This is just a fancy phrase for clicking your left mouse button twice very quickly. The trick is to press the button fast enough. If you click twice too slowly, the computer won't recognize it as a double-click.

Selecting an item gently nudges the computer to wake it up. Dou-ble-clicking jabs it into action. For instance, double-clicking on a desktop icon opens it immediately — no clicking, no selecting, just instant results.

Play it safe ▶ So when do you click, and when do you double-click? Always try clicking first to get the computer to do your bidding. If nothing happens, try double-clicking.

Right-click for options. Compared to the double-click, the right-click is a snap. You simply click on the right mouse button instead of the left. Try it with your middle finger. This gives the computer special instructions. Usually, right-clicking on an object prompts the computer to give you special choices about what you can do with that object.

Drag it and drop it. To move an item on your real desk, you would grab it, pick it up, move it, and set it down. Moving items on your computer screen works the same way.

1 Point at the object to grab it.

2 Click and hold down your left mouse button to pick it up.

3 Keep pressing down on the button as you move your mouse — and the object.

4 Release the button to drop it in place.

Try moving one of your desktop icons across the screen. Point at it, and press down your left mouse button. Keep pressing it down, and drag your pointer across the screen. As your pointer moves, so does the icon. Put the icon where you want it, and lift your finger, releasing the mouse button. This drops it in place. You can use the drag-and-drop technique to move items and to highlight words on your screen.

Fast fix ▶ Did you start dragging the wrong object? No problem. Keep pressing down the mouse button, press the ESCAPE key on your keyboard, and release the mouse button. This cancels any move you were making.

Learning to sew, play an instrument, or use computers takes patience and practice. Allow yourself to make mistakes, and keep trying. Handling a mouse may be frustrating at first, but over time, working with this electronic hand will become second nature.

6 tricks to tame a troublesome mouse

Misbehaving mice cause some of the most common — and frustrating — computer problems. Jerky screen movements, frozen pointers, and mice that won't roll are all signs of a sick mouse. Try these tips to keep yours in top shape.

Clean it. As it rolls around, the mouse collects dirt that can gum up its smooth glide. How you clean the critter depends on what kind you have. Try these cleaning tips and check your mouse's manual for more specific care instructions.

- For roller ball mice, unscrew the cap covering the ball, then remove the ball, rinse it off, and let it air dry. Wipe the rollers inside the ball's cage with a cotton swab dipped in rubbing alcohol, and blow out the fuzz with a can of compressed air. Put the dry ball back in the mouse, screw the cap on, and hook it up to the computer again.

- Optical mice are much lower maintenance — just clean the little feet on the underside with a soft, dry toothbrush. Don't forget to wipe down the surface the mouse sits on.

Play it safe ▶ Remember to turn your computer off before you unplug your mouse. Then, after cleaning it, hook the mouse back up and, finally, turn on your computer.

Check the connection. A loose hookup or a crushed cord can keep your mouse from communicating with the computer. Make sure the mouse is plugged into the correct port on your computer and that the connection is secure. Then look for kinks in the cord or places where it could be squeezed under a heavy object like the monitor. If the cord is damaged, you may need to buy a new mouse.

Shop for a better pad. Roller ball mice work best on a mousepad that has a little texture to it. A slick surface like a desk, or a too-smooth pad won't give the ball enough traction to move properly. Try rolling the mouse on different surfaces to find out what works best.

Test for damage. Dropping your mouse can break the delicate parts inside it. Shake it gently. A rattling sound could mean a piece has broken. If that's the case, you may have to buy another mouse.

Restart your computer. A stuck pointer could signal a computer freeze, or you may have plugged in your mouse while the computer was turned on. In either case, rebooting could provide the cure. See *Dealing with disasters* on page 165 for help doing this.

Reinstall the driver. Your computer could have a simple case of amnesia and may not recognize your mouse. To jog its memory, you'll need to plug in the mouse and reinstall its driver — the software that came with the mouse. The driver is usually on a floppy disk or compact disc. Read *Installation made easy* on page 101 for tips on how to install this software.

Treat your computer mouse like a pet, not a pest, and it could become your best friend.

Enjoy the view with windows

Your computer, like your home, is full of windows. These small, rectangular boxes frame the information that pops up on your computer screen, just as the windows in your home frame the view outdoors.

Facing a plain desktop is like looking at a house with all its curtains closed. You can't see the people — or the information — inside.

With computers, you use your mouse to throw back the curtains and open these windows. Click on the right spots, and windows appear on your screen showing you the folders, files, or programs tucked away in your computer.

The windows in your house may let you look in or out, but they won't let you touch what you see. Computer windows are different. They let you reach inside your computer and make changes.

That said, not all windows look alike. Bay windows look different from attic windows, and a folder window may look different from the one that frames your word processing program. But they do have some features in common. Take a look at this basic window, and refer to it as you learn more.

A typical window

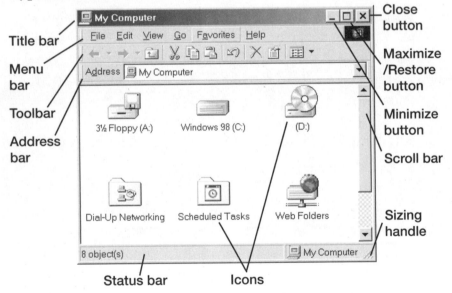

So what do all these parts do? Here's a quick reference table.

Window part	What it does
Address bar	Tells you the window's location in the computer, like a street address tells you the location of a building
Close button	Shuts the window
Maximize button	Enlarges the window so it fills the computer screen; after a window is maximized, this button is replaced by the Restore button
Menu bar	Contains menus with options for the items in that window
Minimize button	Shrinks the window into a button on the Taskbar
Restore button	Returns a maximized window back to its normal size; once a window is restored, this button is replaced by the Maximize button
Scroll bars	Let you move up, down, left, or right in a window to see its full contents
Sizing handle	Lets you make a window larger or smaller by dragging it with your mouse
Status bar	Tells you basic information about the objects in the window
Title bar	Tells you the name of the window
Toolbar	Contains buttons for common options like COPY, PASTE, and UNDO

Become a whiz at windows

Windows may be the simplest yet most important part of your operating system. You'll see them everywhere, and use them constantly. Take time to practice with them and you'll soon be a window whiz.

Throw open a window. Most of the icons on your desktop open into windows when you double-click on them. For now, try opening the MY COMPUTER icon. Double-click on it, and watch as a window opens on your screen.

Fast fix ▶ Can't double-click fast enough to please your computer? The story *Turn on tools for special needs* on page 78 tells you how to make your computer recognize a slower double-click.

Master multiple windows. Windows are a bit like papers. You can have several pages sitting on your desk, neatly stacked or scattered around. The same is true with windows. You can have several windows open at once, neatly stacked on top of each other or scattered across your computer's desktop.

You can only work on one paper — or window — at a time. The one you're using is the one on top of the stack with a colored Title bar. It's called the active window. The inactive windows underneath have Title bars that are gray and dull.

But what if the window that's active now isn't the one you need? In a stack of papers, you would grab the page you want, pull it out, and set it on top. Windows are even easier to switch around. First, you need to open a few more windows.

1   You may have to first move the active MY COMPUTER window to uncover any icons that may be hiding behind it. Use the Title bar like a handle. Click on it, then drag it by holding down your left mouse button, moving the window across the screen. Release the mouse button to drop the window to one side.

2   Now double-click on the MY DOCUMENTS icon on your desktop. A second window should open on top of the one titled MY COMPUTER.

3 Open a third window by double-clicking on the RECYCLE BIN icon. The three windows should overlap. Since you opened the RECYCLE BIN last, it should be the active window.

4 Click once on any part of an inactive window layered underneath the RECYCLE BIN window. It should pop up active on top of the stack, while the RECYCLE BIN turns gray and disappears underneath.

Timesaver ▶ Every time you open a window, a button showing its title appears on your Taskbar. Use these hot buttons to switch quickly between windows. Just click the button once, and its window becomes active.

Line them up. Sometimes you may need to see two windows at once. On a real desk you could pick up the pages and lay them side by side. Use your mouse to do the same thing on your desktop.

1 Drag and drop the active window to one side using the Title bar as you did before.

2 Now click once on one of the gray windows to make it active.

3 Grab the newly active window by its Title bar and drag it to the other side of your screen.

You should now have two windows lined up side by side. Don't worry if they still overlap. You can fiddle with them until you see both windows.

Give your window a workout. Your desktop may start to look crowded with so many windows open, but you don't have to live with a mess. The Minimize and Maximize buttons in the upper right corner of your windows are so tiny you might not notice them at first, but they can help you clean up your screen.

- **Shrink it down.** Minimizing works wonders when you need to clean up your desktop, but still want to find a window fast. Click once on the Minimize button — the one that looks like a long dash — and your window shrinks itself into a button on your Taskbar. Click once on this "hot" button to return the window to its normal size.

- **Super-size it.** Some windows are so small you can't read what's inside them. The Maximize button — the one that looks like a square — offers a simple solution. Click on it once, and your window expands to fill the whole screen.

- **Bring it back.** Look at your enlarged window. The Maximize button has been replaced by a new button that shows two over-lapping boxes. This is called the Restore button. Click on it once to bring a maximized window back to its regular size.

Quick tip ▶ You can also maximize a window by double-clicking on its Title bar. Double-click again on the Title bar to restore the window to its normal size.

Resize it yourself. Minimizing and maximizing are quick window fixes, but you can also stretch your windows out, or roll them up, down, and side to side.

Manually resizing a window lets you stretch it to the exact size you want. You can make a window longer, shorter, wider, or thinner depending on which way you drag it.

1 Put your mouse pointer on the window's edge or on the Sizing handle in the bottom right corner of the active window. When you get it in the right spot, the pointer should change into a two-headed arrow.

2 Click on the Sizing handle and drag it outwards. Drop

the Sizing handle when the window is big enough to show everything.

3 Now make it smaller by dragging the Sizing handle in and dropping it. Shrink the window until you can only see a few items in it, and watch for a Scroll bar to appear along one side.

4 Click on one end of the Scroll bar, and drag it to the other end of its track. Notice how moving the Scroll bar makes the objects in the window roll past.

5 Also, look for the arrows at each end of the Scroll bar's track. Click on the up or down arrow and watch the bar — and the window's contents — move.

FYI ▶ Scrolling in a window doesn't change the size or shape of it. Instead, you use the Scroll bar to roll through a window until you see what you need. Scroll bars only appear when a window is too small to show you everything it holds.

Close the windows. Leaving these windows open won't let the rain in, but it is important to close them before you shut down your computer.

Closing a window is like shutting the drawer of a file cabinet. As long as you saved your files, the information you created, changed, or looked at is still inside, safe and sound — it's just out of sight. To find it again, you retrace your steps, and re-open the window.

Go ahead and close all the open windows on your screen. Just click once on each window's Close button, the one shaped like an X in the upper right corner.

Play it safe ▶ Try to make the last window you open the first one you close. Sometimes, closing the 'parent' window first can cause the other windows to disappear as well.

By learning how to work with windows, you have just taken the first step to finding out how fun and easy computers can be.

Get speedy with keyboard shortcuts

Tired of mousing around your windows? Try these keyboard short-cuts instead. The plus sign (+) means you must press and hold two or more keys at the same time.

To	Press
Maximize the active window	ALT + spacebar, then the X key
Minimize the active window	ALT + spacebar, then the N key
Minimize all windows	Windows key + D OR Windows key + M
Restore a single minimized window	Windows key then TAB to select that window's hot button on the Taskbar, then press ENTER
Restore all minimized windows	Windows key + D
Switch between windows	ALT key then TAB slowly until you see the icon for the window you want to use, then release
Move the active window	ALT + spacebar + M to select the window, release and use the arrow keys to move it, then press ENTER to drop it into place
Close the active window	ALT + F4

The Windows key pictures a flag — the Microsoft logo — and is usually located in the bottom left area of your keyboard, between the CTRL and ALT keys.

Let menus lend a helping hand

Your computer exists to serve you. To do that, it offers you menus, not unlike those in a restaurant. Computer menus won't make your mouth water, but they will offer you lots of useful choices to make computing easier.

You may not notice these menus at first. They stay closed behind buttons and bars until you open them. Point and click in the right spots, and Windows presents you with lots of interesting options. All these choices are organized into different kinds of menus. The three types you'll use most are the START menu, window menus, and shortcut menus.

Start out right with the START menu. The START button at one end of your Taskbar hides your computer's main menu. Clicking once on the START button unfolds the START menu. From here, you can go just about anywhere in your computer, and quickly open hundreds of files, folders, and programs.

This large menu also hides smaller menus behind little black arrows that sit beside the main options. Pointing at these arrows makes the smaller menus unfold down the side like cascading waterfalls. The following picture shows the START menu and two cascading menus open at the same time.

FYI ▶ The START menu lets you choose from several main categories, whereas cascading menus give you more specific choices within those categories.

An open Start menu and its cascading menus

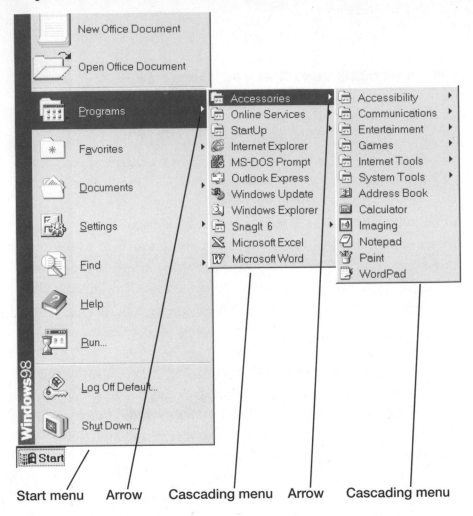

Start menu   Arrow   Cascading menu   Arrow   Cascading menu

Give your START menu a workout with the following exercise.

1 Click on the START button on your Taskbar, and watch as the START menu opens.

2 Move your pointer along the menu, and notice that pointing at each menu option selects, or highlights, it.

3 Point at an option with an arrow beside it to open its cascading menu.

4 Move your pointer along the cascading menu. The options darken here, too, as you point at them.

5 Point at an option on the cascading menu that also has an arrow beside it, and watch as another cascading menu falls open.

6 Look for more arrows in the new menu. You could open even more cascading menus from here, and each would contain more specific choices than the last.

7 Close the cascading menus by moving your pointer back to the START menu. After a moment, the cascading menus should disappear.

8 Close the START menu by pointing to an empty spot on your desktop and clicking.

Timesaver ▶ To open a file, folder, or program you see listed in the START menu, simply click on its icon.

Master window menus. The Menu bar in a window also houses those handy menus — the kind that open or drop downward, just as if you had pulled a windowshade down. In turn, some of these drop-down menus hide cascading menus. You'll get a lot of mileage out of window menus, especially when you begin working with programs. Practice now, and you'll be a menu master later.

1 Double-click on the MY COMPUTER icon on your desktop to open the MY COMPUTER window.

2 Point at the Menu bar, and click on the word VIEW. The VIEW menu should drop down.

3 Move your mouse down the menu and select one of the options in the VIEW menu by pointing at it. The option should become highlighted, just like on the START menu.

4 Look for an option in the VIEW menu with an arrow beside it, like TOOLBARS, and point at it to open the cascading menu hidden there.

View menu in My Computer window

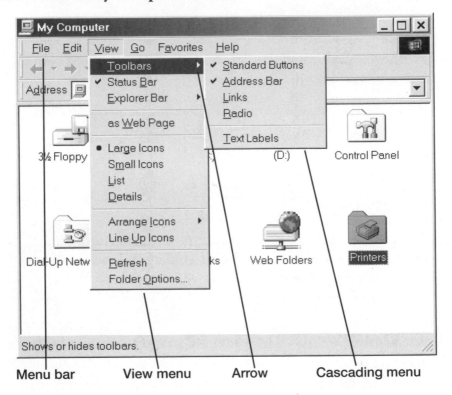

Menu bar   View menu   Arrow   Cascading menu

5 Now switch from one open menu to another. Point back at VIEW on the Menu bar, then move your pointer left to the word FILE. The VIEW menu should close, and the FILE menu should drop open.

6 Point at the CLOSE option within the FILE menu to select it, and then click. The MY COMPUTER window should close.

Timesaver ▸ You can close the menus in a window without closing the window itself. Just click on any empty spot in the window, and the menus you were browsing should close.

Cut to the chase with shortcut menus. Windows provides an easier way to do just about everything. Sometimes, the easy way involves a shortcut — or a shortcut menu. You open these minimenus by right-clicking on an object such as your Taskbar or an icon. They give you quick access to some of the common commands and settings for that object.

Shortcut menus offer different choices for different objects. The options in a shortcut menu for a Taskbar aren't the same as those in a shortcut menu for an icon, as you can see.

A sample Taskbar shortcut menu   **A sample icon shortcut menu**

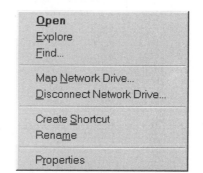

The options in some of these shortcut menus may seem strange now, but they will make more sense as you learn to use your computer.

1 Right-click on a desktop icon to make an icon shortcut menu appear next to your pointer.

2 After you have looked at the menu's options, close it by clicking on a different area of your desktop.

3 Now right-click on an empty spot on the Taskbar to open a Taskbar shortcut menu, and notice how it differs from the one you just saw.

4 Some shortcut menus also hide cascading menus. Look for the tiny arrows next to the menu options, and point at them

to open a cascading menu.

5 Close the shortcut menu by clicking on another part of the Taskbar or desktop.

Many items have shortcut menus. Practice right-clicking on different objects, then click away from them to close any menus that appear.

Quick tip ▶ You'll eventually see menu options that look gray or faded instead of black. These options are unavailable at that time. Clicking on an unavailable option won't produce any results.

Browsing through menus is a great way to learn about your computer and get a feel for the power at your fingertips.

Don't detour around menu shortcuts

Windows has a few tricks to cut the confusion of maneuvering through menus. For instance, there are keyboard shortcuts for many commands. Here are a few examples.

To	Press
Open the START menu	CTRL + ESCAPE
Close the START menu	ESCAPE
Move up and down in a menu	Up and down arrow keys
Open a cascading menu	ENTER
Choose an option from a menu	ENTER
Select the Menu bar in a window	ALT
Move across menus in a Menu bar	Left and right arrow keys
Open a drop-down menu in a Menu bar	ENTER
Close menus in a Menu bar	ALT

Talk back with dialog boxes

Feel like talking to your computer? You can — with dialog boxes, a way to give your computer more instructions. When a click on a menu option isn't enough, a dialog box pops up on the screen asking for more information.

These dialog boxes act like electronic questionnaires. You must check boxes, fill in circles, or indicate a response in other ways. Sometimes your computer automatically fills out some information for you, but you can usually replace it if necessary.

You will use dialog boxes, for instance, to change the way your computer carries out a task — like printing a single page instead of a whole document — or to personalize various settings — like enlarging the font on your screen.

Every dialog box is slightly different, but most contain similar elements. The examples and descriptions that follow will give you the lowdown on dialog boxes, and the know-how to use them.

Title bar. As you might expect, this tells you the dialog box's name, which may give you a clue as to what information your computer is asking for.

Tabs. Some dialog boxes have more than one page. Clicking on these tabs flips the pages. Each tab usually has a title, so you can go straight to the information you need.

Drop-down list box. Like menus, these boxes offer you lists of options to choose from. Click once on the arrow beside the box to open the list, point at an option to select it, then click on that option to make it appear in the box.

Display Properties dialog box

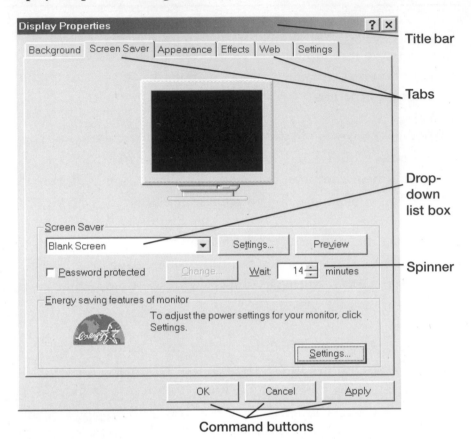

Title bar

Tabs

Drop-down list box

Spinner

Command buttons

Spinner. This little white box has two tiny arrows next to it. Click on the up arrow to raise the value in the box, the down arrow to lower it. You can also type a value directly into the spinner's box.

Command buttons. Clicking on a command button tells the computer to carry out that order. Clicking on the CANCEL button, for instance, cancels any changes you made in the dialog box, and closes it. The APPLY button tells the computer to put the changes you made into effect. The OK command button tells the computer to make those changes, and then close the dialog box. Click on the SETTINGS button for more information about an option.

> **Timesaver** ▶ Some drop-down lists have Scroll bars on the side, so you can scroll through a long list as you would a window. Or type the first letter of an option in the box, and the list will jump to that option.

Settings for FilterKeys dialog box

Check boxes. Use these to turn options on or off. Click on an empty box to put a check in it — turning that option on, and click on a checked box to remove the check — turning that option off. You can turn on more than one option in a group of check boxes.

Option buttons. These are round versions of check boxes. You click once on an empty option button to turn it on. To turn it off, you must click on another option button. Unlike check boxes, you can only turn on one option button in a group.

Text boxes. You can type information directly into these boxes. In some cases, the computer may have filled out a text box for you. To erase it, double-click inside the box to highlight the old information, then start typing. The new text should automatically replace the old.

Tech term ▶ Help system – on-screen assistance or instructions for operating systems and other programs. Usually accessed by a HELP button.

Help button. Dialog boxes can confuse even computer gurus. Click on the HELP button, then click on the puzzling part of the dialog box to get instant help. The computer should show you a message explaining that part. Click again to make the message disappear.

Close button. Clicking on this button — shaped like the letter "X" — closes the dialog box without making any changes.

Quick tip ▶ Like a window, a dialog box must be "active" for you to work in it. You can click once somewhere inside it to make sure the box is active.

Not every dialog box has all of these parts. Many are small and simple, giving you only one or two choices to make. But no matter how basic or detailed the box is, you'll handle it like a pro.

Quick keys can replace your mouse

All that clicking and typing may have you wondering if there's an easier way to fill out dialog boxes. These keyboard shortcuts can lessen the effort of talking to your computer.

To	Press
Move from one field to another	TAB
Open a drop-down list box	ALT + down arrow key
Move up or down in a drop-down list box	Up or down arrow keys
Change the value in a spinner	Up or down arrow keys
Check or uncheck a check box	SPACEBAR
Select a different option button	Arrow keys
Select and open a different tab	CTRL + TAB (to flip forward) CTRL + SHIFT + TAB (to flip backward)
Close a dialog box and cancel any changes	ESCAPE

Add custom touches to your computer

You've arranged your desk at home just the way you like it, so why not your computer desktop? Customizing your computer to meet your needs is easy in Windows.

A simple place to start is the Taskbar. You can make the icons on your Start menu bigger to ease eyestrain, move your Taskbar to a different side of your screen, and even adjust the computer's volume. Use your newfound knowledge of dialog boxes and a few clever clicks to change these settings.

Enlarge the icons on your START menu.

1   Click on the START button to open the START menu, then point at the SETTINGS option.

2   When its cascading menu opens, click on the option for the

TASKBAR & START MENU. A dialog box similar to the one pictured should pop up on your screen with the TASKBAR OPTIONS tab open.

Taskbar Properties dialog box

3 Find the check box that says SHOW SMALL ICONS IN START MENU. If it has a check mark in it, then your START menu icons may be too small.

4 Turn off this option by clicking on this check box to remove the check mark.

5 Click on the APPLY button to tell the computer to keep this change, then click on the OK button to close the dialog box.

6 Click on the START button, and see your bigger, better icons.

Timesaver ▶ Skip the START menu, and take a shortcut to this dialog box. Right-click on an empty spot on the Taskbar, then click on the PROPERTIES option in the shortcut menu that appears. The TASKBAR PROPERTIES dialog box should leap to your screen.

You can also use this dialog box to add or remove the clock, make the Taskbar appear on top of other objects on the screen, or even hide it altogether. Just click on the check boxes under the TASKBAR OPTIONS tab, and remember to click on the APPLY or OK button when you're done.

Not all changes to your Taskbar need a dialog box. Try these other ways to personalize your computer.

Adjust the volume. You should see a small speaker icon in the Taskbar's System tray if your computer came with a sound system. Click on this icon, and a small box will appear with a sliding bar in it that lets you change the computer's volume. Drag the bar to one end of the box to lower the volume and to the other end to raise it. Then click on the desktop to close this box.

Ease eyestrain with larger icons. The tiny Quick Launch icons on your Taskbar need not be tiny any longer. Right-click on an empty space in the Quick Launch toolbar to bring up its shortcut menu. Point at the VIEW option to open its cascading menu, and click on the LARGE ICONS option to put a check mark next to it. Close the menus by clicking on the desktop.

Give your Taskbar a flip. Have trouble seeing your Taskbar across the bottom of the screen? Just move it to the top or the side. Point at a blank area on the Taskbar, and drag it to where you want it. Its shape may change to fit its new home, but it will work the same as before.

These customizing tricks are only the tip of the iceberg. Your computer packs plenty of bells and whistles that can suit it just for you, as you'll see later in this chapter.

Q   **Where is my Taskbar? I don't even see it on the desktop.**

A   Your computer may be hiding it. Hold the CTRL key down on your keyboard and press ESC. Your START menu will pop open and you can then open the TASKBAR PROPERTIES dialog box as you did earlier. Then, uncheck the AUTO HIDE option, and check the ALWAYS ON TOP option. Click on the APPLY button, and close the box. Your Taskbar should leap into the open.

Q   **My Taskbar keeps jumping around the screen. What's happening?**

A   You may accidentally be dragging it when you click on it. Hold your mouse still when you click. If the Taskbar moves again, drag it back to its place.

Q   **I changed something in a dialog box by accident. I haven't closed the box yet. What do I do?**

A   You can cancel any changes you made to an open dialog box as long as you haven't clicked on the APPLY or OK command buttons. You can exit the box one of three ways: click on the CANCEL command button near the bottom of the box, click on the X-shaped Close button in the upper right corner, or press ESC on your keyboard.

Unlock the secrets of My Computer

Without help, your computer could become like a pack rat, storing scraps of information in the attic, the basement, and all the spare closets. It could take a lot of digging to find those scraps.

Fortunately, the MY COMPUTER window organizes all that information in one place, like an electronic file cabinet. From here, you can open each drawer, then each folder, and finally each item filed away in your computer's memory, and browse through them all with ease.

Opening this window is a cinch. Find the MY COMPUTER icon

sitting on your desktop, double-click on it, and a window should appear that looks a bit like this one.

Sample My Computer window

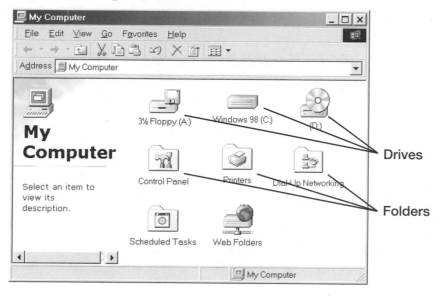

Every icon in the MY COMPUTER window is like a drawer in the file cabinet. Click on each to see more specific information listed in the left frame of the MY COMPUTER window. Generally, the icons in this window fall into two categories — folders and drives.

Fast fix ▶ Do you only see one or two icons in the MY COMPUTER window on your screen? Enlarge the window by clicking the Maximize button, or resize it by dragging the Sizing handle with your pointer.

Folders. Like any file cabinet, the MY COMPUTER window holds a few main folders. The folder you'll open most often from here leads to the CONTROL PANEL. You'll go there to change many of your computer's settings, including how your mouse works, and the color of your desktop.

You'll have a chance to explore the CONTROL PANEL later in this chapter as you continue to personalize your computer.

Drives. You learned in *Getting to know your computer* on page 1 that computers usually come with several different drives. Each has its own icon in the MY COMPUTER window. Double-clicking on a drive icon shows you what information is stored in that drive.

Here's a run-down of the drives you might see in your MY COM-PUTER window.

- **Hard drive.** This drawer of the file cabinet is your computer's main storage area. The files and programs that live permanently in your computer are saved here. You should see essentially the same items stored in the hard drive each time you open it.

- **Other drives.** CD-ROM, DVD-ROM, Zip, and floppy drives all store information on disks that you put in and take out of your computer. Open one of these drive icons, by double-clicking on it, and the computer shows you whatever is stored on the disk currently in that drive.

Fast fix ▶ Your computer may not notice when you take a disk out of a drive and put another one in. To see what's stored on the new disk, click on VIEW in the window's Menu bar, then click on the REFRESH option in the menu.

You may see other icons in your MY COMPUTER window besides the ones described here. For instance, you may have more drive icons, or you may have fewer. That's what makes learning about your computer an adventure.

Which drive is which?

Here are a few tips to tell one drive from another in the MY COMPUTER window.

Check the name. Look back at the sample MY COMPUTER window pictured earlier in this story. The drive icon named 3 1/2 FLOPPY (A:) has the word "floppy" in its name, so it's clearly the floppy disk drive.

Look at the icon. Another drive in that window, however, is simply labeled (D:). When an icon doesn't have a clear name, look at its picture. The circle floating above drive D is shaped like a compact disc (CD) — the disc you put in the CD-ROM drive. So drive D is the CD-ROM drive on this computer.

Know your alphabet. In general, the hard drive is letter C, and the floppy drive is letter A. The other drives could take the letters D, E, F, and so on. Computers are different, however, so don't rely on the letters alone.

Dress up your desktop

From painting the walls to arranging the furniture, decorating makes a new house feel like home. You may not be able to hang curtains in your computer's windows, but you can make it your own with a few colorful touches.

Give your computer a makeover through the DISPLAY PROPERTIES dialog box. Double-click on the MY COMPUTER icon to open its window, then double-click on the CONTROL PANEL icon inside. Finally, double-click on the DISPLAY icon. The DISPLAY PROPERTIES dialog box should open on your screen, looking a bit like this one.

Sample Display Properties dialog box

Timesaver ▶ Open this dialog box the easy way. Right-click on a blank spot on your desktop, and click on PROPERTIES in the shortcut menu that opens. The DISPLAY PROPERTIES dialog box should leap to your screen, ready to help.

Personalizing your computer is a lot like decorating a home, but this dialog box banishes all the work. There are even special preview areas where you can see how changes will look before you make them. Once you've decided what you like, always click on the APPLY button. Otherwise, the computer won't remember your changes.

Also, write down where you made adjustments and note the settings before and after you change them. Then, if you decide to switch something back, you'll have all the information you need.

Tech term ▶ Wallpaper – the background pattern or picture on your computer screen. Most operating systems come with several wallpapers to choose from, or you can download or create your own.

Hang the wallpaper. Tired of staring at a plain desktop? Liven it up with your favorite wallpaper. Click on the BACKGROUND tab in the DISPLAY PROPERTIES dialog box. Here, you can click on a wallpaper from the list at the bottom, and see how it will look on the tiny computer screen in the center of the box. You can even decide how you want it hung. Just click on the arrow beside the DISPLAY drop-down list, then click on one of the options given there.

FYI ▶ Learn how to turn your favorite photo into wallpaper in *Surfing tricks and troubleshooting* on page 236.

Pick a pattern instead. You really need at least 8MB of RAM to hang wallpaper, otherwise your computer may run too slowly. Patterns look a lot like wallpaper, but they take less memory. Use a pattern to fill any leftover space around your wallpaper. If your wallpaper fills the whole screen, it will cover up your pattern, so there's no point in having both.

To switch to a pattern, click on the BACKGROUND tab, then click on the PATTERN button inside. Another dialog box should pop up offering you a list of patterns, and a small preview area next to them. Click on a pattern, look at it, and click on the OK button when you've found one you like. Don't forget, click on APPLY to activate any changes you make.

Fast fix ▶ If your PATTERN button is unavailable, click on the (NONE) option in the wallpaper list. This will turn off the wallpaper, and allow you to set your pattern.

Paint the town red. Or blue, or yellow. Skip the hassle of wallpaper and patterns, and give your desktop a solid color. Click on the APPEARANCE tab, and click on the arrow by the ITEM drop-down list. When the list opens, click on the DESKTOP option. Next, choose a color. Click on the arrow beside the COLOR list to open it, and click on the color you like best.

Beef up your icons. You learned how to make the icons on the START menu bigger in *Add custom touches to your computer* on page 67, but you can also enlarge the icons on your desktop and in windows. Click on the EFFECTS tab, and look for the USE LARGE ICONS check box. If it's empty, click on it to put a check mark in it.

Make boxes and windows easy to read. You can also enlarge the print in windows and dialog boxes, as well as change their colors so they stand out more on screen. Click on the APPEARANCE tab, then click on the arrow beside the SCHEME drop-down list. Each time you click on an option in the list, a preview of it appears in the space above. Try the HIGH CONTRAST options to alter the colors of objects, and the WINDOWS STANDARD LARGE and EXTRA LARGE options to increase the print size.

Super-size it. Still not big enough? Never fear. Under the APPEAR-ANCE tab, you can resize each object to suit your needs. Click on the ITEM drop-down list, and click on the name of the item you want to resize. Nearby, you'll see a spinner labeled SIZE. Use the arrows next to the spinner to raise or lower the number, making the item bigger or smaller. You can also enlarge or shrink the text by adjusting the font size.

Select a screen saver. Screen savers are the moving pictures that fill your screen after your computer sits idle for a while. To choose one, click on the SCREEN SAVER tab, then click on the arrow beside the SCREEN SAVER drop-down list. Click on an option in the list, and preview it on the tiny computer screen in the dialog box. Next, set its timer. Click on the arrows next to the WAIT box to choose the number of minutes the computer will sit idle before turning on the screen saver.

Fast fix ▶ Remember, if you make a mistake in a dialog box and need to cancel your changes, click on the CANCEL button, on the X-shaped Close button in the upper-right corner, or press ESCAPE on your keyboard.

These are just a few of the personal touches you can make to your computer. Have fun as you explore the possibilities for yourself.

Sidestep pesky passwords

At their best, passwords protect your privacy. At their worst, they are pests. Your computer may ask you for one every time you turn it on. But if only one or two people use the computer, you may not really need a password.

Don't let passwords drive you to distraction. Skip them with a few smart steps.

1 Double-click on the MY COMPUTER icon to open its window, then double-click on the CONTROL PANEL icon inside.

2 Double-click on the PASSWORDS icon and the PASSWORDS PROPERTIES dialog box should open on your screen.

3 Click on the CHANGE PASSWORDS tab and then on the CHANGE WINDOWS PASSWORD button in this box. A smaller

dialog box should pop up. In it, you will probably see three text boxes — one for the OLD PASSWORD, one for the NEW PASSWORD, and one to CONFIRM NEW PASSWORD.

4   Click on the OLD PASSWORD text box, and type the old password.

5   Next, click in the NEW PASSWORD text box, and press ENTER on your keyboard. Do this again in the CONFIRM NEW PASSWORD text box. This clears the password out of your computer's memory and allows you to bypass it in the future.

6   If you get a message saying you have successfully changed the Windows password, click on OK, or press ENTER on your keyboard to return to the PASSWORDS PROPERTIES dialog box.

7   Click on the CLOSE command button at the bottom of the box to close it and keep your changes.

If your computer still asks for a password when you turn it on, ignore it and press ENTER on your keyboard.

Play it safe ▶ Passwords make some people feel safer about using a computer. The operating system's Help program can give you instructions on setting a computer password. Check out *Where to go for Help* on page 91 for tips on using Windows Help. Then learn how to *Protect yourself with passwords* on page 252.

Turn on tools for special needs

Computers help thousands of disabled people lead normal lives. But those tricky clicks and hard-to-see pointers can be aggravating even if you suffer from only the normal effects of aging.

You have the power to change that. Whether you have arthritis, or you're just tired of squinting at the screen, make the most troublesome parts of your computer work for you.

Make your mouse mind its manners. Many seniors have trouble getting comfortable with their pointing device. You can fine-tune yours in the MOUSE PROPERTIES dialog box. Remember to set your adjustments by clicking on APPLY before you leave each dialog box.

1 Click on the START button, and point to the SETTINGS option in the START menu.

2 Next, click on the CONTROL PANEL option in the cascading menu that opens.

3 When the CONTROL PANEL window opens, find the MOUSE icon inside, and double-click on it to open this dialog box.

Mouse Properties dialog box

- **Go left.** Mice are automatically set for right-handed people. If you're tired of lefties getting the short end of the stick, click on the BUTTONS tab, and click on the LEFT-HANDED option to switch your mouse to the left side.

Quick tip ▶ The buttons are reversed when you make your mouse left-handed. You'll use your left index finger to click, and your left middle finger to right-click.

- **Fix your double-click.** Double-clicking fast enough to please your computer can pose quite a challenge. Under the BUTTONS tab you can slow it down. In the DOUBLE-CLICK SPEED area near the bottom of the box is a sliding bar. Drag this bar toward the SLOW end of its track to make the computer accept slower double-clicks. Then practice double-clicking in the TEST AREA to the right. Keep adjusting the speed until you're comfortable.

- **Stand out from the crowd.** Make your pointer easier to see. Click on the POINTERS tab, then click on the arrow next to the SCHEME drop-down list. Here, you can click on LARGE or EXTRA LARGE to increase the size of the pointer, or on a color scheme such as BLACK or INVERTED to make the pointer stand out on the screen. Each time you click on an option from the list, you can preview it in the box to the right.

FYI ▶ Some computers have more SCHEME choices than others. If you don't see these size or color options for your pointer, consider other ways to make it more visible — like slowing it down or adding a trail.

- **Reign in runaway arrows.** Sometimes your pointer moves across the screen so fast your eyes can hardly keep track of it. Take a moment to slow this down, too. Click on the MOTION tab of the dialog box, and find the sliding bar labeled POINTER

SPEED. Drag this bar toward the SLOW end of the track to control the pointer's zip.

- **Pin a trail on your pointer.** Give your pointer a trail to make its movements easier to follow. Click on the MOTION tab, then click on the check box that reads SHOW POINTER TRAILS. You can lengthen or shorten the trail by sliding the POINTER TRAIL bar along its track.

Stop getting stuck on your keyboard. Computer keyboards can be impatient. Press down on a key for a second too long, and suddenly you have *zzzz* instead of *z.* Teach your keys some patience.

1 Return to the CONTROL PANEL window, and double-click on the KEYBOARD icon to open the KEYBOARD PROPERTIES dialog box.

2 Click on the SPEED tab.

3 Slide the REPEAT DELAY bar along its track toward the LONG setting. Now your keyboard should give you a little more time to lift your finger before repeating letters.

Customize even more. The ACCESSIBILITY OPTIONS icon in the CONTROL PANEL opens a dialog box that's especially helpful if you have hearing problems, arthritis, or other conditions that slow down your computing. Here, you can turn the computer's sound warnings into visual messages, and use StickyKeys to simplify keyboard shortcuts, among other things.

Fast fix ▶ If you have a hard time hearing your computer's sound signals, learn how to pump up the volume in *Add custom touches to your computer* on page 67.

Accessibility options don't always come loaded on your computer. If you don't see the ACCESSIBILITY OPTIONS icon in the CONTROL

PANEL, you should be able to install it from the operating system (OS) software that came with your computer. See *Installation made easy* on page 101 for tips on loading software. Also, check the manuals that came with your computer for more help.

Your computer was created to help, not hinder, you. Teach it to meet your needs, and experience more enjoyable computing.

Save money with power management

Computers run on electricity, so leaving your computer on all the time, or simply forgetting to turn it off, can inflate your electric bill. Fortunately, Windows provides a smart way to save energy with power management settings.

You learned how computers power down or go to "sleep" in *Best way to shut down your computer* on page 29. Power management is the feature that tells your computer when to go to sleep. It saves energy by gradually turning off parts of your computer — like the monitor and the hard drive — when you aren't using them. The computer is still on, it's just resting. But it won't use nearly as much electricity or battery power asleep as it does awake.

Quick tip ▶ Even a sleeping computer uses power. A laptop can still drain its battery if you leave it asleep too long, so turn your computer off if you know you won't need it for a while.

The POWER MANAGEMENT dialog box lets you turn this feature on and decide how long the computer should wait before going to sleep.

1   Click on the START button and point at SETTINGS in the START menu.

2 Click on CONTROL PANEL in the cascading menu that opens.

3 Double-click on the POWER MANAGEMENT icon in the CONTROL PANEL window to open this dialog box.

Power Management Properties dialog box

Once you've finished fiddling in this box, remember to click on the APPLY or OK button to make the changes stick.

Select a scheme. Windows comes with several power-saving plans already set up. Click on the POWER SCHEMES tab, then click on the down arrow next to the POWER SCHEMES drop-down list. Each option in the list has its own schedule for shutting down the computer's parts. You can choose one of these schedules by clicking on an option such as HOME/OFFICE DESK or PORTABLE/LAPTOP, or you can turn off power management so your computer never sleeps by clicking on the ALWAYS ON option.

Set your own timetable. You can also set how long the computer waits before going to sleep. Under the POWER SCHEMES tab, you should see other options such as SYSTEM STANDBY, and TURN OFF HARD DISKS — you could have many choices here or just a few. Click on the arrow beside each drop-down list and click on the number of minutes you want to set. Usually, the monitor turns off first, then the computer enters Standby mode, and finally the hard disks turn off.

FYI ▶ You may want the computer to start shutting down sooner, say after five minutes, if you are working from a battery-powered system. You could set it for 10 or 15 minutes if you're using a computer that plugs into an outlet.

Computers wake up from their energy-conserving sleep easier than most people do — just press a key on the keyboard or move the pointing device. Although you may have to wait a few seconds for the computer to turn completely on again, eventually the screen should come back to life looking just as it did when it went to sleep.

Most of the time, your computer should wake up without a problem. Occasionally, it may get grumpy and keep on sleeping. Then, you'll have to restart it. Take a look at *Dealing with disasters* on page 165 for help on restarting your computer. If your computer often has trouble waking up, you may want to choose the ALWAYS ON power scheme to keep it from going to sleep.

Play it safe ▶ Don't take risks with your work. Save any changes you've made and close all windows and dialog boxes before walking away from your computer. This way, if you have to restart the computer to wake it up, you won't lose any work. See *Play it smart and save* on page 103 for tips on saving data.

Make — and take — a shortcut

Spend enough time on your computer searching for files or applications, and you may begin to feel like a mouse in a maze, looking for the cheese. Smart mice find shortcuts to the cheese, and so can you — by creating shortcuts to the items you use most in your computer.

Shortcuts are just that — simple ways to save time. Windows lets you place these shortcut icons right on your desktop, on your START menu, or on the Taskbar. So instead of opening window after window to get to the files, folders, and programs stored inside your computer, you can click on an easy-to-find icon.

Speed your work with desktop shortcuts. The desktop is a good place to put shortcuts. Here, they work just like regular icons on the desktop, but they look a little different. Compare these two icons, and notice how the shortcut icon on the right has a small arrow in the bottom left corner. This arrow helps you tell shortcut icons from regular icons on the desktop.

Regular icon **Shortcut icon**

Letters Shortcut to Letters

Working with shortcuts is a snap. Here's how to make the most of them on your desktop.

- **Create.** Dig around in your computer, and find the original icon you want to make a shortcut to. Drag it with your right mouse button — not your left — to a blank area on your desktop, and drop it. A small menu should jump to the screen. Click on the CREATE SHORTCUT(S) HERE option to put the new shortcut on the desktop.

- **Open.** Double-click on the shortcut icon the same way you would open any other desktop icon.

- **Rename.** The computer automatically names desktop shortcuts when you first create them. Luckily, you can change them. Right-click on the shortcut icon, and click on the RENAME option in the menu that pops up. Type in the new name, and press ENTER on your keyboard. You can use this trick to rename regular icons, too.

- **Organize.** Shortcuts are great, but the more you create, the more cluttered your desktop can get. Let Windows do the cleaning. Right-click on an empty area of the desktop to open its shortcut menu, and point to ARRANGE ICONS. Decide how you want them organized, and click on an option in the cascading menu. Or, leave the AUTO ARRANGE option unchecked in this menu, then drag and drop the icons wherever you want on the desktop.

- **Delete.** Clean up your desktop by deleting old shortcuts. Right-click on the shortcut icon, and click on DELETE in the menu that appears. When the computer asks if you're sure you want to delete this icon, click on YES.

Play it safe ▶ Look before you delete. Deleting a shortcut icon only erases the quick pathway to a real item. Deleting a regular icon erases the actual file, folder, or program it represents. So check for the arrow that makes a desktop shortcut different from a regular icon.

Start fast with START menu shortcuts. All of the icons you see on the START menu are actually shortcuts. You may already have some here since many programs automatically place a shortcut on your START menu during installation. However, you can add more — to particular files or folders, and to other programs.

- **Create.** First, check the START menu to make certain the shortcut you need isn't there already. If not, open the window containing the original icon of the item you want. Press and hold your right mouse button and drag the original item to the START button, then wait for the menu to open. Just drop the icon here to store the shortcut on the main START menu. Or point at an option to open the cascading menus, and drop the icon in one of these. Then click on the CREATE SHORTCUT(S) HERE option in the small menu that appears.

- **Open.** You can now open this shortcut as you would any other item on the START menu. Click on the START button, and click on the new shortcut in the menu.

- **Delete.** Click on the START button, and right-click on the shortcut icon in the START menu. Then click on the DELETE option in the small menu that pops to your screen.

Play it safe ▶ Think carefully before you delete a shortcut that your computer put on the Start menu. Some items, like the calculator, can be hard to find without a shortcut.

Track shortcuts with the Taskbar. Desktop shortcuts can disappear behind open windows, and the START menu still requires some maneuvering. The Taskbar, however, should always be visible, and opening a shortcut from here takes just a click.

Taskbar shortcuts appear in the Quick Launch area of your Taskbar. In fact, you may have a few there already. Learn how to manage those you have and add more. Since the Quick Launch area is small, add only those shortcuts you'll use the most.

FYI ▶ Check out *Add custom touches to your computer* on page 67 if you can't find the Quick Launch toolbar, or if you don't see the Taskbar on your screen.

- **Create.** Find the item you want to create a shortcut to. With your right mouse button, drag it to the Quick Launch area of your Taskbar, and drop it. Click on CREATE SHORTCUT(S) HERE. The new shortcut should take its place among the other Taskbar icons.

- **Open.** Click on the shortcut icon on the Taskbar.

- **Delete.** Right-click on the shortcut icon, and click on DELETE in the menu that pops up. When the computer asks if you're sure you want to delete the item, click on the YES button.

Fast fix ▶ If you get an error message when you click on a shortcut, maybe you've moved the original item it opens. The shortcut becomes a dead end when the program or file isn't where it used to be. The fast fix? Create a new shortcut.

Get the specs on your PC

Owning a computer is like owning a car — eventually you have to learn how to open the hood and check the oil. When the time comes to buy new software or upgrade your computer system, you'll need to know details like how fast the modem is, or how big the hard drive.

You can check the sales order, packing slip, and other paperwork that came with your computer to find this information. But if you've misplaced them, Windows can help out.

The SYSTEM PROPERTIES dialog box can give you most of the information you'll need.

1 Click on the START button.

2 Point at SETTINGS in the START menu, and click on CONTROL PANEL in the cascading menu that opens.

3 Double-click on the SYSTEM icon in the CONTROL PANEL window to open the SYSTEM PROPERTIES dialog box.

FYI ▶ These instructions are for computers that use the Microsoft Windows 98 operating system (OS). Some of this information may not apply if your computer has a different OS.

Basics. Click on the GENERAL tab and you'll discover these fundamentals about your computer.

- Operating system. Learn what type of OS your computer uses, such as Windows 98 or Windows XP.

- RAM. See how many total megabytes (MB) of RAM are installed on your computer.

Peripherals. Click on the DEVICE MANAGER tab to discover all about the extras your computer system may have.

- CD-ROM. Click on the option button at the top of the box labeled VIEW DEVICES BY TYPE. Click on the plus sign (+) next to the CD-ROM icon in the list of computer peripherals. The CD-ROM option should expand, showing you the make and model of your computer's CD-ROM drive.

- Other drives. Click on the plus sign (+) next to the DISK DRIVES icon to see what other drives your computer houses — such as floppy, ZIP, or DVD drives.

- Modem. Some computers use modems to connect to the Internet, and others use network cards. Clicking on the plus sign (+) by the MODEM icon in the list should tell you what kind of modem your computer uses — if it has one.

- Network card. Not all computers come with a network card. To see if yours does, click next to the NETWORK ADAPTERS icon in the list. When it expands, you should see information about the computer's network card.

- Sound card. Click on the plus sign (+) next to the SOUND, VIDEO, AND GAME CONTROLLERS icon. You'll see the make and model of your computer's sound card.

Unfortunately, SYSTEM PROPERTIES can't tell you everything. You still need to find out about a few other nuts and bolts in your computer.

Video. Head for the DISPLAY PROPERTIES dialog box to learn about your video card.

1 Right-click on a blank area of the desktop, and click on PROPERTIES in the shortcut menu that appears.

2 The DISPLAY PROPERTIES dialog box should pop up on your screen.

3 Click on the SETTINGS tab in the box, then click on the ADVANCED button in the lower corner.

4 A new dialog box should appear with many tabs inside it. Click on the ADAPTER tab.

Here you'll see a list of information about your video card, including its name, manufacturer, type, and how much memory it holds.

Hard disk space. You can find details about your hard disk with the help of MY COMPUTER.

1 Double-click on the MY COMPUTER icon to open its window.

2 Right-click on the hard drive icon — generally drive C.

3 Click on the PROPERTIES option in the shortcut menu.

You'll now see a dialog box with a pie chart showing how much used and unused storage space you have on your hard drive.

Processor. Finding your processor's speed in Windows can be confusing and the resulting number — called COMPSPEED — is not always accurate. Nevertheless, it's an important piece of information to have. The most reliable way of finding the processor's speed is to check the paperwork and manuals that came with your computer.

Get the basics about your computer now and save yourself from a headache later. Write down the details you find, and keep a copy with the computer's other paperwork. Someday, you'll be glad you did.

Where to go for Help

From useful hints to step-by-step instructions, your computer packs tools that can save you from frustration. While the tips here are for the Windows 98 operating system (OS), other versions of Windows have similar assistance.

Meet your computer tutor. For those times when a manual just isn't enough, Windows comes with a built-in instructor — a tutorial, or interactive training program — that walks you through the basics of computing, step by step, and even offers advanced tips. You can get to this tutorial through the START menu.

1 Click on the START button, and point to PROGRAMS in the START menu. A cascading menu should open.

2 Point to ACCESSORIES and another cascading menu should open.

3 Point to SYSTEM TOOLS in the new menu, and watch as a final cascading menu opens.

4 Click on WELCOME TO WINDOWS in this last menu. The WELCOME TO WINDOWS 98 dialog box should appear.

5 Click on DISCOVER WINDOWS 98.

6 For basic lessons, click on the words COMPUTER ESSENTIALS. For advanced tips, click on the words MORE WINDOWS 98 RESOURCES.

Follow the directions on the screen, and you're on your way to mastering Windows. You can quit the tutorial at any time by clicking on the CLOSE command button in the window.

Fast fix ▶ In order to access this tutorial, you may have to insert into the CD-ROM drive the operating system CD that came with your computer. See *Installation made easy* on page 101 for help installing computer software.

Ask the Windows expert. For even more assistance, the Windows Help system covers almost every possible computer question.

Open this program by clicking on the START button, then click on

HELP in the START menu. The Help system window should look a bit like this one.

Sample Windows Help system window

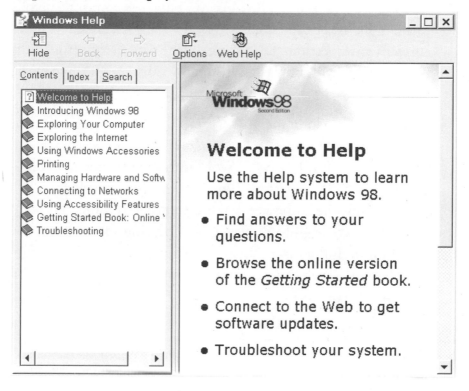

From here, you can browse and learn a little about everything, or search on a specific problem. Notice the three tabs on the left side of the window, and the separate viewing pane on the right. Each tab lets you search a different way, while the right pane shows you information about a topic.

- **Contents tab.** Click on the CONTENTS tab, and you'll see a list of topics organized like the Table of Contents in a book. Click on the book icon next to a topic to open a topic's "chapter" and click again to close it. You'll also see icons that look like pages with question marks on them. Click on one of these, and information about that subject appears in the pane on the right. Use the CONTENTS tab when you want to know more about a general topic, such as printing or the desktop.

- **Index tab.** To search by subject, click on the INDEX tab and type a word into the text box. As you type, the computer scrolls through its list of topics. Click on one that looks like it might answer your question. Then click on the DISPLAY button, and the computer will show you information about that topic in the pane on the right.

- **Search tab.** Click on the SEARCH tab when you want information on a broad topic, or when you aren't exactly sure what you're looking for. Just type a word into the text box, and click on the LIST TOPICS button. Type in the word *Taskbar*, for instance, and the computer will list every Help topic that mentions the Taskbar — from hiding it to putting shortcuts on it. Scroll through the list, click on a topic that fits your problem, and click the DISPLAY button to see helpful information in the right-hand pane.

Quick tip ▶ Clicking on an underlined word in the right-side pane causes a message to appear next to your pointer explaining the word. Click on the message after you've read it to make it disappear.

Let help in through the window. You can get quick help from inside any window, as well.

- Inside a folder window, click on HELP in the Menu bar, then click on the HELP TOPICS option in the menu. This opens up the larger Windows Help system discussed earlier.

- Program windows, on the other hand, offer help for just that specific program. Click on HELP in the Menu bar of a program window, and click on one of the options listed. Clicking on the CONTENTS AND INDEX option opens a help dialog box with three tabs like the Help system window. Click on MICROSOFT

WORD HELP or MICROSOFT EXCEL HELP, for instance, and an animated paper clip friend will offer to answer your questions. For more information on specific program help, see *Good help is easy to find* on page 105.

Timesaver ▶ Skip all the clicking. Press F1 on your keyboard to call up Help on the desktop or in a window.

Clear up confusion in dialog boxes. You've probably noticed dialog boxes don't have Menu bars the way windows do, but they do have a tiny question mark button in the upper right-hand corner. Click on this Help button, then click on the area of the dialog box you have a question about. A message should appear next to your pointer with helpful information.

Sign on to save headaches. Find the latest answers to computer problems on the Internet. First, brush up on your web-surfing skills in the Internet essentials chapter later in this book. Then visit Microsoft's special Web page at **http://support.microsoft.com** for help troubleshooting Microsoft products. If you need assistance with hardware or software made by other companies, look for an Internet address in the paperwork that came with these items, and then visit the manufacturers online.

Call for help. Once upon a time, telephone technical support was free. Now, having a live person talk you through a computer problem may cost a hefty fee. Before you place that call, try other ways of troubleshooting — read the manual, check out the Windows Help system, visit the manufacturer's Web site, or call the dealer who sold you the product.

If you're still stuck, read the fine print in the computer paperwork to find out if you get free telephone tech support, or if you have to pay. Be prepared to tell the technician basic details about your computer, especially the part that's giving you problems. *Get the specs on your PC* on page 88 can help you find the information you'll need.

With so much help available, no matter what your problem, you'll never be stranded for long.

Software survival

Understanding applications

You need more than just your hardware and Operating System (OS) to get the most from your computer. You need software like a word processor, a spreadsheet, an Internet browser, and a virus shield.

To understand why, imagine that your computer is a factory. You are the president and owner. Your OS is the factory manager. Just like a real manager, your OS can't run the whole "factory" by itself. It needs employees — the software programs — to do the work.

Programs carry out different tasks, just like factory employees have different jobs. You will find some programs very useful, while others won't be used at all. It just depends on what you want your computer to do.

Quick tip ▶ Software, applications, and programs all refer to the same thing. They are tools that allow your computer to carry out specific jobs, like writing letters or organizing your finances. Note — these three words will be used interchangeably in this chapter.

Here are the main types of software you'll come across:

Word processor. This is like your computer's secretary. It whips up letters, to-do lists, party invitations, resumes, and anything else you can type up.

Spreadsheet. Like your computer's bookkeeper, this program is great with math. It can build monthly budgets and help organize your bills.

Other valuable programs. An application called a database acts like a recordskeeper and builds computer file cabinets. Another type of application puts together slideshows. Others play games, broadcast music, figure out your taxes, and protect your computer from viruses and hackers.

Bundles, suites, and offices

Amazingly, new computers often come with a bunch of programs included in the purchase price. Together, these programs are called a bundle, a suite, or an office.

When you shop for a new computer, look for bundles that offer the most programs, or the best quality programs. The two most common bundles — Microsoft Office and WordPerfect Suite — have the best of both worlds. They come with top-of-the-line word processing and spreadsheet applications, as well as personal organizers, e-mail programs, and slideshow makers.

These bundles include all the programs an average computer user needs. They are a great bargain, especially since the programs are worth hundreds of dollars by themselves.

Nevertheless, you may need newer and more advanced programs as you become a computer whiz. That's when knowing how to buy software will come in handy.

How to buy the best software

Buying new software is a big step. Remember — programs are the "employees" that transform your computer into a productive "factory." So learn the steps to buying the best software for your system.

Know your needs. Start by making a list of what you want to accomplish with your computer. Think up specific projects, like creating a party invitation or balancing your budget. Then find out what kind of programs will get these jobs done.

If you plan to write letters and keep a journal, a word processor like Microsoft Word would be your best bet. A more expensive publishing program could come with too many unnecessary features. Buying it would be like hiring Picasso when all you need is someone to paint your garage.

Talk to friends. It's smart to ask advice from experienced computer users you know and trust. Find out about the programs they have, what they use them for, and if they're happy with them.

Play it safe ▶ Have your computer's measurements handy when you shop. This means knowing about its RAM, processor, OS, hard drive, sound card, CD-ROM, modem, network card, and video card. (See *Get the specs on your PC* on page 88 to learn how to locate this information.) This list is important because all programs have system requirements, which can be found on the software packaging or Web site. Your computer needs to match or outdo these requirements to run the program properly.

Seek professional advice. Next, flip through computer magazines to find software reviews. Browse technology Web sites like **www.zd net.com** and **www.cnet.com**. And talk to the gurus at your local computer store, too. With all this help, you should be able to single out the application that's the best fit for you.

Buy the latest and greatest. Before you buy this perfect program, make sure you're purchasing the most recent edition. Software makers constantly tinker with their work, developing newer, and usually better, versions of their software.

These versions are named for the year they come out, like Microsoft

Word 2002. Or they have numbers and decimals, like WordPerfect 10.0. Either way, find out which version is the latest and grab it.

Quick tip ▶ Many software makers offer free or low-cost trial versions of their programs on their Web sites. You either download the program from the Internet, or send for it in the mail. Then you try it out on your computer for a limited time and judge for yourself. Check out *Get the lowdown on downloading* on page 247 for more information.

Shop around. Now comes the fun part of buying software — saving money. It takes a little effort, since you need to hunt down price quotes from several stores to do it. But you'll find a lot of leeway in those prices, so the work pays off in the end. Don't forget to compare warranties, return policies, and technical support, too. Here are the major types of stores to visit.

Software store	Pros	Cons
Local computer store	Knowledgeable staff	Small selection
	Allows test runs of software in the store	Higher prices
Chain superstore	Good selection	Less knowledgeable staff
	National store dependability	
Online or catalog outlets	Low prices	Shipping wait and costs
	Wide selection	Impersonal and sometimes difficult customer service

After following these steps, you can have your cake and eat it, too. You'll get the best software for your needs — at a great price and with great customer support.

Installation made easy

Installing software sounds complicated, but it's actually a snap.
You are simply copying the program onto your computer's hard
drive. This makes the program a part of your computer, which
means it's always there when you need it. If you don't install it, you
have to insert the software disks every time you use the program.
That's a hassle.

Play it safe ▶ Some experts recommend scanning new software with
an anti-virus program before you install it. Even store-bought software can
have a computer-crashing bug hidden in it.

So set aside five minutes for installation when you buy new software.
Sit at your computer with the entire software package — its floppy
or compact disks, manual, and box. And follow these steps.

1 Start up your computer if it's not already on.

2 Check that your hard drive has enough available memory for
   the software. (Remember — the system requirements are on
   the back of the software's packaging.)

3 Quit all applications except your OS.

Now it's time to actually install. Please note — the following
instructions are for Windows 98. They may be different for other
systems, but the general idea is the same.

1 Click on the START menu, select SETTINGS, and click on
   CONTROL PANEL.

2 Double-click on the ADD/REMOVE PROGRAMS icon.

3 Click on the INSTALL/UNINSTALL tab in the dialog box and
   then on the INSTALL button.

4 Insert the compact or floppy disk into the correct drive. (If more than one disk came in the package, insert the disk with the number one, or the word "install" or "installation" printed on it.)

Timesaver ▶ **If you have a newer computer, it may automatically ask if you want an installation after you insert the disk. Just click on** OK. **If this doesn't happen, click on** NEXT. **Your computer should then begin installation.**

---

5 Provide any information the computer asks for, such as the software registration number. Look for this information in the manual or on the box.

6 Choose the express setup, which allows the OS to pick the best storage place for the program.

The computer will do all the work from this point on. When it's finished, it will recommend a reboot. Make sure to first remove the installation disk. Next, click on FINISH and restart your computer. The program will be easy to find and ready to use when your computer starts up again.

Opening an application

Your "factory" is stocked with "employees" now you've installed your software. But how do you put these employees to work? The answer is simple. Just ask your manager — or operating system — to do it.

In other words, instruct Windows to open your application or program of choice. If you want to write a letter to a friend, for instance, tell Windows to start the word processor. It's a simple point-and-click process. And there are several ways to do it.

For the easiest way, follow these instructions. Remember, these steps are for Windows 98. The process may be similar — but not exactly the same — if you use another OS.

1 Click on the START menu and select PROGRAMS.

2 Browse the different application folders and individual icons until you find the program you're looking for.

3 Click on that program's icon.

For practice, try finding the icon for your word processor, such as Microsoft Word. Then click on it. Word's introductory screen should appear, followed by a new word processing document. It's like a blank sheet of typewriter paper on your computer monitor.

Keep reading this chapter to learn all the amazing things you can create with this one document.

Timesaver ▶ Don't forget about shortcut icons on your desktop. They are one of the fastest ways to open an application. Flip back to *Make — and take — a shortcut* on page 85 for more details.

Play it smart and save

Now that you know how to start a computer project, you better know how to save it. And it's easy to save your work on your hard drive. When you close the application or turn off your computer, your project will always be there when you're ready to tinker with it again. If you don't save your work, it could be gone — forever.

Scary as it sounds, you also can lose projects even though they're saved. This can happen if your computer crashes or your hard drive is damaged. That's why a backup copy of your work can come in very handy. It's a duplicate file you store in a safe location.

Here are the best ways to save and make backup copies of your work. Please note — almost all programs feature SAVE and SAVE AS, but only some have CREATE BACKUP and AUTOSAVE.

Function	When to do it	Why?	How?
SAVE	When you first open a project. Every five minutes while you're working.	To store an up-to-date version of your project.	Click on the FILE menu and then on SAVE.
SAVE AS	When you're finished working on a project.	To save a backup copy to a separate location. (A floppy disk, for instance.)	Click on the FILE menu and then on SAVE AS. Type in a file name and choose a location.
AUTOSAVE	When you first open a project.	To set the program to automatically save in case the computer freezes.	Click on SAVE AS and then on OPTIONS. Check AUTOSAVE or AUTO RECOVER. Set for five minutes.
CREATE BACKUP	When you first open a project.	To set the program to automatically save a backup copy.	Click on SAVE AS and then on OPTIONS. Check BACKUP.

Play it safe ▶ There's one time when saving is not a good idea — if you wreck your project and don't know how to fix it. In this case, just close the file. The program will ask you if you want to save. Click on NO. Then re-open your project. It will appear like it did before, although you may lose some of your work.

Good help is easy to find

Dive right into your new software once you have it set up. If you're a little unsure of yourself, don't worry. Almost all programs come with a safety net — the HELP menu. There you'll find the answer to any question you may have about the software.

Different programs have different versions of this menu. Each one works only for the particular program it's in.

But all HELP menus basically run the same way. So if you know how to use one, you'll know how to use them all. The key is asking the right questions.

A typical Help menu

Q How can I find out the name of a Toolbar button?

A Try balloon help. Just point your cursor on a button. Wait a moment, and the name of the button may pop up in a "balloon." Balloon help comes on automatically in some programs, like Microsoft Word and Excel. In other programs, you need to turn it on.

Tech term ▶ Balloon help – on-screen information available for some operating systems or programs. When you place your cursor over an object, a helpful message will appear in a cartoon-like balloon.

Q How do I turn on balloon help?

A Check for this function in the HELP menu and click on it. Please note — some programs give this tool a different name, like FLYOVER HELP or SCREEN TIPS. They also may give it a different location, such as the TOOLS menu under CUSTOMIZE, or in the EDIT or OPTIONS menu.

Balloon help at work in a Microsoft Excel Toolbar

Q How can I get more details about a button?

A Open the HELP menu and click on WHAT'S THIS? Next, point the cursor at a button and click on it. A super-sized balloon appears and gives a full description of the button's function.

Q What if WHAT'S THIS? isn't there?

A Some programs don't have WHAT'S THIS? in their menu, but they could still show the information automatically. In this case, keep an eye on the bottom of the program window. When you place the cursor on a button or Toolbar function, its description may appear there.

Q What if I need more help than that?

A Click on the HELP menu. You should see CONTENTS AND INDEX or HELP TOPICS, depending on what program you're using. Click on whichever one shows up. It will provide a listing of almost every help subject imaginable. Find the topic that best matches your question and double-click on it.

Help Topics dialog box

Help Topics: Microsoft Excel [?][X]

Contents | Index | Find

Click a book, and then click Open. Or click another tab, such as Index.

- Key Information
- Getting Help
- Installing and Removing Microsoft Excel
- Creating, Opening, and Saving Files
- Working with Workbooks and Worksheets
- Entering Data and Selecting Cells
- Editing Worksheet Data
- Formatting Worksheets
- Printing
- Creating an Online or Printed Form
- Creating Formulas and Auditing Workbooks
- Working with Charts
- Displaying Data in a Map
- Creating Drawings and Importing Pictures
- Managing Lists

Open | Print... | Cancel

Q What if I still have questions?

A Visit the software's customer support Web site where you can e-mail your questions to a company rep. Or search through their extensive online help files. First, click on the HELP menu and look for the command that mentions "Web" or "online." Click on it. Just remember you need to be hooked up to the Internet to use this.

Q What if I don't have Internet access yet?

A Contact the customer service center the old-fashioned way — with a telephone. Look for the number in the software manual.

Work wonders with a word processor

The word processor may be your most important program —
besides the OS — simply because it helps you do so many different things.

Take typing, for instance. Your word processor makes it easy. If
using a typewriter is like cleaning clothes in a river, then using a
word processor is like doing laundry in a washing machine. The
program takes care of carriage returns, finds your spelling and grammar mistakes, and allows you to print your project as many times as
you want.

Tech term ▶ Word processing – a software program that lets you write,
edit, store, and print text.

But a word processor also goes far beyond what an old-fashioned
typewriter can do. For example, the program allows you to rearrange
the order of words or whole paragraphs. It allows you to change the
size, color, and style of your text. And it helps you add fancy tables,
pictures, and cartoons.

In short, your word processor helps you create the perfect project,
store it forever, and print it as many times as you want. It does all
this without a hitch, while you just point and click your mouse.

But here's the catch — you need to know the program's tools and
tricks, and this is a good place to start.

Document. This is the general name for an individual word processor project. A document looks like a blank sheet of paper at first, but
you can type in it any way you want.

Menu bar. Click on the headings, such as FORMAT and INSERT, to open a menu. There you'll see what commands, or tools, your word processor has to offer.

Toolbars. These contain buttons, which are quick ways to turn on or turn off a command.

Tech term ▶ Button – a small rectangular graphic you can click on with your mouse to tell the computer to do something.

Title bar. This is the location for the title of your document. It will say DOCUMENT1 until you save your project and give it a name.

Ruler. This is where you set your margins, which mark where a line of text begins and ends.

Insertion point. Look for this blinking vertical line to see where your typing will go. If you don't see it, click anywhere in the document. The insertion point will appear there.

Page number and location. These tell you what page you're working on, and exactly where on the page your insertion point is.

Direction bars and arrows. Use them to scroll up and down and left and right.

View buttons. Click on these to see your document in different ways. For instance, the NORMAL view is the easiest to work in. The PAGE LAYOUT view, on the other hand, allows you to see how your document will look when you print it.

It will soon be time to try your hand at a word processor project. The step-by-step lessons in this chapter will help you become an expert. These lessons are geared for Microsoft Word 97, but the idea will be similar for other word processors.

A Microsoft Word document

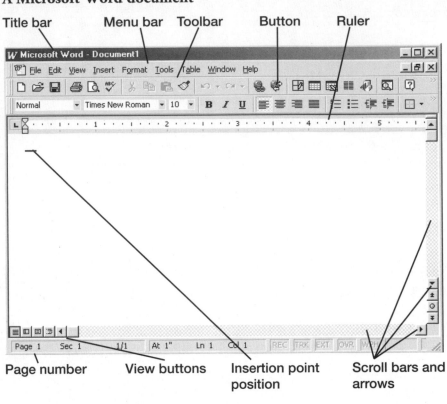

Title bar   Menu bar   Toolbar   Button   Ruler

Page number   View buttons   Insertion point position   Scroll bars and arrows

Meet your personal office assistant

Microsoft Word has a special feature that could save you time and a lot of anguish. It's called the Office Assistant, and it pops up when you open the application.

At first glance, you might not take Office Assistant seriously, since it's a comical cartoon paperclip. But get to know this little helper. The Office Assistant is there to answer your questions, give you tips, and help prevent problems.

Fast fix ▶ Don't fret if your Office Assistant is nowhere to be found when Word starts up. Activating him is as easy as 1-2-3. Just click on the Toolbar button with the question mark in it. Then click on the Office Assistant's face to open the dialog box.

The Office Assistant

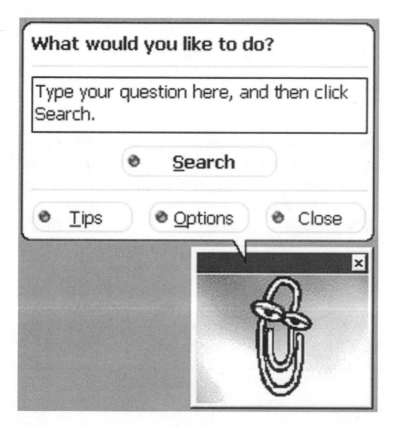

Here are the main ways the Office Assistant can come to your rescue.

Daily tips. The Office Assistant can offer a tip every time you open up Word. They range from the fastest way to change your text color, to the easiest way to put together a 100-page document. Click on CLOSE after you read it.

Anytime you want to read the tip again, click on the TIPS button in the Office Assistant dialog box.

To make sure you get your daily tip, click on the OPTIONS button in the dialog box. Then click on the check box for SHOW TIP OF THE DAY AT STARTUP.

Off-the-cuff tips. The lovable paperclip can offer help while you work, too. When you see a light bulb above its head, click on the bulb, and the Office Assistant will suggest a better way to do what you're doing. To turn on this feature, click on the OPTIONS button. Then check the three boxes under SHOW TIPS ABOUT.

Quick answers. Ask the Office Assistant a question and receive its advice right when you need it. Highlight in the dialog box where it says *Type your question here.* Next, type your question. Finally, click on SEARCH. The Office Assistant will then come up with a list of subjects that may answer your question. Click on the one that sounds like the closest match. If you aren't satisfied with the answer, click on HELP TOPICS for more options.

Quick tip ▶ You can give your Office Assistant a facelift if you get tired of the paperclip. Click on the OPTIONS button. In the GALLERY tab, click on NEXT to see all your choices. You can pick from an Einstein look-alike, a dog, a flying robot, and other wacky cartoon characters.

Become a wizard at writing letters

Now that you have a computer, why not write a friend so you can brag about it? The quickest and easiest way to get started is to familiarize yourself with Word's Letter Wizard. It can help you build a letter step by step.

The Letter Wizard will ask what information you want to include in your letter. Then — like magic — it inserts this data into a pre-made document called a template. Templates are like order forms with empty spaces where addresses, names, and other information need to go. The Wizard simply fills in the blanks for you.

To write your friend a snazzy-looking letter, open your word processor program. Click on the FILE menu and then on NEW. A dialog box opens that looks like this:

New dialog box

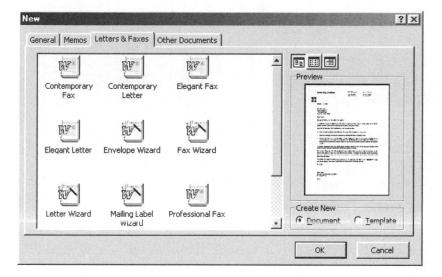

Next, follow these steps to begin the Letter Wizard.

1 Click on the LETTERS & FAXES tab.

2 Double-click on the LETTER WIZARD icon.

3 Choose to send one letter.

The LETTER WIZARD dialog box opens. This is where you type the information for your letter.

Letter Wizard dialog box

4 Click on the DATE LINE check box to tell the Wizard you want, or don't want, the date in your letter.

5 Pick the way you want the date to appear. Click on the arrow in the drop-down list box and then click on your choice.

6 Choose a page design and a letter style from the drop-down list boxes, and see how these will look in the preview areas.

Quick tip ▶ You can still use paper stationery for your correspondence, thanks to a special feature in Letter Wizard. Just click on the PRE-PRINTED LETTERHEAD check box in the dialog box. Make sure to fill in the extra information for your stationery letterhead.

---

7 Click on NEXT when you are finished.

8 Type in your friend's name and mailing address as you want them to appear in the letter.

9 Choose a salutation style from the option buttons and then one from the drop-down list box.

10 Click on NEXT.

11 Browse these fancier letter options. Most of them, like a subject line and an attention line, are for business letters. Click on any of them if you decide to use them. Also, pick specific styles from their drop-down list boxes.

12 Click on NEXT.

13 Type in your name and return address, or click on OMIT.

14 Click on the drop-down list box and select a complementary closing.

15 Click on FINISH.

Amazingly, a letter will appear on your screen with all of the information you just entered. A dialog box will also appear. It asks whether you want to create an envelope, a label, or another letter. Click on CANCEL. This leaves the body of the letter to do. But first, save your work.

1 Click on the FILE menu and then on SAVE.

2 Enter a file name — like LETTERTOFRIEND — or whatever you want to call your document.

3 Pick the location where you'll save it from the choices in the SAVE IN drop-down list box. (The MY DOCUMENTS folder is a smart spot for now).

4 Click on SAVE or SAVE AS, and the following dialog box will appear.

Save As dialog box

Now that your letter is safe and sound on the hard drive, get writing.

1 Highlight the line in the document that starts *Type your letter here.*

2 Start typing your letter. Notice how the word processor knows when you are at the end of a line. It will automatically wrap your sentence to the beginning of the next line, so don't add carriage returns.

3 Press the ENTER key after each paragraph. You are still in charge of carriage returns here.

Fast fix ▶ What if you've made it this far only to realize you entered the wrong address for your friend? No need to scrap the whole thing. Just click on the TOOLS menu and then on LETTER WIZARD. The dialog box reappears, so you can change addresses, dates, or any other information.

---

4 Remember to save your work every five minutes or so while you're writing. And save your letter one last time when you are through.

5 Click on the FILE menu and then on CLOSE to stop writing for now.

Building a letter with the Wizard was a snap. For an easy way to create memos, resumes, and other documents, check out Word's other Wizards. In the meantime, read on to discover how you can gussy up the letter you just created.

Fine tune your letter with formatting

Your letter looks fine just as it is, but why not improve on the job the Wizard started? You have the power to personalize and perfect your document, thanks to your word processor's formatting commands.

These tools allow you to change the size and the style of your letter's text. You can also space out the lines to make them easier to read — or adjust the way the word processor carries out carriage returns or wraps words around the margin. Before you tinker with your letter, you need to open it and bring the letter onto your screen. Make sure your word processing program is open and follow these steps:

1 Click on the FILE menu and then on OPEN. A dialog box will appear. Click on the LOOK IN drop-down list box.

2 Scroll down until you see MY DOCUMENTS, the folder you saved the letter in, and click on it.

3 Double-click on your letter's icon or name. Depending on your computer's settings, your file name may contain a period or dot followed by three letters. This is called an extension. For more information, see *Bring your files to order* on page 169.

Timesaver ▶ Skip a few steps by opening your letter the speedy way. When you click on the FILE menu, look down at its bottom. The name of your letter should be there, as well as any other documents you recently worked on. Click on the name. Your letter will appear on the screen.

4 Highlight the text starting with the date at the top, down to your name at the bottom.

5 Click on the FORMAT menu and then on FONT.

The FONT dialog box will appear. This is your tool for changing almost anything about your text.

Font dialog box

| Font | | | ? | X |

Font | Character Spacing | Animation

Font:

Calisto MT
Century Gothic
Comic Sans MS
Copperplate Gothic Bold
Copperplate Gothic Light

Font style:

Regular
Italic
Bold
Bold Italic

Size:

8
9
10
11
12

Tabs for more commands

Font list box

Underline:

(none)

Color:

Auto

Effects

☐ Strikethrough ☐ Shadow ☐ Small caps
☐ Double strikethrough ☐ Outline ☐ All caps
☐ Superscript ☐ Emboss ☐ Hidden
☐ Subscript ☐ Engrave

Effects check boxes

Preview

computer maestro

Preview area

Default...   OK   Cancel

6 Scroll through the FONT list box and click on CALISTO MT, which is the font used for the sample letter at the end of this story.

7 Look in the preview area to see how this font would look in your letter. If you don't like it, click on other fonts until you find one you like.

8 Make sure REGULAR is selected in the FONT STYLE list box. Clicking on BOLD would make the font look thicker and darker, while ITALIC would make the letters look slanted.

9 Click on 12 in the SIZE list box. The Wizard set the font at 10, but 12 is much easier to read. You can even test a larger font size in the preview area.

10 Get adventurous and click on the EFFECTS check boxes. Or try changing the text color or adding an underline. You can always switch them back if you don't like what you see in the preview area. Click on OK when you're through.

To make the highlighting disappear, click on any spot in your letter. Next, highlight only the body of your letter. Now you can adjust the way your paragraphs look.

Paragraph dialog box

11 Begin by clicking on the FORMAT menu and then on paragraph. The PARAGRAPH dialog box will pop up.

12 Click on the ALIGNMENT drop-down list box and then on LEFT. This setting has a more informal feel. It will keep the left margin of your letter straight, while leaving the right margin ragged. The Wizard automatically sets the alignment on JUSTIFIED, which makes both the left and right margins line up neatly.

Fast fix ▶ All of the changes you made in the dialog box now take effect in your actual letter. If at any time you decide you don't like any of the changes you made, just re-open the FONT dialog box and change your selections.

---

13 Click on the LINE SPACING drop-down list box and select 1.5 LINES. This will put more space between your lines of text, making them easier to read. If you want to add more space, preview DOUBLE line spacing.

14 Click on OK.

15 Click on the FILE menu and then on SAVE. Don't forget to save!

After making these formatting changes, your letter will be more pleasing to the eye. Not only to yours, but to your friend's, as well.

Just remember, if you decide you don't like one of your changes, simply open the appropriate dialog box and tinker with the settings.

Tech term ▶ Font – typeface of a particular style and size.

A sample letter after Wizard and formatting

```
LetterToFriend                                        _ □ ✕

  Mr. Matt Livingstone
  110 Clover Street
  Magnolia, GA 34567


  Dear Matt,

  I just bought a computer, and I'm well on my way to becoming a computer expert.
  Learning to use a computer is really a cinch.  The word processor is especially easy.
  It has a feature called the Letter Wizard, which helped me write this letter.

  It's about time I wrote to say hi.  I'm sorry I haven't written in a while, but now I
  don't have an excuse for not keeping in touch.

  You should think about getting a computer.  I can use it to write letters to friends
  and family, as well as balance my checkbook and send e-mails to my grandkids.  On
  top of all that, I can do research on the Internet to uncover my family roots and find
  the best way to invest my money.  A computer has so many possibilities!

  Well, enough about my computer.  Take care, and I hope to hear from you soon.


  Best wishes,


  Joe Sharpe








              232 COMPUTER EXPERT LANE
              WORD PROCESSOR, PA 12345
```

Rearrange your letter to read better

Now that you have your letter looking perfect, make sure it reads perfectly, too. Scan over it to see if your sentences are all in the order you want them.

If they aren't, don't worry. Your word processor makes this proof-reading chore a snap. You just need to learn the tricks to moving text around in a document.

BACKSPACE key. Press this key when you find something you want to delete, or remove, from your letter. First, click on the text directly to the right of what you want to delete. The insertion point will appear there. Then press BACKSPACE as many times as it takes to remove the troublesome text. (Please note — on some keyboards, this key may be called DELETE or have a left-pointing arrow on it.)

For instance, pretend this page is a document on your computer screen, and you want to delete the word *computer* from this sentence. To do this, you would click on the right side of the *r.* Then you would press BACKSPACE nine times to erase the word and the extra space.

Timesaver ▶ To delete something in one fell swoop, highlight everything you want gone — like the entire word *computer.* Press the BACKSPACE key once. And voila — the word will vanish.

Cut and paste. You're ready for the next trick — moving words from one section of your letter to another. In word processor lingo, this technique is called cut and paste.

To see how it works, imagine that the sample letter from the previous lesson is yours. After proofreading it, you decide the first paragraph would read better as the second, and vice versa. Instead of deleting the whole thing and re-typing it, follow these steps:

1 Highlight the whole first paragraph, going left to right from *I just* all the way down to *letter.*

2 Click on the EDIT menu and then on CUT. The paragraph will disappear.

The sample letter — before cut and paste

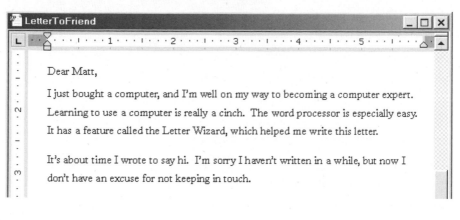

3 Click on the end of the new first paragraph. (To the right of the words *in touch*.) Press ENTER once.

4 Click on the EDIT menu and then on PASTE. Abracadabra, the missing paragraph will reappear in its new spot.

5 Press BACKSPACE once to get rid of the extra line created during the cut and paste.

The sample letter — after cut and paste

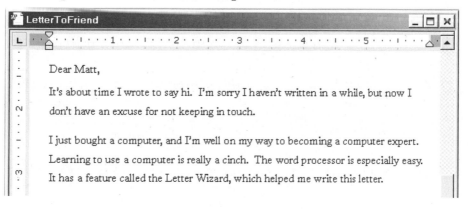

If you make a change you don't like, use the Undo command. Look for it in the EDIT menu, or as the Toolbar button with the counter-clockwise arrow in it. When you click on it, the word processor undoes the change you just made.

Copy and paste. It's also possible to move words without having to delete the original ones. Let's say you wanted to insert more of your friend's name into the sample letter. In the sample letter, for instance, why not put Matt's name at the end of the first sentence in the third paragraph? This would make the letter sound more personal.

To do this, highlight *Matt* in the salutation. Next, click on the EDIT menu and then on COPY. Position the insertion point directly to the right of *computer.* Then click on the EDIT menu and then on PASTE. The name will appear. Paste it in as many places as you like.

Quick tip ▶ Cut, copy, and paste are also buttons on the STANDARD Toolbar. To locate them, first click on the VIEW menu and then select TOOLBARS. Make sure STANDARD is checked. Look at the Toolbars afterward. You'll see a button with scissors in it (cut), a button with two documents in it (copy), and a button with a clipboard and document in it (paste).

All these commands work like magic when you are making changes to your document. That's why it's important to remember them, even if you didn't find a reason to use them now in your letter.

It's also key to learn to use the other editing tools in your word processor. Read on to find out more.

Check your spelling and grammar

You've done everything you can to spruce up your letter. Now let your word processor do the rest. It has editing tools that can help you scan your letter for grammar and spelling mistakes and can even correct them for you.

Spelling and grammar checker. You don't need to dig up your old grammar book to check your command of the English language. Just click on the TOOLS menu and then on SPELLING AND GRAMMAR.

The checker will go through your letter word by word. When it finds a possible mistake, it will alert you with this dialog box:

Spelling and Grammar dialog box

Misspelled word

Correction suggestions

Most times, the checker will be correct, and the word will be misspelled. In this case, select a replacement word from the SUGGESTIONS text box. Click on CHANGE. But if you think the word should be spelled the way you have it, click on IGNORE.

Fast fix ▶ Your decisions in the SPELLING AND GRAMMAR dialog box are not set in stone. If you clicked on CHANGE and you decide you should have clicked on IGNORE — or the other way around — then click on UNDO. The checker will go back to your original version.

Your word processor also points out possible grammar mistakes while it checks spelling. The Office Assistant explains why the grammar may be wrong. If you agree, fix the problem by following the same steps previously mentioned. If you disagree, leave it alone.

Timesaver ▶ The program can also point out mistakes while you're working. To see how this works, click on the OPTIONS button in the SPELLING AND GRAMMAR dialog box. Next, click on the check boxes for CHECK SPELLING AS YOU TYPE and CHECK GRAMMAR AS YOU TYPE. Then click on OK. Afterward, you may notice wiggly underlines in your letter. A red line shows a spelling mistake, and a green one shows a grammar error.

Find and replace. Believe it or not, your word processor is not perfect. It may miss some spelling errors, especially if they occur in the names of people and places.

For an example, let's return to the sample letter from the past lessons. This time, pretend you forgot that your make-believe friend Matt actually likes to be called Matthew. The spellchecker didn't know this, so it left *Matt* throughout the letter. That means you have to make all the changes, right? Actually, that's where the find and replace command comes in handy.

To turn it on:

1 Click on the EDIT menu and then on REPLACE.

2 Type *Matt* into the FIND WHAT text box.

3 Type *Matthew* into the REPLACE WITH text box.

4 Click on REPLACE ALL.

The word processor will then make all the changes for you, and it will tell you how many changes it made.

Find and Replace dialog box

```
┌─────────────────────────────────────────────────────────────┐
│ Find and Replace                                    ? │ × │
├─────────────────────────────────────────────────────────────┤
│                                                             │
│    Find    │ Replace │  Go To                                │
│                                                             │
│  Find what:     [Matt                        ▼]  [ Find Next ]│
│       Options: Search Down                                   │
│                                                  [  Cancel  ] │
│  Replace with:  [Matthew                     ▼]  [  Replace  ]│
│                                                             │
│                                                  [ Replace All ]│
│                                                             │
│                                                  [  More ▼  ] │
└─────────────────────────────────────────────────────────────┘
```

Now that your letter is perfect, you can see how powerful and useful your word processor can be. Still, you've only touched the tip of the iceberg. There's more to discover about this incredible software.

A lesson in creating labels

Your word processor can spare you from hand addressing a mountain of envelopes. It may even have a Wizard that can whip up the mailing labels for you.

This comes in handy around Christmas time, or any occasion that leaves you with a big stack of letters to mail.

To conquer that stack, open your word processor. Click on the FILE menu and then on NEW. In the LETTERS & FAXES tab of the dialog box, double-click on the MAILING LABEL WIZARD icon.

Next, click on CREATE LABELS FOR A MAILING LIST. When the MAIL MERGE HELPER dialog box opens, follow these steps.

Create Data Source dialog box

```
┌──────────────────────────────────────────────────────────────┐
│ Create Data Source                                    [?][X]   │
├──────────────────────────────────────────────────────────────┤
│  A mail merge data source is composed of rows of data. The     │
│  first row is called the header row. Each of the columns in    │
│  the header row begins with a field name.                      │
│                                                                │
│  Word provides commonly used field names in the list below.    │
│  You can add or remove field names to customize the header row.│
│                                                                │
│  Field name:              Field names in header row:           │
│  ┌──────────────────┐     ┌────────────────────┐  ┌──┐         │
│  ││                 │     │Title            ▲│  │ ↑ │         │
│  └──────────────────┘     │FirstName        │  └──┘         │
│  ┌──────────────────┐     │LastName         │  Move          │
│  │ Add Field Name ≫ │     │Address1         │  ┌──┐         │
│  └──────────────────┘     │Address2         │  │ ↓ │         │
│                           │City             │  └──┘         │
│  ┌──────────────────┐     │State        ▼│                 │
│  │ Remove Field Name│     └────────────────────┘              │
│  └──────────────────┘                                          │
│                                                                │
│  ┌──────────────┐      ┌──────────┐      ┌──────────┐         │
│  │ MS Query...  │      │    OK    │      │  Cancel  │         │
│  └──────────────┘      └──────────┘      └──────────┘         │
└──────────────────────────────────────────────────────────────┘
```

1 Click on GET DATA and then on CREATE DATA SOURCE. The CREATE DATA SOURCE dialog box will appear. Here you'll see a list of field names. Fields are the categories of information that go in your labels, like name and address.

2 Click on OK.

3 Save your fields in the SAVE AS or FILE NAME dialog box that automatically pops open here. Give the file a name like *Label Fields*. Select MY DOCUMENTS in the SAVE IN drop-down list box and click on SAVE.

4 Click on SET UP MAIN DOCUMENT.

FYI ▶ To buy the sticky labels you'll use with your printer, go to your local office supply store. Find the right size and type for your envelopes. When it comes to brands, Avery is the most popular and works with most word processors.

The LABEL OPTIONS dialog box will open. This is where you start building a label template.

5 Give the Wizard technical information to help it design the template. This includes your printer type, your brand of labels, and the labels' product number. Look for this last bit of information on the label packaging.

6 Click on OK.

The CREATE LABELS dialog box will open. You'll arrange the fields in your template here.

Create Labels dialog box

7 Click on INSERT MERGE FIELD.

8 Click on the field you want to appear first on your label. TITLE or FIRST NAME is a good choice. Whichever field you pick, it will appear in the SAMPLE LABEL preview area with chevrons (<< >>) around it.

9 Press the space bar.

10 Click on INSERT MERGE FIELD again and click on your second field. Press the space bar.

11 Repeat this for each field you want in your label, and press ENTER when you want to start a new line. And don't forget to type in a comma between the city and state fields.

12 Click on OK when your sample label looks something like the preceding illustration.

The MAIL MERGE HELPER dialog box will appear again. This time click on the EDIT button that's to the right of the big number 2. Then click on LABEL FIELDS, the name of the file you just saved. A document will appear containing all of your fields.

13 Look for the smallest Toolbar at the top of your screen. This is the DATABASE Toolbar. It should look like this:

The database Toolbar

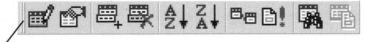

The DATA FORM button

14 Click on the button that has a pencil and a grid in it.

Yet another dialog box will appear — the DATA FORM dialog box. It's a database where you'll store all of your mailing list information.

15 Type the name and address of the first person on your mailing list into the corresponding fields.

16 Click on ADD NEW when you are through. A new blank data form will appear.

17 Type in the information for the next person on your address list. Click on ADD NEW. Repeat for everyone on your list.

18 Click on OK after you type in the information for the last person on your mailing list.

Timesaver ▶ To skip having to input all of this label information, use the address book from your e-mail program. In the MAIL MERGE HELPER dialog box, click on GET DATA and then on OPEN ADDRESS BOOK. For more information about e-mail and address books, see *Keep friends at your fingertips* on page 279.

---

19 Click on the TOOLS menu and then on MAIL MERGE. This will re-open the MAIL MERGE HELPER dialog box one last time.

20 Click on EDIT and then on DOCUMENT2.

21 Click on MERGE.

22 Click on MERGE again.

The label templates will appear again, but this time they'll be filled with your mailing list information. Remember to click on SAVE right away. Give this document a name like FINISHEDLABELS.

Your labels are now ready for printing, or you can wait until later to print. Whatever you do, the computer will eventually ask if you want to save DOCUMENT2, which is the template. Click on SAVE and give it a name like LABELTEMPLATE. Then you can use it the next time you have a stack of letters to mail.

Design a to-do list

Now it's time to try word processing without the Wizard's help. This may sound scary at first, but it's actually fun. You'll have the power to design your own special document. And you'll be able to perform nifty style tricks, like adding bullets and columns.

To take your first step toward formatting freedom, create a make-believe practice document — a to-do list for an upcoming vacation.

Begin by launching a new word processor document by clicking on the FILE menu and then on NEW. This time, however, click on the BLANK DOCUMENT icon under the GENERAL tab. This opens a plain document you can use for any word processor project.

Play it safe ▶ Don't forget to click on SAVE. **Type in a name, like** *ToDoList,* **and save the file to the** MY DOCUMENTS **folder. Save the document often while you're working on it, too.**

The insertion point will blink at the top left corner of the document, waiting for you to start typing.

1 Type in a title for your to-do list, such as *My vacation to-do list.*

2 Press ENTER twice and then begin typing your list.

3 Start with clothes you'll need to pack. Then include toiletries, as well as documents you want to take. Add people you want to talk with before your departure, and items you need to buy. At the end, tack on last-minute chores.

4 Make sure to press ENTER after typing in each entry.

After you type a few lines, the software may automatically add numbers to your list. This tool may be useful in the future. But to practice formatting on your own, turn off this command for now.

Click on the TOOLS menu and then on AUTOCORRECT. Under the AUTOFORMAT AS YOU TYPE tab, uncheck the boxes for AUTOMATIC BULLETED LISTS and AUTOMATIC NUMBERED LISTS. Click on OK.

Now it's time to have some fun with formatting. Instead of the old way to format, try something new — use the FORMATTING Toolbar.

Click on the VIEW menu and then select TOOLBARS. Click on FOR-MATTING. This Toolbar will appear.

The Formatting Toolbar

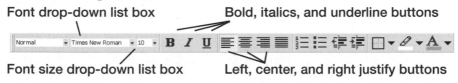

Font drop-down list box   Bold, italics, and underline buttons

Font size drop-down list box   Left, center, and right justify buttons

5 Highlight the title of your to-do list.

6 Use the drop-down list boxes in the Toolbar to increase the font size to 16. Then change the font to TAHOMA.

7 Click on the button with the B in it to make the title bold. To center the title in the middle of the page, click on the button with the six centered lines in it.

8 Highlight the entire document, from the title down to your last list item.

9 Click on the FORMAT menu and then on PARAGRAPH. Click on the LINE SPACING drop-down list box and then on DOUBLE.

This will add space to your list so it's easier to read. But this may also make it longer than one page. Trim it back down to one page by arranging your list into columns.

10 Highlight everything in the document except the title of your list.

11 Click on the FORMAT menu and then on COLUMNS.

12 Click on the TWO button, which has two columns of lines in it, under PRESETS. Click on OK.

Your list is almost complete. Just one last step is left — to add check boxes to it.

1 Make sure your list is still highlighted, and click on the FOR-MAT menu and then on BULLETS AND NUMBERING.

2 Click on the BULLETED tab in the dialog box that opens.

3 Look for the button with empty square bullets in it. Click on it. These empty square bullets make great check boxes for a to-do list. Or try another bullet design, like checkmarks or diamonds. It's your list, so design it your way. Click on OK.

A sample to-do list

My vacation to-do list

☐ Pack shorts	☐ Bring Bible
☐ Pack pants	☐ Call the kids
☐ Pack shirts	☐ Call the neighbors
☐ Pack swimsuit	☐ Call cousin Ethel
☐ Pack belts	☐ Buy bug spray
☐ Pack socks	☐ Buy sunscreen
☐ Pack shoes	☐ Buy disposable cameras
☐ Pack ties	☐ Buy a hat
☐ Pack T-shirts	☐ Buy sunglasses
☐ Pack dinner jacket	☐ Clean up house
☐ Remember toothbrush	☐ Leave food out for pets
☐ Remember toothpaste	☐ Turn on automatic timers for lamps
☐ Remember floss	☐ Unplug all other outlets
☐ Remember soap	☐ Empty the refrigerator
☐ Remember shampoo	☐ Say goodbye to my computer
☐ Remember shaving cream	☐ Set booby traps for would-be robbers
☐ Remember razors	

Your list should look something like the example. If you're not going on vacation — no problem. Your new list-making skills will make a difference whenever you take a trip — even if it's just to the store.

Start a party with your computer

You can create a festive, professional-looking party invitation with the tips in this next lesson. It's easy once you learn how to add an eye-catching border to your document and line up your text perfectly.

To begin, open up a new, blank document in your word processor. Save it with a name like PARTYINVITE.

Next, change the margins of the document. It'll make the invitation appear like it came right from a printing shop.

1   Click on the FILE menu and then on PAGE SETUP.

2   Change the settings for the left, right, top, and bottom margins by clicking on the spinner arrows. Set the margins to 2 inches, and click on OK.

Now that you set up the edge of the document, wrap a border around it. A border can make your invitation appear zany or elegant — whatever suits the kind of party you're having.

3   Click on the FORMAT menu and then on BORDERS AND SHADING. Go to the PAGE BORDER tab.

4   Click on the ART drop-down list box and choose a border, like balloons. Peek at your selection in the PREVIEW area.

5   Set WIDTH to 20 PT by clicking on the spinner arrows, and click on the OPTIONS button.

6 To guarantee that your border fits perfectly around your invitation, click on the MEASURE FROM drop-down list box and click on TEXT.

7 Click on OK to close each dialog box.

Borders and Shading dialog box

FYI ▶ With a border, your invitation will come out full of color — if you have a color printer. If not, print your invitations in black and white or e-mail the invitation, color and all. See *Form healthy e-mail attachments* on page 289 to learn more about sending attachments.

---

8 Type in an announcement, like *You're invited to a graduation party*, on the top line. Highlight it and format it anyway you want. Be creative and make it stand out.

9 Press the RIGHT ARROW on your keyboard to un-highlight the announcement text.

10 Press ENTER as many times as it takes to move the insertion point to the middle of the document.

11 Set the format for your party information text ahead of time. It's a good idea to stick with a readable font size like 14 point and switch back to left justify. Change the color and font style, too, if you like.

Quick tip ▶ Here's yet another way to format. Right-click on highlighted text and click on font or paragraph. The corresponding dialog box will open.

Now type in the party information so everybody knows when and where to attend the festivities. You could just enter it in willy-nilly, or you could line up everything neatly — with a table.

12 Type in your first bit of information, like *Day.* Press the TAB key and type in the day it's to take place, like *Saturday.* Press ENTER.

13 Type your second bit of info, like *Time.* Press TAB, followed by the actual time it's to take place. Press ENTER.

The TAB and the ENTER keys are crucial to building a table around the text. Imagine a table to be like a bookshelf. Pressing the TAB and the ENTER keys are like putting in the shelving that keeps the books in their places.

14 Repeat this for all of your information and highlight it when you're through typing.

15 Click on the TABLE menu and then on CONVERT TEXT TO TABLE. In the dialog box, set the NUMBER OF COLUMNS to 2. Click on OK. Rectangles, or cells, will box in your party information and organize it.

16 To remove the table border, click on the FORMAT menu and on BORDERS AND SHADING. Then click on the NONE button under SETTING. Finally, click on OK. On your screen, you'll still see a faint table border. It's only for your reference and won't show up when you print.

17 Position the insertion point below and out of the table. Press ENTER as many times as it takes to move the insertion point near the bottom of the page.

18 Type your R.S.V.P. information and format it however you like.

A sample invitation

Play it safe ▶ To make sure the invitation turns out like the one pictured, do what's called a print preview. Click on the FILE menu and then on PRINT PREVIEW. Your document will appear as it would if you printed it. If you need to make changes, click on the CLOSE button, and your document will go back to its normal view.

Add pizazz with clip art

You can guarantee a packed house at your next party with eye-catching invitations using clip art. This professional artwork usually comes free with your word processor. It's great for jazzing up an invitation and other documents.

To learn how to do it, open your invitation. Next, position the insertion point just below the first line in the document.

1   Click on the INSERT menu and then select PICTURE.

2   Click on CLIP ART. The clip art gallery will open. Select one of the pictures and click on the INSERT button. If the clip art is too big, click on the FORMAT menu and then on PICTURE to shrink it. Then look for the SCALE spinners in the SIZE tab. Set them to 50 percent for starters. Click on OK.

Timesaver ▶ If the clip art is still too large, try the quick way to change its size. Click on the clip art picture in your document. Move your cursor onto one of the little squares surrounding it. Your cursor will turn into a two-headed arrow. Click on it, hold it, and drag in the edge of the clip art until it's the size you want.

3   Center the clip art in your document. To move it, click on the middle of the clip art, hold it, and drag its dotted outline. Move it so it's still below the first line of text.

Your document should still be one page long at this point. If it's not, you can get rid of extra space in your invitation.

4 Highlight the blank space between the clip art and your party information. Just click on the space, hold the mouse button down, and drag the highlight over the space. Press BACKSPACE.

5 Highlight the space between the party info and the *Regrets only* line if you need to delete more. Press BACKSPACE.

An invitation with clip art

You're invited to a
graduation party

Day	Saturday, October 10
Time	12 p.m. to 5 p.m.
Place	123 Oak Lane
Guest of honor	Matt Livingstone

Regrets only
(123) 555-7890

When you are finished, your invitation should look something like the sample pictured.

FYI ▶ You can also insert your own pictures and photographs into documents. Instead of clicking on CLIP ART in the INSERT menu, click on FROM FILE. For more on storing and using photos on your computer, see *Digital photography: It's a snap* on page 358.

Save time using shortcuts

You're close to becoming a word processor wiz. You only need to take one more step — learn the shortcut keys. These "shortcuts" are the quickest ways to perform common commands, like undo, cut and paste, and save. Here's a handy chart of the most useful ones.

Press these keys at the same time	Command
CONTROL + A	Select all the text in a document
CONTROL + B	Bold the selected text
CONTROL + C	Copy the selected text
CONTROL + E	Center a selected paragraph
CONTROL + F	Find and replace words
CONTROL + I	Italicize the selected text
CONTROL + L	Left-justify a selected paragraph
CONTROL + N	Open a new document
CONTROL + O	Open a saved document
CONTROL + P	Print a document
CONTROL + R	Right-justify a selected paragraph
CONTROL + S	Save a document
CONTROL + U	Underline the selected text
CONTROL + V	Paste the selected text
CONTROL + W	Close a document

CONTROL + X	Cut the selected text
CONTROL + Z	Undo the last command
CONTROL + 1	Single-space a selected paragraph
CONTROL + 2	Double-space a selected paragraph

That's how easy word processing can be. By holding down two keys at the same time, you can carry out numerous commands. What's even better — many of these shortcut keys work for other programs, too, like spreadsheets.

Get acquainted with a spreadsheet

Nothing can match a spreadsheet program when it comes to doing finances and other math-related jobs. Spreadsheets make organizing and calculating numbers as easy as pointing and clicking.

You could do your finances the old-fashioned way — using ledger paper and a calculator, but that can take forever. Instead, hand over your figures to your computer's "accountant" — the spreadsheet.

This program can crunch your numbers in a fraction of a second, and it can build neat tables and graphs, too. And just like a word processor, a spreadsheet program allows you to store and print out your work. Meanwhile, you won't even break a sweat.

So get to know what's in a spreadsheet. It'll pay you back dividends for years to come.

Workbook. This is the general name for a spreadsheet file. Each workbook is like a project folder, which can contain three or more worksheets.

Worksheets. Filled with a crisscrossed grid, these look like pieces of graph paper on your screen. Space out your work in as many

142

worksheets as you need. Tabs at the bottom of the screen allow you to flip between them.

Cells. Insert numbers, words, and math problems into the rectangles, or cells, in the grid. The cells help you line up all of your work into columns and rows.

Cell coordinates. Cells are labeled alphabetically going left to right, and numerically going down. These coordinates help you locate cells and their information quickly.

Title bar. This is where you'll find the title of your workbook. It will say BOOK1 until you save and name it.

Menu bar. Click on these headings just as you would in the word processor. Just remember — some of the menus and commands are different in a spreadsheet.

Name bar. This text box tells you the name of the cell you are currently in.

Toolbars. Don't forget the buttons located here. They are still some of the fastest ways to carry out commands.

Formula bar. Here you can type what you want inserted into a cell. It's also where you can carry out adding, multiplying, and other math problems.

Now that you're familiar with a spreadsheet, don't hesitate to dive right into the following step-by-step lessons. However, please note — these lessons are tailored to Microsoft Excel 97. The idea will be similar for other spreadsheet applications, but the details won't be exactly the same.

A typical spreadsheet workbook

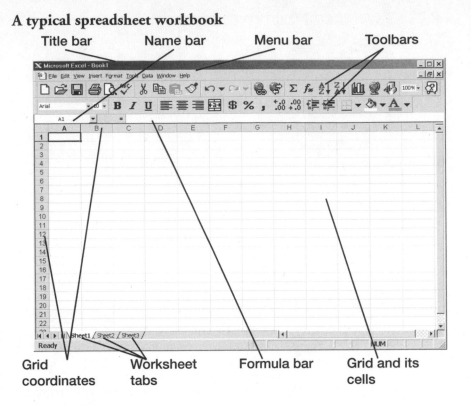

Title bar   Name bar   Menu bar   Toolbars

Grid coordinates   Worksheet tabs   Formula bar   Grid and its cells

Simplify your household budget

A spreadsheet can transform your household budget from a guessing game to a sure thing. All it takes is a little know-how on your part.

For starters, learn how to get around in a workbook and input figures into cells. This may seem as tricky as moving pieces on a chessboard, but it's more like a checkerboard, where jumping around is simple.

It's also a snap to enter information into a cell. Find out how easy it is by creating your own monthly budget.

1 Start your spreadsheet program. A blank workbook will automatically open.

---

2   Type *Monthly Budget* into cell A1, which is always the cell you start in when you first open a workbook.

3   Press the DOWN ARROW key. Your text is now set in cell A1.

4   Click on cell A4 and type *Bottom Line*.

5   Press the RIGHT ARROW key to enter it. Then press the key twice until you highlight cell D4. Type *Amount.*

FYI ▶ There's more than one way to move around in the grid. You can simply click on a particular cell. Or press the ARROW keys to skip from one cell to another until you reach the one you want. Once you're there, the cell will become highlighted. Then type in your information. Afterward, press an ARROW key to move out of the cell. Pressing ENTER works, too. Or just click on another cell when you're through typing.

---

6   Click on cell A5, type in *Income,* and then press ENTER.

7   Type *Total Expenses* into cell A6.

8   Move to cell A7 and type in *Savings.*

9   Click on cell A10 and type in *Individual Expenses.*

10   Press the RIGHT ARROW three times to get to cell D10 and type in *Amount.*

Now it's time to record each of your individual expenses. Include rent or mortgage payments, utilities, insurance, car payments, groceries, credit card bills, medication, and miscellaneous.

11 Type the first expense, *Rent* or *Mortgage payment*, into cell A11.

12 List the rest of your expenses below it. Each expense should be in its own cell. After you type the last one, skip over the cell below it, which is cell A19.

13 Type *Total Expenses* into cell A20.

You just completed the hardest part of building a spreadsheet — designing and typing in the column and row headings. But don't stop here. You still need to plug in the numbers for your income and expenses.

14 Start by typing the amount of your monthly income into cell D5.

15 Type your first individual expense amount into cell D11. Then type the figures for each of your other individual expenses into their matching cells in column D.

Fast fix ▸ It's easy to correct typing mistakes in a spreadsheet. If you catch them while you're still in the cell, press the BACKSPACE key to delete them. If you've already moved out of a cell, move back into the cell. Press BACKSPACE to erase everything in it. Or click on the Formula bar and edit the information there. Press ENTER when you're through.

Just like that, your spreadsheet is almost complete. You only need to do one more thing. Tell the spreadsheet what numbers you want added and subtracted. To do this, you need to insert functions, which are like the math formulas you learned in high school.

16 Highlight cell D20.

17 Click on the INSERT menu and then on FUNCTION. The PASTE FUNCTION dialog box will open.

Paste Function dialog box

18 Click on ALL in the FUNCTION CATEGORY list box. In the FUNCTION NAME list box, you'll see every function that your spreadsheet has to offer.

19 Scroll down to SUM and double-click on it. The SUM dialog box will open.

The sum function allows you to add together a range or string of cells. In this case, you want to add up the numbers in column D. Amazingly, the spreadsheet can guess this ahead of time.

In the NUMBER 1 text box, it may have already inputted D11:D19. That means it knows to add the numbers in all of the cells from D11 to D19. All you need to do is click on OK.

If the function's not there, type it in yourself. Make sure it matches the following illustration.

Sum dialog box

```
┌─ SUM ──────────────────────────────────────────────┐
│   Number1 │D11:D19                          │▼│ = {650;320;425;325;1 │
│   Number2 │                                 │▼│ = number             │
│   Number3 │                                 │▼│ = number             │
│                                                = 2470                │
│  Adds all the numbers in a range of cells.                           │
│                                                                      │
│      Number2: number1,number2,... are 1 to 30 numbers to sum. Logical values and │
│               text are ignored in cells, included if typed as arguments.         │
│   [?]      Formula result =2470               [   OK   ]  [ Cancel ] │
└──────────────────────────────────────────────────────┘
```

20 Move to cell D6 and type in: *=D20*. This is a simple function that will copy the contents of cell D20 into cell D6.

That way, it will be easier to keep track of your bottom line — the total amount you make and spend. Subtract those two figures, and you can find out how much money you save.

21 Move to cell D7. Type in *=D5-D6*. The equal sign tells the spreadsheet you're typing in a function. And the rest is your own homemade formula, which tells the program to subtract your total expenses from your income. Press ENTER.

Notice how the spreadsheet now shows a number in cell D7. If you want to see the function again, click back on the cell. Look in the Formula bar. There you'll see and change the function.

The total in cell D7 is the amount of money you saved that month. You can use your budget spreadsheet to save next month, as well as every month of the year. Here's how:

1 Save the spreadsheet and then close it. Re-open it when the next month rolls around and you want to plan your budget.

2 Click on the FILE menu and then on SAVE AS. Change the file name to FEBRUARYBUDGET, and click on SAVE.

Remember, you won't lose last month's budget. With the SAVE AS command, you will make a duplicate of it, which you can change without affecting the original.

3 Switch the figures in this new budget. Let's say you plan to spend $25 less on credit card bills this month, but $50 more on groceries. Click on cell D15 and adjust your grocery costs. Do the same in cell D16 for your credit card amount.

The spreadsheet will re-do your math. In cell D20, it will show the new total for your expenses. Like a chain reaction, the new expense total will appear in cell D6, too. The spreadsheet will also recalculate your total savings. It will do this anytime you change your numbers.

When you are finished with your new budget, save it. Come next month, you can change the numbers all over again.

A finished budget

	A	B	C	D	E	F
	JanuaryBudget					
1	Monthly Budget					
2						
3						
4	Bottom Line			Amount		
5	Income			3500		
6	Total Expenses			2470		
7	Savings			1030		
8						
9						
10	Individual Expenses			Amount		
11	Rent			650		
12	Utilities			320		
13	Insurance			425		
14	Car payments			325		
15	Groceries			100		
16	Credit card bills			50		
17	Medication			200		
18	Misc.			400		
19						
20	Total Expenses			2470		
21						
22						
23						

Sheet1 / Sheet2 / Sheet3

149

Enhance your budget with formatting

Your monthly budget will work fine just as it is. But your spread-sheet software offers so many formatting options, it's a shame not to use them.

With the formatting tools, you can take your plain budget and get creative. Add a border and color to make one section of your spread-sheet stand out from another. Change the fonts of your letters and numbers so they're larger and bolder. And widen the grid columns or lengthen the rows.

To learn how to do all this and more, follow these steps.

1 Start your spreadsheet program. Click on the FILE menu and then on OPEN. Click on the icon for your budget workbook.

JanuaryBudget.xls

2 Highlight cell A1.

3 Click on the FORMAT menu and then on CELLS. The FOR-MAT CELLS dialog box will appear. This dialog box is similar to one in the word processor.

4 Click on the FONT tab.

5 Change the font, size, and style of your spreadsheet's title (MONTHLYBUDGET) so it stands out. Then click on OK.

Notice how your cell will expand when you increase the font size. The top of the cell will stretch to make room for the bigger letters. Meanwhile, your words will appear to stray into the cell next door. No matter how far they go, your words are still in cell A1, or their original cell. You'll need to click on that cell to change them.

FYI ▶ You can set your cells to stay the same size no matter how large your font is. **Click on the** FORMAT **menu and then on** CELLS. **In the** ALIGNMENT **tab, check the box for** SHRINK TO FIT **or** WRAP TEXT.

---

6 Highlight row 4. To do this in one step, click on the row's coordinate button located on the left side of the spreadsheet.

7 Format these two headings so they're easy to notice. Then highlight row 10, then row 20. Format these the same way.

Timesaver ▶ The FORMATTING **Toolbar can handle all of your font and style jobs, too. If it's not already showing, click on the** VIEW **menu, select** TOOLBARS, **and click on** FORMATTING. **Or try another quick trick — right-click your mouse when you have cells selected. Then click on** FORMAT CELLS.

The Formatting Toolbar

To make your spreadsheet's headings even fancier, whip them into shape in two other ways. First, increase the size of their cells.

1 Move your cursor onto the bottom line of the coordinate button for row 1. The cursor will become a two-headed arrow with a line through it.

2 Click on the button, hold it, and drag down. The bottom line of the row will become a dashed line. Move it down as far as you like.

3 Do the same with rows 4, 10, and 20. To make them all the same size, keep an eye on the height measurement. Set the rows' heights to be the same.

Making a row bigger

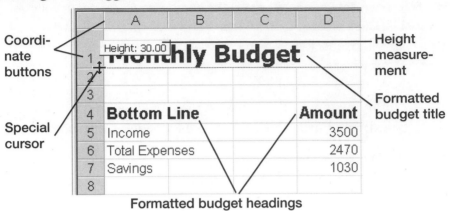

Coordi-
nate
buttons

Special
cursor

Height: 30.00

Height
measure-
ment

Formatted
budget title

Formatted budget headings

Next, draw a border around these rows and shade in their cells.

4 Highlight cells A1 through D1.

5 Open the FORMAT CELLS dialog box. In the BORDER tab, click on the OUTLINE button. This will draw a line around the outside of those cells.

6 Click on the PATTERNS tab and pick a color for your cell shading. A light color, like yellow or aqua, works best. That way, you can still read the text in the cells. Click on OK when you're through. Repeat for the first four cells in rows 4, 10, and 20.

Quick tip ▶ Here's the fastest way to copy the border and cell shading onto those other rows. Highlight the cells. Click on the EDIT menu and then on REPEAT FORMAT CELLS.

Now your spreadsheet can balance your budget, and it looks great, too. But why stop there? For instance, if you're proud of how much money you save each month, show off that part of your budget.

To do this, separate it from the other rows of your spreadsheet.

1 Click on cell A7. That's the row for your savings information.

2 Click on the INSERT menu and then on ROW. This will place a new blank row of cells between rows 6 and 7. You can also do the same thing with the columns.

3 Make your savings information even easier to read. Change its font, style, and size any way you like.

Add extra rows to your spreadsheet if you need to include more individual expenses — like clothes, shopping, and entertainment. Create the new rows, type in the expense name in column A and the amount of the expense in column D. Don't worry. The spreadsheet will take care of re-calculating your bottom line.

Fast fix ▶ To delete one of your new rows, highlight a cell in that row. Then click on the EDIT menu and on DELETE. Select ENTIRE ROW and click on OK.

There's one last styling trick you should know. Since you're dealing with money, it makes sense to add dollar signs to your spreadsheet.

1 Highlight column D.

2 Open the FORMAT CELLS dialog box. Click on the NUMBER tab. Click on CURRENCY in the CATEGORY text box. Then click on OK.

With all these additions to your budget, it will look like a professional accountant handled your finances. Your computer's accountant, that is.

The budget after formatting

	A	B	C	D	E	F
JanuaryBudget					_ □ ×	
1	**Monthly Budget**					
2						
3						
4	**Bottom Line**			**Amount**		
5	Income			$3,500.00		
6	Total Expenses			$2,470.00		
7						
8	**Savings**			**$1,030.00**		
9						
10						
11	**Individual Expenses**			**Amount**		
12	Rent			$650.00		
13	Utilities			$320.00		
14	Insurance			$425.00		
15	Car payments			$325.00		
16	Groceries			$100.00		
17	Credit card bills			$50.00		
18	Medication			$200.00		
19	Misc.			$400.00		
20						
21	**Total Expenses**			**$2,470.00**		
22						
23						
24						

Sheet1 / Sheet2 / Sheet3 /

Chart a course for your budget

Your spreadsheet program offers several ways to build a graph using the numbers from your budget. You don't need a ruler or an art degree to make one. And you end up with a chart that's fit for an important business meeting.

To start, re-open your monthly budget. Then follow these steps to chart your expenses.

1   Click on the INSERT menu and then on CHART. The CHART WIZARD dialog box opens. Like the other Wizards you've used, this one will help you every step of the way.

2   Pick a type of chart and click on it. Then choose a chart sub-type, or design. A simple column or bar graph is probably the best bet for your budget. Click on NEXT.

The Chart Wizard will ask what numbers you want included in the chart.

3   Type *D11:D18*. This range will tell the Wizard you want to use cells D11 through D18, which are your individual expense costs. Click on NEXT.

A new dialog box will appear with a preview of your chart in it.

4   Type in a chart title, like *Expense Report.*

5   Name the X, or horizontal, axis *Individual Expenses.* Type it into the CATEGORY (X) AXIS text box.

6   Give the Y, or vertical, axis a label, too, like *Amount.* Type it into the VALUE (Y) AXIS text box. Click on NEXT.

7   Pick a chart location. Try clicking on the AS NEW SHEET option button. This will place your chart in its own work-sheet. Click on FINISH.

Just like that, your new chart will appear in your spreadsheet. It will have its own worksheet tab (CHART1) at the bottom of the screen. Toggle between it and the SHEET1 tab to move from your graph to your budget.

To make your chart easier to follow, label each bar in the chart with the name of its matching expense.

1 Click on the CHART menu and then on SOURCE DATA. The SOURCE DATA dialog box will appear. Then click on the SERIES tab.

2 Type in the names of the individual expenses in order into the CATEGORY (X) AXIS LABELS text box. Put a comma between each one. For a reference, see the following illustration. Click on OK.

Source Data dialog box

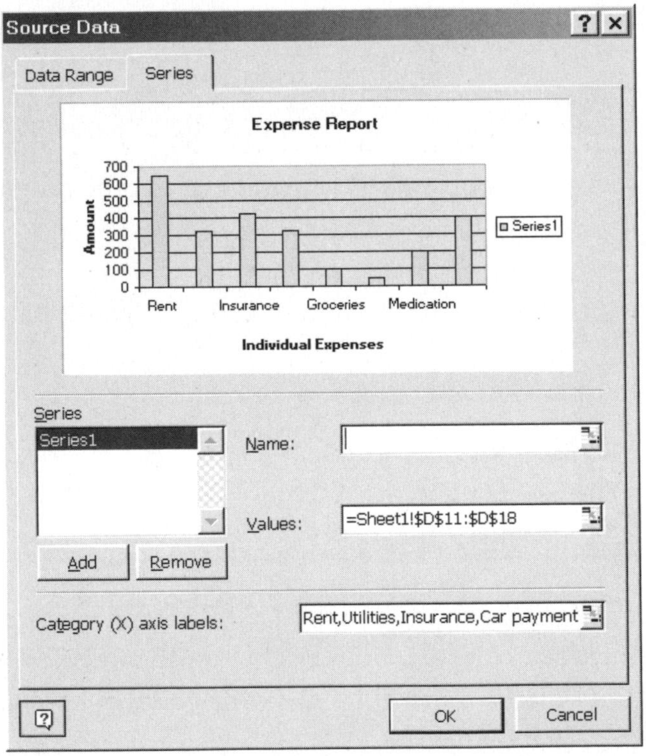

Quick tip ▶ As with anything in a spreadsheet, you can make your chart as creative as you want. The Chart Wizard has a formatting dialog box that will give you the tools. Double-click on one of the bars in the chart to open the FORMAT DATA SERIES dialog box. For instance, in the PATTERNS tab, change the colors in your chart. Or change the width of the bars in the OPTIONS tab.

A sample chart

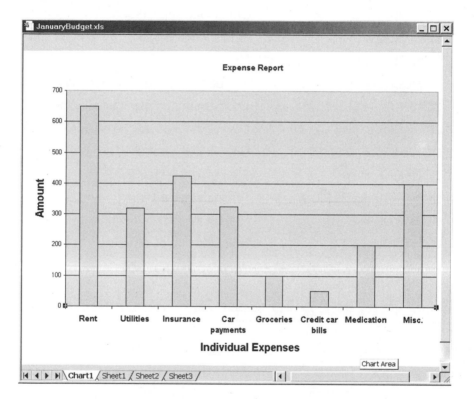

Shortcuts for spreadsheets

Spreadsheet programs have shortcut keys just like word processors. That means important commands are only one simple step away. Just remember to press the keys at the same time to "take" these shortcuts.

Press these keys at the same time	Command
CONTROL + 1	Display the FORMAT CELLS dialog box
CONTROL + B	Bold the selected cells
CONTROL + C	Copy the selected text
CONTROL + F	Find and replace words
CONTROL + I	Italicize the selected cells
CONTROL + N	Open a new workbook
CONTROL + O	Open a saved workbook
CONTROL + P	Print a workbook
CONTROL + S	Save a workbook
CONTROL + SHIFT + $	Add dollar signs to selected cells
CONTROL + SHIFT + %	Add percentage signs to selected cells
CONTROL + SHIFT + &	Outline the selected cells with a border
CONTROL + U	Underline the selected cells
CONTROL + V	Paste the selected text
CONTROL + X	Cut the selected text
CONTROL + Y	Repeat the last command
CONTROL + Z	Undo the last command

The first step to printing your work

You've created a budget, party invitation, and several other eye-catching documents. But right now, they're all trapped on your computer screen. It's time to learn how to print them.

Before you can do this, however, you need to install your printer. First, make sure the printer is attached to your tower with the printer cable. This cable allows the two components to "talk." See *Simple steps to successful setup* on page 21 for more information.

Next, install the printer software, or driver, onto your computer.

Imagine this driver to be like a translator. Even though your computer and your printer speak different "languages," the driver helps them communicate and work together.

To install the driver, follow these steps.

1 Click on the START menu, select SETTINGS, and then click on PRINTERS.

2 Double-click on the ADD PRINTER icon.

3 The ADD PRINTER WIZARD will greet you. Read its message and click on NEXT.

4 Make sure LOCAL PRINTER is selected. Then click on NEXT.

Most likely, your printer will come with its software on a CD or floppy disk. If you have this disk, follow these instructions.

1 Click on the HAVE DISK button in the ADD PRINTER WIZARD dialog box.

2 Next, insert the disk into the appropriate drive — either the CD-ROM or the disk drive.

3 The driver will start up on its own. Then follow the software's directions. When it's finished, your printer driver will be installed and ready to go.

4 Just click on CANCEL to exit the Wizard.

If you don't have a disk, you'll need to use one of the drivers already installed on your OS. They're listed in the ADD PRINTER WIZARD dialog box by the printer's make and model. Just follow these steps.

Add Printer Wizard dialog box

```
Add Printer Wizard

    🖨   Click the manufacturer and model of your printer. If your printer came with an
         installation disk, click Have Disk. If your printer is not listed, consult your printer
         documentation for a compatible printer.


   Manufacturers:                    Printers:

   Agfa                ▲           Digital DEClaser 5100/Net          ▲
   Apple                            Digital PrintServer 17/Net
   AST                              Digital PrintServer 17/12mb/Net
   AT&T                             Digital PrintServer 17/600/Net
   Brother                          Digital turboPrintServer 20/Net
   Bull                             Digital PrintServer 32/Net
   C-Itoh              ▼           Digital PrintServer 40 Plus/Net    ▼

                                                    Have Disk...


                        < Back       Next >          Cancel
```

1 Scroll down in the left text box and click on your printer's manufacturer. Then click on your printer's model in the text box on the right.

Fast fix ▶ If you can't find your exact printer in the list, look in the printer's manual for a possible substitute, or call the manufacturer's customer service hotline and ask them which one to use.

---

2 Click on NEXT after you've set the printer brand and type.

3 Click on parallel, or printer, port. This is the name of the socket on the back of your tower where the printer cable goes. Click on NEXT.

4 Set your newly installed printer as the default by clicking on the YES option button. This means it will be your computer's first choice for printing. Once again, click on NEXT.

To try out your new printer, allow the Wizard to print a test page.

Click on FINISH to start the process. It should work without a hitch. But if it doesn't, follow your computer's directions or read *Solutions for printing problems* on page 163.

Now you're ready to print

Here's the moment you've been waiting for — printing those impressive documents you've created. All it takes is familiarizing yourself with the PRINT dialog box.

To open the dialog box, click on the FILE menu in your word processor or spreadsheet program and then on PRINT. Or press the shortcut keys — CONTROL and P — which work in most programs.

Print dialog box

Once you're ready to print, follow these steps to set up the dialog box for perfect printing.

1   Click on the NAME drop-down list box and click on your printer's name. If you set it as your default printer, it will automatically show up here, and you won't need to do anything.

Play it safe ▶ It's a good idea to use the PRINT PREVIEW command to double-check your document before you print it. Click on the FILE menu and then on PRINT PREVIEW. You'll see exactly how your document will print up — without having to waste paper or ink on a test run.

---

2   Click on the PROPERTIES button for advanced printing features. You'll need these to change the type of printing paper — from standard letter size to envelope, for example. Or switch from normal vertical printing (portrait) to a horizontal version (landscape).

3   Pick a page range. Clicking on the ALL option button will be your best bet most of the time, since it will print your entire document. If you only want to print the page you're working on, click on CURRENT PAGE. Or print a string of pages by clicking on PAGES and typing the page numbers — separated by commas or dashes — into the text box.

4   Click on the NUMBER OF COPIES spinner arrow if you want more than one copy of your document. This tool is great if you want to print 15 copies of your party invitation or two copies of your to-do list. It will save you the trouble of having to use the PRINT dialog box over and over.

These basic pointers will help you print virtually any document. Once you master them, you can move on to expert printing commands, like collating and the OPTIONS button.

Timesaver ▶ To print without opening your document or the PRINT dialog box, right-click on your document's icon in the MY DOCUMENTS folder. Then click on PRINT. This will automatically print one copy of your document on the default printer.

Solutions for printing problems

Your printer may work perfectly nine out of 10 times. But for that one time when it goes haywire, here are some fast fixes for the most common printer problems.

Q   Why won't my printer start printing?

A   It could be one of several problems. First, make sure the cable between the printer and the computer is attached securely. Then see if your printer is plugged in and turned on. Next, check whether the ink cartridge and paper are inserted correctly. If your printer still won't work, it's time to consult your manual or call the manufacturer's customer service hotline.

Q   What can I do to stop smudges on my inkjet printouts?

A   Wait until your printouts are dry before handling them. In addition, make sure the paper slides out of your printer without brushing against anything.

FYI ▶ With a laser printer, you don't need to worry about smudging. That's because laser printers use a dry powder called toner. When the toner is heated, it fuses images on paper, just like a copy machine. Inkjets, on the other hand, spray tiny dots of wet ink onto the paper to form letters, shapes, and even photographs.

Q   Why do my documents print out splotchy, blurred, or faded?

A   If this happens, your inkjet cartridge may be almost empty. Some printer software includes a gauge that lets you know if your cartridge has ink. When it shows your cartridge is low, it's time to buy a new one. Also, if you haven't used your printer in a while, dried ink can form a blockage in the cartridge tubes causing the ink to spurt out in the wrong

163

direction — or not at all. To fix this, look in your manual for information about running the printer's self-cleaning process. Most times, the printer can clean the clog on its own.

Q   **Why won't my old printer work with my new computer, or vice versa?**

A   Your printer cable may not be installed in the correct port. To check, click on the START menu, select SETTINGS, and click on PRINTERS. Then right-click on your printer icon and click on PROPERTIES. In the DETAILS tab, it will say which port you're using. It should be set to the printer, or parallel, port. If that's not the problem, your driver software may be outdated. Visit the printer manufacturer's Web site to see if there's a newer version.

Q   **What kind of ink cartridge should I buy when I need to replace the old one?**

A   Save the box from the old cartridge so you can use it as a reference. No matter what type of cartridge it is, buying a new one is your safest bet. Some people recommend using refurbished ink cartridges, or refilling your old ones, but most printer manufacturers warn against this.

Quick tip ▶ When shopping for standard-size printer paper, buy paper that says it's safe for laser and inkjet printers. If you need to use a different size paper, be sure to tell the printer ahead of time. Just click on the PROPERTIES button in the PRINT dialog box. Click on the type of paper you're using and click on OK. If you want specialty paper — like paper for printing photographs or transparencies — it's best to buy the same brand as your printer. This will prevent jams and guarantee the best looking finished product.

Q   **What can I do if I printed the wrong document or too many copies of the right document?**

A   Cancel the print job. Click on the START menu, select SETTINGS, and click on PRINTERS. Double-click on your printer's icon. The print queue will appear, which lists the print jobs that are running at the moment. Look for the document's name in the list, right-click on it, and then click on CANCEL.

Q   **What should I do if the paper gets jammed?**

A   Turn off the printer and unplug it. If the paper is sticking out, gently but firmly pull it free. If you can't get at the jammed paper, read the manual to learn how to open your printer's case and clear the jam. In the future, stack the paper in the loading tray neatly, and don't put too much paper in the tray.

Dealing with disasters

Sooner or later, your computer will "crash" — in other words, a software program will suddenly and unexpectedly quit. You may even "freeze" — when nothing will move on your computer or respond to your mouse or keyboard.

It's frustrating, but you don't need your computer manual just yet. Slow down, take a deep breath, and learn how, with just a few quick clicks, you can fix and even prevent these problems.

Put the brakes on computer crashes. An application usually bombs because something in the software confuses the computer. While these failures aren't your fault, you can help prevent them.

- Don't have too many programs open at once. Just as with too much traffic on the highway, you increase your chances of crashing.

- Install only one program at a time. If you have a lot of new software, you may be tempted to install it all quickly. But work with one new program for a while before you install another. If your computer crashes, you'll have a better idea about what caused it. Always shut down the computer completely and start it up again before you install another program.

- Limit the amount of software on your computer. It's hard to resist all those exciting plug-ins, games, and utilities — especially when so many are free. But the fact is, there's a limit to what your system can support. So be selective.

- Say "no" to prerelease and pirated software. Prerelease software is distributed for testing before it's released to the general public. If all the bugs were worked out, it would be on the regular market. Pirated copies, besides being illegal, are more likely to have problems. And you won't have a reliable source of support to help you when trouble arises.

- Protect your system against viruses. To learn how to keep these invasions from bringing your computer down, see *Keep viruses from bugging you* on page 255.

Tech term ▶ Blue Screen of Death (BSOD) – when a computer locks up and the screen turns blue. It usually requires a reboot.

"Thaw" a frozen computer. These solutions to application lock-ups are listed from the simplest — pressing a single key — to the most drastic — rebooting. So try them in the order they are given.

- Press the ESCAPE key. This easy step can work like an emergency escape hatch to get you out of a jam.

- If you're stuck in one application while others are also open, press ALT + TAB to switch to another program. Give the problem application a few minutes to work through its confusion.

- Save your work and quit as many of the open programs as you can. This will free up memory for the computer to work through its problem and will protect you from losing more work.

- If the troublesome application is still stuck, press CONTROL + ALT + DELETE once, and click on END TASK to quit the program.

- Click on the Windows START button. From the START menu select SHUT DOWN and then RESTART. Your computer will reboot. Sadly, you may lose some work.

- Force a restart if necessary. It's always best to restart from the START menu, but if you're frozen, try these as last resorts. Press the restart button if your computer has one. Or press CONTROL + ALT + DELETE twice. This should automatically restart the computer.

Restarting will probably solve 95 percent of your computer glitches. But to save more of your work — and your time — always try the less extreme options first. A few quick clicks or pressing a few "magic keys" may be all it takes to get you happily computing again.

Computer housekeeping

Bring your files to order

It's virtually impossible to find anything on your desk if you allow letters, bills, and work papers to pile up haphazardly. The same is true of your computer desktop. Once you start creating and saving documents, you'll need an efficient filing system to keep them all in order.

In this chapter you'll learn how to organize your files and folders. You'll move, copy, delete — even undelete — them. Pretty soon you'll be an organizational whiz.

Divide and conquer your info. Think of your monthly gas bill. You may file this at home in a hanging folder, labeled Utilities, in a drawer inside your file cabinet. You may even put it in a Manila folder, labeled Gas, inside your Utilities folder — a folder within a folder.

Computer files work the same way. Each file is a piece of information — like June's budget, a favorite recipe, a digital photo of the grandkids, or a personal letter. You can organize each piece of information by placing it inside a digital folder within your virtual file cabinet.

Look inside your file cabinet. Your computer comes with many folders and files already set up and you've probably created some files of your own by now. Take a quick peek inside to see how this filing concept works.

Double-click on the MY DOCUMENTS icon on your desktop. Think of this as one drawer within your file cabinet.

Identify your icons. Remember, icons are little pictures that give you a clue to the type of computer element you are dealing with. They can help you tell files from folders, or quickly recognize a file by the program used to create it. Notice the difference between icons.

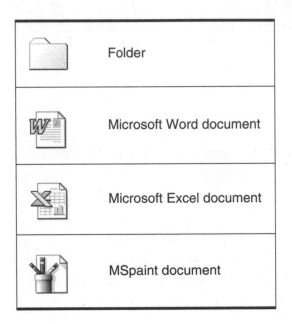

	Folder
	Microsoft Word document
	Microsoft Excel document
	MSpaint document

Call your files by name. Each file not only has a name, but a last name, too, called a file extension. This is generally a period and a three-letter suffix. Extensions come right after the name of the file and tell the computer which program created that file. The computer needs this information to open, read, and format each file.

Sometimes your computer will show you the icon for your file, but not its extension. It's easy to tell your computer you want to see the extension on all your files.

1 Open MY COMPUTER and click on VIEW on the Menu bar.

2 Choose FOLDER OPTIONS from the drop-down menu.

3 Under the VIEW tab, uncheck the box called HIDE FILE EXTENSIONS FOR KNOWN FILE TYPES.

4 Click on APPLY and then OK.

File extensions can be very helpful. If you're browsing through your files and want to find only letters you wrote in Microsoft Word, you can look for the extension .DOC and know these are word processing documents. Here are some of the more common extensions you'll come across.

File type	Extension
Word processing	.doc
Microsoft Excel	.xls
Internet	.htm or .html
Photographs or graphics	.bmp or .tif or .gif
Temporary	.tmp
Program	.exe

Find folders and files with ease

There are many roads to one destination — often you can choose the path you'll take. It's the same with your computer. You can choose between two file management programs — MY COMPUTER and Windows Explorer — to view and access your files. Just remember, no matter which path you choose, you'll wind up at the same files.

If you'd rather follow written directions to get from one place to the next, you'll enjoy using MY COMPUTER. But if you travel better map-in-hand, Windows Explorer will give you just the bird's-eye view you need. The choice is yours.

Make your way with MY COMPUTER. This is the most immediate way to get to your files since you see each of your folders in its own window. While it is simple and familiar, MY COMPUTER doesn't give you a general overview of your filing system.

1 Double-click on the MY COMPUTER icon. Note how this window is visually separated into two panes. The narrower left pane gives the name of the folder you are currently in. The right pane shows icons of the objects within that folder.

2 In the right pane of MY COMPUTER you will see icons for various drives and folders. This is a very general location on your computer. Think of it as being in the right town, but still far away from your street. You don't want to save your files way out here, so double-click on the (C:) icon.

3 This is your hard drive. It's sort of like being on the right street, but not yet in your own yard. Most of what you do on your computer will end up somewhere in here. Let's get a little more specific still. Take a peek into MY DOCUMENTS by double-clicking on its icon.

My Documents by way of My Computer

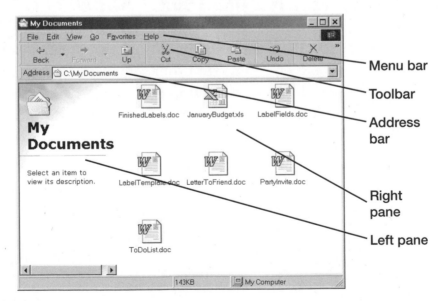

4 You have finally arrived. MY DOCUMENTS is your own private office, where you will store most of your files. In fact, the documents you created in the previous chapter should already be lined up in the right pane of this window.

Chart your course with Windows Explorer. This program works just like MY COMPUTER, but lets you see the relationship between your files all in one place — instead of forcing you to flip through various windows.

FYI ▶ Windows Explorer is not the same program as Internet Explorer. The first shows you what information you have on your hard drive, and the second helps you roam around the Internet.

---

1 To find Windows Explorer, click on the START menu.

2 Point to PROGRAMS with your mouse, then move across to WINDOWS EXPLORER and click on it.

3 Notice this screen is also separated into two panes. In the left pane is a list of folders and files neatly staggered under the drive they are stored in. Every indented layer sits inside the previous layer. This view is often called the filing tree. The main trunk is your desktop, and each folder is a branch. Off these branches are other folders and files.

4 You can tell which folder has subfolders by the little plus (+) or minus (-) sign to the left of its name. Click on the minus sign next to MY COMPUTER to collapse the open list. Click on the plus sign to see it again.

5 If (C:) is not open, click on the plus sign by (C:), and then click on the MY DOCUMENTS icon under it. All the files and folders within MY DOCUMENTS should appear in the right pane. Now you are exactly where you ended up in the MY COMPUTER exercise — you just didn't have to click through windows to get here.

6 In the right pane, Windows Explorer lists the contents of the folder you have highlighted in the left pane. In this view you see not only the name, but also the size, date, and program used to create your file.

My Documents by way of Windows Explorer

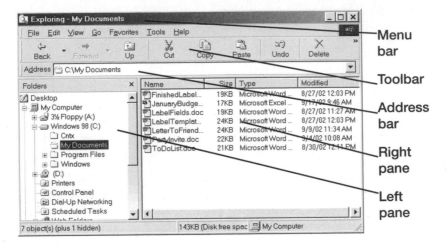

Speed up filing with shared features. Before you leave your chosen file manager, take a look at what these two programs have in common.

- **Toolbar.** Below your Title bar and above your Address bar is your Toolbar. This strip of buttons will help you manipulate your files. You can cut, copy, delete, and paste files — just like you can in word processing applications — move back and forth between filing levels, and change the view of your files. Take a few minutes to get comfortable with these shortcuts. They will save you time down the road.

- **The Address bar.** The computer automatically gives each file an address — but backwards. It begins with a file's general location and becomes more specific. Each location is followed by a backwards slash (\). If you know it, you can type in a file's address and go directly to it. The system will even help you get there. Once you start typing, you'll see a drop-down list of all your recent destinations. Highlight the one you want, press ENTER, and the computer will take you there.

FYI ▶ You may not use it now, but get familiar with the Address bar anyway. Windows uses it extensively in other programs and you will use it all the time when you are on the Internet.

In both MY COMPUTER and Windows Explorer you can easily create new folders, move files around, and reorganize your filing system by dragging and dropping files from one pane to the other. The rest of this chapter will take you through these actions step by step.

Choose the view that suits

You can change the way your files look by clicking on the VIEWS icon on the far right of your Toolbar. Here are your VIEWS menu options.

LARGE ICONS. How you usually see files — as icons with a name typed underneath.

SMALL ICONS. Identical to your LARGE ICONS view, just smaller. You can fit more files in your window with this view.

LIST. Lines up your files in a list, with a small icon beside each.

DETAILS. Shows the location, file type, and modification date of each file in your folder. This view is ideal for identifying mystery files.

Fast fix ▶ If you can't see the VIEWS icon, click on the tiny double arrow in the upper right corner of the Toolbar.

Get organized with new folders

Gone are the days of steel filing cabinets, Manila folders, peel-and-stick labels, and bulging file drawers. Computer folders are free and plentiful — so use them to keep your files in perfect order.

Know your destination. Your computer automatically opens MY DOCUMENTS any time you choose to save a file. Creating personalized folders within MY DOCUMENTS will, therefore, make saving files simple and fast. It will also make it easier to find files later on — at least you'll know where to start looking — and making a backup will be a snap. (Learn more about creating backups in the story *Don't get caught without a backup* on page 190.)

Plan your folder structure. Before you start making folders, however, take a moment to think about the kinds of files you need to organize. Will you be writing a lot of letters? Keeping track of your finances? Storing photographs? Try to map out a simple folder structure so all your files fit in very specific folders grouped within more general folders.

Quick tip ▶ If you have more than one person using the computer, create a folder for each user and keep everyone's files separate.

Group files by content. Perhaps the most logical way to organize your files is to keep like items together. For instance, group all your financial documents — your expense and earnings worksheets, your bank correspondence and statements — in one general folder named FINANCES. Then create a subfolder (a folder within a folder) for each year or even each month.

Try the same strategy with a folder called CORRESPONDENCE. You could create a subfolder for family, one for friends, one for business, etc.

FYI ▶ You can create new folders just as easily using Windows Explorer. The steps are almost exactly the same and the logic is identical.

Create new folders. It's so easy to make a new folder, you just might become addicted. Open MY COMPUTER, double-click on (C:), then double-click on MY DOCUMENTS. Notice how cluttered your folder has become. Perhaps it's time to create some general folders — like one for correspondence and one for celebrations.

1 In MY DOCUMENTS, click on the FILE drop-down menu and point to NEW. A second drop-down menu will appear to the right. Choose FOLDER from your options.

2 You will see a folder icon pop up in the right pane of your folder window. The generic title NEW FOLDER is highlighted. You can rename it by simply typing over the old name. Rename it CORRESPONDENCE and press ENTER to save the name.

3 Repeat steps 1 and 2 to create another new folder and call it CELEBRATIONS.

New empty folders

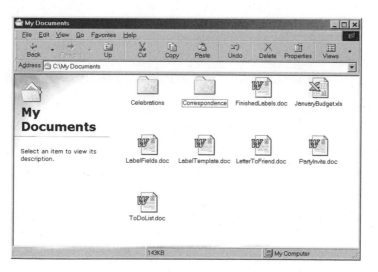

4 Now double-click on CORRESPONDENCE. A blank window will appear since this is an empty folder. Repeat the previous steps to create two subfolders in here. Name one folder PERSONAL and one BUSINESS. In the next story you will learn how to move your files into these new folders.

Change a folder's name. Perhaps you already have a folder, but the name you originally chose no longer fits. It's easy to rename the folder to match its contents.

1 Click once on the icon of the folder you want to rename.

2 Now click on the name of the file. A small rectangular box will appear around the name, and it will be highlighted.

3 Type in a new name and press ENTER to save it.

Quick tip ▶ You can also select a folder by clicking on it and then choosing RENAME from the FILE menu.

Avoid naming no-no's. When you choose a name for your file or folder, stay away from these common mistakes.

- Don't give your file a long name. Keep it short, and try to include a unique word from your text that you might use later to find this file.

- Don't get too general. If you need more than a couple of words to describe a file, create a new folder for files like it, and be detailed with your name. For instance, don't name your document BIRTHDAY LETTER TO JOHN 2003. Instead, create a folder called LETTERS TO JOHN, and label your document BIRTHDAY03.

- Don't use strange characters. The computer uses the characters " * / : ? \ | for specific functions.

- Don't identify files by the name of a month. Use numeric dates if you want to file by date. This way the computer, which likes to sort alphabetically, will keep your files in chronological order.

Your filing system may not be perfect right now but don't worry — just develop a blueprint you can start with.

Put files in their place

Pack your bags, it's time to move — your files, that is. You need to bring some order to all those files sitting in MY DOCUMENTS. But don't worry, rearranging things is a snap and all your data will end up tidy and easy to find.

Drag files about. The simplest way to move a file is to literally drag it from one location to the next using Windows Explorer.

1 Open Windows Explorer and look in the left pane. Click on the plus sign next to (C:). Next, click on the plus sign next to MY DOCUMENTS.

2 Get your destination folder open by first clicking on the plus sign by the folder CORRESPONDENCE (if it's not already open). You should see the folder titled PERSONAL underneath it.

3 Still in the left pane, click once on the MY DOCUMENTS icon to select it. This lets you see all the files and folders within MY DOCUMENTS in the right pane of Windows Explorer. Now you simply select the file you want to move.

4 Find the file LETTERTOFRIEND.DOC that you created in the last chapter. Click on it, and, holding the mouse down, drag it over to the left pane and down the list until you are hovering over the folder PERSONAL.

5 When PERSONAL turns dark, release the mouse and the file should disappear from the right pane.

6 Now click on the folder icon for PERSONAL and check the list in the right pane to make sure the file you moved is in its new location.

Word document in Personal folder

Window title: Exploring - Personal

Menu: File Edit View Go Favorites Tools Help

Toolbar: Back Forward Up Cut Copy Paste Undo Delete

Address: C:\My Documents\Correspondence\Personal

Folders:
- Desktop
- My Computer
  - 3½ Floppy (A:)
  - Windows 98 (C:)
    - Cntx
    - My Documents
      - Celebrations
      - Correspondence
        - Business
        - Personal
    - Program Files
    - Windows
  - (D:)
  - Printers
  - Control Panel
  - Dial-Up Networking
  - Scheduled Tasks
  - Web Folders

LetterToFriend.doc

1 object(s)   23.5KB (Disk free space: 9.1   My Computer

Quick tip ▶ If the file you just moved doesn't seem to be in the proper folder, take a peek in the adjacent folders. You may have accidentally dropped it in the wrong one.

Make a copy. Another way to move a file is to copy and paste it to a different location. This takes a little of the anxiety away from the whole moving process since you have the original safe and sound in its old location until you're convinced the move was a success.

1 Using either Windows Explorer or MY COMPUTER, find the file PARTYINVITE.DOC you created in the previous chapter. It should be sitting in MY DOCUMENTS. Click on it and then choose COPY from the EDIT drop-down menu.

2 In the left pane, click on the folder CELEBRATIONS so that it is highlighted, and choose PASTE from the EDIT drop-down menu. A copy of PARTYINVITE.DOC should now appear in its new location.

3 After you are sure your file is in the proper folder, go back to MY DOCUMENTS and drag the original PARTYINVITE.DOC file into the RECYCLE BIN on your desktop. (You'll learn more about throwing away files and folders later in this chapter.)

Play it safe ▶ Don't use the cut and paste commands when moving a file. It's too easy to make a mistake and lose your file. For your peace of mind, stick to the copy-and-paste or drag-and-drop methods instead.

Avoid filing foul-ups

Never move files you didn't create even if you don't recognize the file extensions — they may be part of a software program. When you move them, the computer has trouble finding these vital files, and your application may no longer work.

If you dropped a file in the wrong folder, or regret your latest move, you can restore everything to the way it was. Simply keep pressing the UNDO button on the Toolbar until the file is back where it started.

Find files and folders fast

Try to find a file when you're in a hurry and you'll not only get frustrated, but you'll probably waste a lot of time. Don't hit the panic button, use the FIND command, a Windows mini-program that will hunt down files for you.

1 From the START menu, point to FIND. Then click on FILES OR FOLDERS.

2 You'll now see a FIND dialog box. The simplest way to search is on the name of a file. In the text box next to NAMED, enter your file name. For instance, type in *lettertofriend.doc*.

3 If you can't remember the whole name of your file, just type in a word you do remember, and add an asterisk (*) before and after the word. In this case, type *friend*. The asterisk is a type of wildcard that tells your computer to look for any file with this string of letters in it.

Find dialog box

Find: Files named *friend*			_ □ ×

File   Edit   View   Options   Help

Name & Location	Date	Advanced	

Named: *friend*   ▼   **Find Now**

Containing text: **Stop**

Look in: Windows 98 (C:)   ▼   **New Search**

☑ Include subfolders   Browse...   🔍

Name	In Folder	Size	Type	Modified
LetterToFriend.doc	C:\My Docum...	24KB	Microsoft Word ...	9/9/02 11:34 A

1 file(s) found   Monitoring New Items

4 If all the details of the name slip your memory, don't worry. Probably the most useful feature of this program is its ability to search for a word in the contents of your files. In the

CONTAINING TEXT box, type in a term you know is in your document. Since you used your return address in the letter you created, enter your street name for instance.

5 If you followed the filing tips earlier in this chapter, you know that all your files are in the MY DOCUMENTS folder. You can also narrow your search by choosing this folder from the drop-down list below the LOOK IN text box.

Play it safe ▶ For the most general search, choose drive (C:) from the drop-down list beside the LOOK IN text box, and check mark the box INCLUDE SUBFOLDERS.

---

6 Click on FIND NOW. The computer will work for a few seconds, and a window of options will pop up below the main text window. This window should list all the files on your hard drive that match your search.

7 Scroll down the list until you see LETTERTOFRIEND.DOC. To open it, simply double-click on the icon by the file name.

Sometimes the computer will bring up a list of results longer than your arm. Instead of sorting through them, start a new search and narrow your parameters. You can add another word in the CONTAINING TEXT box, or use the advanced search options — like setting a date range, file type, or file size. This will keep your hit list short.

Quick tip ▶ Make sure you click the NEW SEARCH button to reset all your options before running another search.

The more boundaries you give your search, the more likely you are to find your file. Just be careful not to get too specific or the computer won't find anything that matches your request.

It's time to take out the trash

Old or useless files take up valuable space on your hard drive and slow your system down. That's why you need to clean up the clutter on a regular basis. It's easy to throw files away, but before you begin, learn what to toss and what to keep.

There are typically three types of data you can delete to free up some disk space.

- **Regular trash.** Documents you create by accident or no longer need are the easiest files to identify as trash.

- **Temporary files.** Most of the time you'll never even know you have temporary — or temp — files. These are a sort of backup copy your computer automatically makes of certain files and Internet sites. Usually, your computer automatically deletes them, as well. Sometimes, however, temp files hang around taking up valuable space and slowing down your system. Look for files with a .TMP extension. It's almost always safe to delete them.

- **Miscellaneous.** You may want to throw away other items you no longer need, like empty folders, shortcuts to old programs or files, certain backup files — with a .BAK extension — or .ZIP files you've already unzipped.

Play it safe ▶ Don't ever delete program files — like those with .EXE as a file extension. These files can be critical to a program you use frequently. If you delete them you may damage the whole application.

Clean house. The RECYCLE BIN is really a holding area for files you think you don't need. Imagine it's like your household trash can — you can put a piece of paper in it, but you can always get it back out again. Once you empty the can, however, your data is gone.

There are several ways to drop your files into the RECYCLE BIN. One basic way is to click on the name of the file and choose DELETE from the FILE menu. But there are other ways to send these files into document limbo.

From MY COMPUTER, open (C:), then double-click on MY DOCUMENTS, for instance. Click on the file you no longer need, then:

1 Hold down your mouse while you drag your pointer — and the file — to the desktop and hover over the RECYCLE BIN icon.

2 Wait until the RECYCLE BIN turns dark then release the mouse.

3 The computer will ask if you are sure you want to move this file into the RECYCLE BIN. Confirm by clicking on YES.

Quick tip ▶ Make sure you can see the RECYCLE BIN before you start dragging files. If you can't, move the bin or minimize the window so both are showing.

Through Windows Explorer, open (C:) then, again, MY DOCUMENTS, for instance. In the right pane, find the file you want to delete and click on it once to select it, then:

1 Drag it to the left pane.

2 Still holding down your mouse, scroll down the list until you find the RECYCLE BIN. If it's not visible, hold the file at the bottom of the list and the computer should continue scrolling. This can be a little tricky, so practice holding your pointer in different areas until the list begins to scroll.

3 Wait until the RECYCLE BIN is highlighted and release your mouse button to drop the file in.

4 Confirm that you want to send this file to the RECYCLE BIN by clicking on YES.

Timesaver ▸ Single-click on a file you want to trash, then right-click on it and choose DELETE from the drop-down menu.

Rescue that trashed file

If you accidentally throw away the wrong file, don't despair. Before you empty your RECYCLE BIN, you can still retrieve it.

1 Double-click on the RECYCLE BIN icon.

2 Scroll through the list of files and click on the file you wish to recover.

3 Under the FILE menu, click on RESTORE. The file will disappear from the RECYCLE BIN. Look for it in its original location.

Play it safe ▸ To make sure you don't accidentally delete an item while moving it around, drag your RECYCLE BIN to the bottom right corner of your desktop, away from other folders.

Empty the trash. Remember, until you actually clean out your bin and permanently erase files in the trash, they will continue to use up computer memory — and slow your system down. Regularly empty your RECYCLE BIN and you may notice your computer picks up speed.

1 Double-click on your RECYCLE BIN icon and take a quick look at its contents. Some of the files may be unfamiliar since the computer automatically trashes program temporary files.

2 To empty the bin, point your mouse on the FILE menu option and click on EMPTY RECYCLE BIN from your drop-down menu.

3 If you are sure you want to delete these files, click on YES in the next dialog box.

4 The window showing the contents of your RECYCLE BIN should now be empty.

The computer has set aside about 10 percent of your hard drive space for your RECYCLE BIN. This may seem like a lot, but it fills up quickly. If you don't empty it and the bin goes over its allotted space, the computer will automatically delete files in it. Make sure you look in your RECYCLE BIN periodically. By emptying it yourself, you won't lose a file you might need to recover later.

Uninstall — remove programs properly

Getting rid of a program is not as simple as throwing out an old file. Simply moving an application to the RECYCLE BIN doesn't mean you've deleted all the smaller files it uses that may be scattered across your hard drive. Instead, you must uninstall it.

Uninstalling takes exactly the same steps as setting up the program — but in reverse. Your computer winds up deleting every trace of that program from your hard drive.

1 To uninstall, open the MY COMPUTER window and double-click on the CONTROL PANEL icon.

2 Double-click on ADD/REMOVE PROGRAMS and make sure you are in the INSTALL/UNINSTALL tab.

3 Scroll down the list until you find the program you want to

remove and click on it. Then click on ADD/REMOVE.

4 This launches the uninstall process and you must simply respond to various dialog boxes that appear.

Play it safe ▶ The computer may post a warning if you are trying to remove a file used by other programs. You should only uninstall files that are not shared by other applications.

Keep your original program disk handy for the possibility your computer will ask you to insert it into your disk drive. At the end of the uninstall process, your computer may or may not confirm the program is gone.

In fact, when you are through, the program may still show up in the START menu under PROGRAMS. Don't worry, the program is probably gone and only the shortcut remains. Double-click on this shortcut to make sure — nothing should happen and you can safely delete the shortcut.

Fast fix ▶ To remove the shortcut from your START menu, refer to *Make — and take — a shortcut* on page 85.

If you can't find your application listed in the ADD/REMOVE PROGRAMS list, search for the program folder using your favorite file manager. Peek inside — if it has its own uninstall file, double-click on it to launch a customized uninstall.

12 speedy filing shortcuts

Filing isn't usually fun. But if you try some of these shortcuts, you'll enjoy the chore a bit more and your files and folders will be tidy in a snap. The plus sign (+) means you hold the first key down while pressing the second key.

Keys	Action
Hold ALT; type F N F	To create a new folder in the window you currently have open
F3	To launch the FIND menu
F2	To rename a file
Hold CONTROL	And drag a file with your mouse to a different folder, leaving a copy in its original location
Hold CONTROL	And click on files with your mouse to choose more than one file in a folder
CONTROL + C	To copy a file or a folder
CONTROL +V	To paste a file or folder
BACKSPACE	To move back to the parent folder of your current active folder or file
ALT + ENTER	To open the PROPERTIES dialog box of a file
DELETE	To move a folder or file into the recycle bin
SHIFT + DELETE	To permanently delete a folder
CONTROL + Z	To undo your last action

Learn to flip a floppy

A floppy disk fits in the three and one-half inch slot on the front of your computer tower. You can buy disks that say Preformatted for PC (IBM) or you can format them yourself. This step is necessary for your computer to be able to put information on or read data off of a floppy. Check your computer manual if you need help formatting a floppy.

Don't get caught without a backup

A backup is basically a copy of your files stored separately from your computer. It comes in handy in case you lose or destroy files on your hard drive. You should make decisions about backing up based on how you use your computer.

Decide what files to back up. You can make an emergency backup disk of your entire system — including the operating system, software, and all your personal files. This will take quite a bit of time and tons of storage space, or memory.

Since you probably have all your original system and software disks, you might choose to back up only your personal files — like word processing documents, an address database, etc.

Or you can make a full copy of your files and then only back up those you change or update on a regular basis. Just remember that while it will save you time and disk space to do partial backups, it will be time-consuming if you ever have to restore all your files from partial backups.

Time your backups wisely. Now you need to set up a schedule. Experts recommend you make a list of all the things you do frequently on your computer. Then write down the files you use for these tasks. Back up these at least once a month — preferably once a week.

Then consider an immediate backup of anything you've just spent time on. For instance, if it took you all day to work out a financial plan or to write two pages of your autobiography, you'll probably want to back up these files before you shut down for the night.

Tech term ▶ Megabyte (MB) – a measure of computer memory equal to 1 million bytes.

Choose a backup method. Just like everything else you accumulate, you have to decide where to store your saved data. There are options that can save you time, space, or money.

Disk type	Pros	Cons
3.5" Floppy disk	Floppies are cheap and easy to find The disk drive may already be installed on your computer	Each disk holds very little information (1.44MB) so you need many Disks are easy to damage, and the technology is dying out
ZIP and JAZ disks	You can store plenty of information on one disk (100-250MB) Also a fairly common drive on personal computers	Both drive and disks are somewhat expensive You may need more than one disk to back up a whole system
CD-RW	Long-lasting disks hold a whopping 600MB of storage CD drives come on most new computers	Drives are moderately expensive if you must add one to your system Can be somewhat confusing to use
DVD	10 times the storage capacity of a CD Reliable, long-lasting medium	Disks and drives are expensive The technology is still evolving

Start the habit now. Once you have a disk and drive chosen, it's time to make your first backup. Microsoft Windows comes with its own simple utility program called Microsoft Backup. You can start with this program and update to a more complex program later on.

Install Microsoft Backup

You may find this program was not loaded on your computer when it was first set up. To load it yourself, slip the Windows 98 system disk or CD into your drive.

1 On your desktop click on the START button.

2 Point to SETTINGS then click on CONTROL PANEL.

3 Double-click on the ADD/REMOVE PROGRAMS icon.

4 Under the WINDOWS SETUP tab, click on SYSTEM TOOLS to check-mark it.

5 Click on DETAILS.

6 Select BACKUP from the list to check-mark it.

7 Click on OK, then APPLY. The computer should begin installing the program.

To find and use Microsoft Backup the first time:

1 Insert a blank, formatted disk into the correct drive. This will become your first backup disk.

2 Click on START, point to PROGRAMS, then ACCESSORIES, SYSTEM TOOLS and then click on MSBACKUP.

3 Select CREATE A NEW BACKUP JOB since you are creating a backup from scratch. This should bring up a Wizard that will take you though the process step by step.

When it's time to save and exit, give your backup an explicit name. This will make finding data on it easy later on. Don't worry about adding a date to the title since your computer automatically tags each file with a date and time.

Make sure you also write the name and date of your backup on the disk label, and note whether it was a full or partial backup.

Play it safe ▶ Once created, make sure you store your backup files away from your computer so they can't be destroyed in any incident that could affect your system.

Recoup your losses. It's an awful day when you realize you have lost a file or a folder. But now you can make use of your careful backups.

1 Make sure you have the correct backup disk in the drive and access Microsoft Backup through the START menu as instructed before.

2 Select RESTORE BACKED UP FILES from the first Wizard dialog box.

3 Then simply follow the Wizard's instructions to restore your lost data.

If your computer crashes and you don't have a backup, don't despair — there are companies that can successfully recreate data from a corrupted hard drive. However, you may spend as much money getting the old drive back as you would spend on a new computer. Take the time now to make a backup — a day will come when you will be glad you did.

Q My computer says A: IS NOT ACCESSIBLE. THE DEVICE IS NOT READY. What should I do?

A Check to see if your disk is properly inserted in the disk drive. Try inserting it again.

Q Why does my computer gives me a GENERAL FAILURE message when I try to save a file to my disk?

A Your computer may not be able to read your disk if it is unformatted or formatted for a different operating system. You can reformat the disk but you will lose all the information currently on it.

Q My computer says DESTINATION DISK DRIVE IS FULL when I try to create a backup. What does that mean?

A This means you don't have enough room — or memory — on your disk to hold the information you are trying to save. Free up some space by deleting old files. Or use a brand new disk, perhaps with more memory, instead.

Q I just inserted a disk and I don't see the files I expected in the MY COMPUTER window. What can I do?

A Refresh the contents of the window by pressing F5.

Keep a spare startup disk

If you ever power up your computer and nothing happens, something might be terribly wrong with your startup file — a kind of key you need to unlock your system. You'll need an emergency startup disk to put things back in order.

You may already have one if you followed the instructions when you loaded your Windows software. If not, create one right now, before disaster strikes.

1 Click on START.

2 Point to SETTINGS and choose CONTROL PANEL.

3 Double-click on ADD/REMOVE PROGRAMS and click on the STARTUP DISK tab.

4 Slip a new disk or CD into your disk drive, click on CREATE DISK, and follow the on-screen instructions. Soon you'll have your own spare key.

Clean out computer clutter

Your hard drive can get cluttered with lots of temporary or corrupted files. To clean up your drive and keep your system running smoothly, try some of these maintenance programs that are already installed on your computer.

1 Open your START menu by double-clicking on the START button.

2 Point to PROGRAMS, then ACCESSORIES and finally SYSTEM TOOLS.

3 The last cascading menu has several options for cleaning up your computer.

Find all your cleanup utilities here

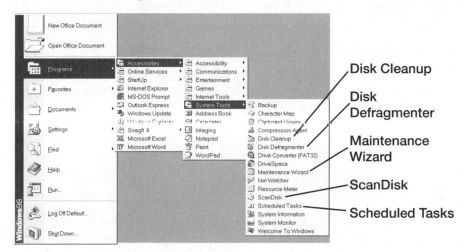

Disk Cleanup

Disk Defragmenter

Maintenance Wizard

ScanDisk

Scheduled Tasks

Scan everything. ScanDisk is your computer watchdog. It checks both your files and your hardware to see if there are any glitches or problems. When it finds one, it solves the problem for you.

To begin this maintenance program, click on the SCANDISK icon in the last cascading window. Choose the drive you want to check — probably your hard drive (drive C:) — and mark the THOROUGH option. Click on START and the computer will go to work.

If the program finds errors, it will open a dialog box asking what you want to do about a particular file. You can ignore the problem, fix it, or delete the file.

It's very important you run this program about once a month. You may not be able to access the rest of your computer while ScanDisk is in action, so run it when you can walk away for a while.

Timesaver ▶ If you don't want to receive a notice every time ScanDisk finds an error, mark the AUTOMATICALLY CORRECT ERRORS option in the program's dialog box.

Find the fragments. Think of the memory on your hard drive as a book. When your computer is new, your programs and files start on the first page and run in order. All the empty pages at the end of the book represent free memory. Pretty soon you start to add and save files, and your long continuous block of free memory fills up. Then you change and delete files, creating blank pages here and there — scattered chunks of free memory.

Eventually, a new file can't be stored all in one space because you don't have enough empty pages all together. So your computer automatically splits — or fragments — the file. Fragmentation slows down your computer because to access a file, it must go hunting for each piece.

Click on Disk Defragmenter to have this program look at all your files and try to reorganize them. First it moves files to create larger chunks of free memory, then it reconnects as many fragments as possible. This could take awhile — up to a few hours — so plan to do something else while it runs. You'll be surprised how much faster your computer can operate.

Quick tip ▶ Make sure your screen saver is turned off while you run this utility, or Disk Defragmenter will have to restart each time your computer goes into this mode.

Clean up your hard disk. Disk Cleanup will hunt down useless files, like temporary Internet records and old updates, which can clog up your computer. But you decide if you want to get rid of them.

Click on DISK CLEANUP and select your hard drive (probably C:) and click OK. The program will bring up a dialog box listing the various files you can choose to delete.

Disk Cleanup

Select one at a time by clicking on its name and read a short description in the text box below it. Click in the check-box to select those you want to delete and click on OK.

Play it safe ▶ Make a backup of your hard drive before you run Defragmenter or Disk Cleanup in case one of these programs accidentally throws out an important file.

Put it on automatic. Remember, just like a car needs regular tune-ups, your computer needs maintenance periodically to stay in tip-top condition. But if you think you might forget, Windows 98 comes with a special program called the Maintenance Wizard. It can help you set up an automated schedule for regular cleanups. Just choose a date and time when you know your computer will be on, but not in use. To personalize your timetable, open SCHEDULED TASKS. Double-click on each task to see a dialog box that lets you customize the schedule.

Help your PC hurry up

If your computer seems suddenly slow, here are a few tips to restore its zip.

- Close all programs you aren't using.

- Empty the recycle bin.

- Press F3 and search for temporary files by typing *.tmp* in the NAMED text box and clicking on FIND NOW. Select those files you don't need and press DELETE.

- Uninstall programs you don't use anymore and old versions of your newer software.

- Run the Disk Defragmenter at least once a month.

- Buy and install more RAM (Random Access Memory).

Quick fixes for annoying problems

You've heard the expression, "Don't sweat the small stuff." Unfortunately, it's often the little things that are the most annoying when it comes to your computer. Here are the best ways to solve the 10 most annoying computer problems.

Q   How can I stop my keys from sticking?

A   Crumbs, dust, and other debris can cause keyboard keys to stick. Dust can also create havoc in a computer system, clogging ventilation and overheating components. Keep a can of compressed air handy, and use it to periodically clean off your computer equipment.

Q   Why is my mouse acting crazy?

A   If your mouse gets sluggish and jerky, it probably needs a good cleaning. After months of rolling around on your mouse pad, it can collect a lot of dust and grit. Flip the mouse over and remove the ball from inside. Use a soft, clean cloth to clean the ball and the inside of the mouse. You may also want to dip a cotton swab in alcohol to clean the little rollers that the ball touches. If you find that you have to clean your mouse often, you may need a new mouse pad.

Q   Why is everything on my screen so small?

A   If your eyesight isn't as good as it once was, and you have to squint at your screen, simply enlarge your text. Click on your START button, then select SETTINGS and CONTROL PANEL. Double-click on DISPLAY to open the Display panel. Click on the tab that says APPEARANCE, and you can choose the font size you want. You can also make the icons on your desktop bigger. In the DISPLAY panel, click on the EFFECTS tab and check the box that says USE LARGE ICONS.

Q   How do I slow down my mouse?

A   If you're having trouble controlling your mouse because it's just too zippy, you can change its speed. Double-click the mouse icon in the CONTROL PANEL. You can change the speed of the mouse itself under the MOTION tab and the speed of the double-click under the BUTTONS tab.

Q   Where did my Taskbar go?

A   Move your mouse toward one of the edges of your screen — the top, bottom, left, or right — and it should reappear. To prevent your

Taskbar from hiding again, click on your START button, then select SETTINGS. Click on TASKBAR & START MENU, and uncheck the AUTO HIDE box.

Q   Why is my monitor giving me a headache?

A   If your flickering monitor gives you headaches, change its refresh rate — how many times per second the graphics system redraws the image on your screen. Right-click on your desktop, and click on PROPER-TIES. Click on the SETTINGS tab, then click on ADVANCED. Click on the ADAPTER tab, and choose a higher refresh rate from the drop-down list.

Q   Why does my computer keep falling asleep on the job?

A   This happens when you have your computer on, but you haven't typed or moved your mouse in a while. After a certain amount of time, the monitor will go into standby, or "sleep," mode. Just jiggling your mouse or pressing any key will bring your computer back to life. To change the setting so your computer waits longer before taking a nap, click START, SETTINGS, CONTROL PANEL, and POWER MANAGEMENT. Choose your new setting from the drop-down lists.

Q   Where did my file go?

A   Your natural instinct is to panic when you can't find a file. Relax. Maybe you saved it to the wrong folder or deleted it by mistake. Do a search for the file by name or browse through Windows Explorer. If you think you might have deleted it, open the RECYCLE BIN. If the file is there, click on FILE in the Menu bar then on RESTORE to return it to its proper place.

Q   Why did my computer freeze?

A   Freezes, or crashes, happen for mysterious reasons. It could be a faulty program or hard drive — or just a fluke. If all else fails, restarting the computer will usually solve the problem. For more information on com-puter crashes, see *Dealing with disasters* on page 165.

Q   What happened to my work?

A   After a crash, you might lose the latest updates to the file you were working on. Limit the damage by playing it safe. Save your work regu-larly, and remember to make backup copies. If the program has an AUTOSAVE feature, set it for more frequent saves.

Internet essentials

Explore the world of cyberspace

The Internet can put the world at your fingertips. And in doing so, it can make your life a whole lot easier. For instance, how often have you found yourself scrambling for a gift just before a friend's birthday? Now you can relax, pull up a chair, and let the Internet do all the work for you. Find the perfect present in one of the many online stores, and have it wrapped and shipped that same day. Then, send your friend an instant birthday card from one of the free greeting sites. Presto, you're through, and you did it all from the comfort of your living room.

Far from being a sinister computerized monster, the Internet is much more like a huge floating library of information, shopping resources, and entertainment. Once you understand the basics of using this library, you'll discover just how much it can benefit you.

Picture a system of roads. That will give you an idea of how the Internet works. This communication phenomenon developed in the 1960s, when government organizations and universities created a network of computers that could communicate with each other. The ARPANet, as it was called, soon spread around the world, and in the 1990s it became available to the public.

What we know as the Internet (international network) is actually a huge web of large computer servers connected to smaller computers with cables, phone lines, satellites, and other devices. If you could see them on a map, they would look like our system of roads, which is one reason the Internet is called the "information superhighway."

FYI ▶ Because the Internet resembles a web of interconnected sites, it is often nicknamed the Web, the Net, or even cyberspace. However, sometimes the Web refers specifically to the World Wide Web, so check your context.

Get familiar with the World Wide Web. The World Wide Web (WWW) is often confused with the Internet, but it is actually only a part of the bigger system that includes e-mail and newsgroups. The World Wide Web simply organizes massive amounts of text into beautiful pages, or Web sites, full of colorful illustrations and for-matted text. You can move from one page to the next by clicking on text that is highlighted in a different color. This is called a hyperlink, or link for short.

Since the World Wide Web is a major part of the Internet, you will spend most of your time there, and you'll be zipping from page to page in no time.

Quick tip ▶ Today, almost anything can be a link. Click on pictures on the Web, and they enlarge. Click on an advertising box, and you will go straight to the advertised company's Web page.

Understand how information travels. When you ask to see a Web page, either by typing its address or clicking on a link, your com-puter sends a request over your telephone or cable line. Your request travels through a maze of computers until it arrives at the one stor-ing the page you asked for. That computer then sends the page, in bits and pieces, back through the pipeline and into your computer. Here it is reassembled to pop up, full of life, on your screen.

You'd think this process would take days or weeks, but the beauty of the Internet is that you can see the site you asked for almost instantly. This is why the Internet is changing how we see the world.

With it, you have immediate access to anything you might need.

Play it safe ▶ Web sites are constantly changing and evolving. A site you visited last month may no longer look the same or even exist. Since no one controls who is qualified to write a Web page, the content of the Internet is also uncensored. So use common sense and an ounce of caution when you choose what to believe.

Learn the lingo. One thing for sure, the Web is full of strange terms and concepts. Here are a few basic ones to get you started.

- **Web site.** An area on the World Wide Web that contains a collection of electronic documents, called Web pages, bound together with links. These documents can be written by a company or an individual and generally cover a common subject. Just like a library is full of books, the Web is packed with Web sites.

- **Home page.** The introductory page of a Web site. When you type in the address of a site, the first page you go to is the home page. It's similar to a table of contents but with pictures and other graphics. It will tempt your interest with bits of information and give you links to the actual page that holds the data you want.

- **Surf.** Move from site to site or page to page in a relatively random way, using links and search engines. This is known as "surfing the Web."

- **Online.** Connected to or located on the Internet. When you are connected to the Internet, you are online. When you view a document on the Internet, that document is online.

- **Download.** To move data from the Internet or another computer to your computer. When you request a document from the Internet, and then copy it to your computer's hard drive, you have downloaded a file.

With this basic information in hand, you are now ready to explore the exciting world of the Internet.

Meet the modern modem

By now you are revving your engine, ready to cruise the Internet. Before you can get on the information superhighway, you need three things — a piece of hardware called a modem, a phone or cable line, and a company willing to sell you access to the Internet.

You have a choice of many different modems to get you on the Web. The three big ones are dial-up, cable, and DSL. The cheapest, but slowest, of these is the dial-up modem.

Place a call. A dial-up modem is a piece of hardware installed on your computer that allows you to communicate with the outside world. Every time you log on to the Internet, your dial-up modem places a call to a local Internet access company and connects you. When you are through, you hang up the modem. This is why it's called a dial-up.

Play it safe ▶ If you recently bought a computer, it probably already has a modem installed. If not, make sure you have it installed by a technician. This is one piece of hardware you don't want to deal with on your own.

Speak to be understood. In order for your computer to talk to another computer on the other end of the phone line, you need a translation service. You see, your computer speaks a language called digital, which is made up of long strings of ones and zeros. But a phone line only transfers sound waves, a series of tones called analog. Your modem translates digital into analog, and then this modem song travels over the phone line just like your voice does.

Fine-tune for speed. Since phone lines are so thin, they can only transfer so much information at a time. That's why your Web pages may take a few moments to appear on your screen.

If you want an Internet page to pop up within seconds, you need to get the fastest modem available and use every possible trick to speed up your reception. Most home users are happy with a dial-up service. But if you find you need more speed, you can always switch to a faster service later on.

Set your modem on full speed ahead

Sometimes you can fiddle with your existing modem settings to speed up your Internet connection. Before you start changing your settings, though, check to make sure you have a modem installed and ready to go.

1 Click on the START button. Find the SETTINGS option and choose CONTROL PANEL from the drop-down menu.

2 Double-click on the MODEMS icon. You will see a dialog box called MODEMS PROPERTIES with a large text window at the top. If you have a tiny icon and the name of a modem in that box, you already have a modem installed. Go ahead and set it up for 10-digit dialing.

If you live in an area where you dial the area code just to order pizza, you need to set your modem to dial all 10 digits instead of just the local seven.

1 From the MODEMS PROPERTIES box, click on the DIALING PROPERTIES button. The dialog box that pops up will look like the following illustration.

Dialing Properties dialog box

Dialing Properties [?] [X]

My Locations

I am dialing from:
[Home ▼] [New...] [Remove]

I am in this country/region: Area code:
[United States of America ▼] [   ] [Area Code Rules...]

When dialing from here

To access an outside line:

For local calls, dial [ ]

For long distance calls, dial [ ]

[✓] To disable call waiting, dial: [*70 ▼]

Dial using: ( ) Tone dial   (•) Pulse dial

[ ] For long distance calls, use this calling card:

[None (Direct Dial) ▼] [Calling Card...]

[OK] [Cancel] [Apply]

2 Click on the NEW button at the top of the box. In the I AM DIALING FROM text box, type in a new name like *home* or *work*.

3 In the text boxes below, choose your country from the drop-down list, and fill in your area code.

4 Before you exit this window, click on the AREA CODE RULES button. Check the ALWAYS DIAL THE AREA CODE (10-DIGIT DIALING) option, then press OK.

5 Back in the DIALING PROPERTIES box, click on APPLY. You are now set up to dial the area code.

Now you're ready to improve your Internet connection. Here are a few adjustments that will help you get the most from your modem.

Disable call waiting. Because your phone and your Internet connection share a line, your Internet link can cut off the minute someone tries to call you. Disable call waiting, so incoming calls will not disrupt your Internet session.

1   First, call your phone company and ask for the code to turn off call waiting.

2   On your computer, follow the steps at the beginning of this story to locate the DIALING PROPERTIES box (see illustration).

3   Click the box marked TO DISABLE CALL WAITING, DIAL at the bottom of the DIALING PROPERTIES window, and choose the correct code from the drop-down list next to it. Click APPLY and exit.

Match your computer speed. Sometimes your computer is set to process information at a slower speed than your modem can send it. To make sure you are getting your money's worth out of a fast, 56Kbps modem, match your computer and modem speeds.

1   Right-click on the MY COMPUTER icon on your desktop, and choose PROPERTIES from your options. Click on the DEVICE MANAGER tab.

2 Click on the plus sign next to the MODEM option and double-click on the listed modem that shows up.

3 Under the MODEM tab, check to make sure the MAXIMUM SPEED window is set to 115,200 bps.

4 Make a note of the location of your modem port, which is listed in the text box in the center of the screen. It should be something like COM2 or COM3. Press OK.

5 Back in the DEVICE MANAGER tab, click on the plus sign beside the PORTS option. Double-click on the COM option that matches your modem, and choose the PORT SETTINGS tab. The first item in the text box marked BITS PER SECOND should read 115,200. If it doesn't, choose it from the drop-down menu. Press OK, and exit all open windows.

Download modem drivers. Every six months, your modem needs updated instructions to interact quickly with your computer. These little bits of software, called drivers, can be downloaded directly off the Internet.

1 Find the paperwork that came with your modem to determine the manufacturer and model number. Or follow the instructions at the beginning of this story for identifying the modem on your computer. The name of your modem is in the text box of the MODEMS PROPERTIES box.

2 Go to the manufacturer's Web site to download an updated driver for that particular modem. If you can't find your manufacturer's Web site, go to **www.driverguide.com** and use its search engine.

3 Once you have downloaded the new driver, follow steps 1 and 2 from the previous paragraph about matching your computer speed to open your modem information window.

4 Click on the DRIVER tab and choose UPDATE DRIVER from the bottom of the window.

5 The computer will bring up a Wizard to walk you through the update.

Tech term ▶ Wizard – a computer help file that gives you step-by-step instructions to complete a process.

If your connection is still too slow, ask your local telephone provider about Integrated Services Digital Network lines, or ISDN for short. ISDN can double your hookup speed and free up your phone line at the same time — but it requires special telephone wiring that might not be installed in older homes.

Enjoy life in the fast lane

If you feel the need for speed, you have several other modem options. Collectively called "broadband," they are noted for their use of high frequency signals resulting in incredibly fast connections. Be warned that once you cross over into broadband-land, you may never be happy with a dial-up modem again.

Digital Subscriber Line (DSL). This high-speed connection may be your first choice if you live in an urban area. DSL takes advantage of unused space on your telephone line and uses a special modem that processes information so fast, your pages load almost instantly. Your Internet connection stays on continuously, but you can still use your telephone while you're online.

The tradeoff is cost. First, you have to buy, or lease, the special modem, which can run a couple of hundred dollars. Then, you'll pay a monthly rate of about $50 compared to $20 for a dial-up modem connection. Yet many happy DSL customers find these costs well worth it when they see their Internet pages load in less than a minute.

To set up DSL in your home, call your local Internet Service Provider and ask about its DSL options. Large communication companies like AT&T and Earthlink, and your telephone company, may offer DSL in addition to their regular dial-up access. If you live in the suburbs, this service may not be available since you have to live within three miles of a DSL station to use it.

Cable modem. The same cable that brings 100-plus TV channels into your home can bring the Internet to your computer. After the cable enters the house, a modem separates the television signals from the computer data and sends them to their proper places.

Tech term ▶ Bandwidth – a measurement of how much information can be transmitted at a time. The higher the bandwidth, the faster you can receive information.

Because cable uses fiber optic lines instead of phone lines, it can transfer Internet data up to 30 times faster than a dial-up connection. Plus, cable won't tie up your phone, and it saves you the hassle of dialing in every time you want to go online.

At the moment, cable seems to be the most popular broadband Internet option, probably because it is so available. But this may also be its biggest drawback. If you and your neighbors hook up to the same cable line, then log on to the Internet at the same time, everyone's connection will slow down. Still, even at its slowest, cable is faster than a dial-up modem.

Like DSL, a cable Internet subscription can cost you up to $50 a month, and you may need to pay for modem rental and installation costs. Still, if you regularly download large files like photographs, news video clips, and music, or just surf the Web extensively, cable is the way to go.

Call your local cable provider to see if this service is available in your area. Don't forget to ask the cable company if the package includes the modem or if you have to buy the modem separately.

Play it safe ▶ One problem with a continuous connection is that you leave your computer open to anyone on the Internet who wants to get into your system and cause mischief. Block them out with a piece of software aptly called a firewall. It will protect your files from tampering.

Wireless Internet: wave of the future?

Forget telephone and cable wires. The next generation of wireless connectors is pulling the Internet out of thin air.

- **WISP.** Touted as the wave of the future, this wireless Internet Service Provider sends Internet communication over radio waves picked up by an antenna on your roof.

- **Wi-Fi.** Take your Internet connection on the road. Wi-Fi providers set up hot spots in major cities, so your laptop antenna can pick up an Internet signal when you come close to their base stations.

- **Satellite modem.** Just like satellite TV, this system uses a dish to connect you to the Internet.

- **Airborne Internet.** This unusual system sets unmanned airplanes with satellite dishes and modems into orbit over major cities. While in orbit, these planes provide wireless Internet service to users below.

Keep your eye out for new wireless options, especially if you live in rural areas where DSL and cable are not available.

Hitch a ride on the Internet highway

You are now ready to cruise the Internet, but you may not know how to get there. Internet Service Providers (ISPs) are your answer. They are like taxicabs transporting you all over the Internet super-highway. You pay a fee, and they take you where you want to go.

ISPs have large computers that are connected to the Internet with fast and thick cables. They buy points of presence (POPs) — local telephone numbers in your area — to link you through their net-work directly to the Internet. Most ISPs will provide you with at least one e-mail address, space on the Web to store or build your own Web site, and unlimited access to the Internet. You connect to them through your modem or cable line, and they coordinate all your incoming and outgoing traffic.

Take your pick. You can choose from three types of ISPs. The larg-est are commercial services like America Online (AOL), Microsoft Network (MSN), Earthlink, CompuServe, and Prodigy. You can also select national telecommunication services such as AT&T, Bell telephone, and cable; or small local providers like mom-and-pop operations and community services. All three have pros and cons.

- **Commercial providers.** Joining a commercial service is a bit like taking a guided tour of the Internet. It has a simple start page with links to custom-built sites your ISP hopes will inter-est you. You can tailor this start page to your tastes and join thousands of newsgroups and chat rooms to meet people within the safety of your ISP's site. But because these providers are so popular, you may have trouble connecting to the Internet, or get disconnected when you pause to read or write e-mail. Cus-tomer service also can be a problem. If you find yourself more offline than online, you may want to seek a different service.

Tech term ▶ Start page – the first page you see when you connect to your Internet Service Provider.

- **National providers.** If you want full exposure to the wild Web frontier, this is the place for you. National providers don't worry about choosing sites for you. They supply you with a basic start page and let you range free. Because this service is offered by national telecoms, the connection is usually fast and reliable. They are stable and not prone to disrupted service. These larger services also have extensive technical support to help you solve problems — that is, if you can get to them. Because they cover such a large area, customer service may be impersonal and hard to access.

- **Local providers.** If you are interested in supporting your community and keeping up with local interests, this is a good provider to choose. Even though local services are small and sometimes slow, they often provide you with excellent, personal customer service. They usually include local sites and events on their start page. Because they have a small customer base, local ISPs may not survive the swiftly changing world of the Internet. Yet surveys show they have the highest rate of customer satisfaction of the three types of providers.

Check out your options. Here are some tips to help you find a provider in your area.

- If you get a free Internet offer in the mail, go ahead and give it a spin. Just make sure you read your contract carefully. And if you decide you don't want it, remember to disconnect before they start charging for the service.

- Ask around. Your friends and neighbors are the best references for a good service in your area. You can also check ISP ratings in consumer and computer magazines.

- Check the listings under Internet in your local paper, or check the Yellow Pages. Call your phone company, and ask if it offers online service.

- Most libraries offer free access to the Internet. Log on to these Web sites to research and order your ISP software.

The List of ISPs	http://thelist.internet.com
All Free ISP	www.all-free-isp.com
Find an ISP	www.findanisp.com

Ask before you sign. You need to ask a potential ISP at least six crucial questions before you sign on. If their answers line up with your needs, sign up and join the millions already on the Web.

- **Will my access be limited or unlimited?** Don't get unlimited access if you'll only be on the Internet a few hours a month. Many companies will sell you a cheaper service that restricts the number of hours you can surf on the Web. When you first start out, the 10 hours a month they offer may be just what you need to test the waters. Then, as you grow more confident, you may want to switch to unlimited access.

- **How much will this service cost including setup?** Is the software package free? Most ISPs provide free disks or CD-ROMs with their Internet service. Make sure you order the format that is compatible with your computer.

- **Do you have local access numbers, and if so, what are they?** Don't assume 1-800 numbers are free — some can cost up to $6 an hour. Also, some numbers that look local actually transfer to a long-distance number. Call the phone company to confirm your access number is local before signing up.

- **Do you have a free 24-hour customer support line, and what is that number?** Call your ISP outside regular business hours to make sure the service has a courteous and helpful staff.

- **Do you offer a trial period?** Don't sign a year-long contract with an ISP before trying it out for a few months.

- **How many modems do you have available at peak hours?**
  Many small Internet providers don't have enough modems to
  go around during peak hours. If too many people log on at the
  same time, you will get a busy signal every time you try to connect. As a general rule, seven customers per modem is excellent,
  12 is good, but 20 customers per modem can be a problem.

Now that you have chosen your Internet provider, all that remains is
the adventure of discovering resources and friends online.

Get the scoop on free ISPs

If you're thinking about signing with a free ISP, make
sure you examine the pros and cons.

Services like **www.juno.com**, **www.netzero.com**,
and **www.dotnow.com** offer free access to the
Internet for a limited number of hours a month. But in
return, you fill out a long marketing questionnaire,
allow them to track your movement on the Internet,
and put up with an endless stream of advertisements
flashing on your screen. These services are often
slow and have high customer service fees. Some
charge you for software, lock you into a yearly contract for other services, or pressure you to join their
paid service for more storage space.

In short, read the fine print carefully before commit-
ting to a free ride. You may be better off finding a relatively inexpensive, but more reliable, Internet provider.

Link up with your ISP

After you've picked an Internet Service Provider, the next step is to
open an account and set up your Internet connection. Once that's

done, the Internet will be available to you. In other words, you'll officially be "online."

To get started, contact your ISP for details on how to connect. Each ISP has its own process. For example, EarthLink and AOL send software CDs to help you sail through account setup. Their software also creates your dial-up connection automatically — so getting online is simple and quick. Other ISPs may provide step-by-step paper instructions (or software) to help you get online. Some DSL or cable connections may even need to be handled by the ISP's professional installer. Follow these tips, and your ISP connection will be up and running in no time.

Be prepared before you begin. A little advance preparation will simplify your job.

- Close all other software programs on your computer.

- Make sure no one is online. If you have a dial-up connection, keep everyone off the phone.

- If you plan to install ISP software on your hard disk, check that you have enough free hard-disk space available.

- For connections requiring a modem, be sure the modem is connected and — if external — turned on.

- Gather any information your ISP has sent you just in case you need it during the setup process. Also, gather any files, CDs, or instructions your ISP requires for setup.

If you have a dial-up connection, find out:

- whether you need to dial an outside line before connecting.

- whether your area requires 10-digit dialing.

- the code needed to turn off call waiting (if you have it) while you are online. Often the code is simply *70.

- which cities are covered by your local calling area. Consider checking your local phone book for this. If your ISP asks you to pick a local access phone number, this will come in handy. If you can choose the number(s) located closest to you in your local calling area, you'll avoid long-distance charges.

Know what to expect. Remember these helpful hints when opening your ISP account.

- Be prepared to set up billing through your credit card or checking account.

- When you are asked to agree to a Terms of Service (TOS) Agreement, read it carefully first. Your member agreement tells you what your ISP's policies and rules are. It also describes your rights as a user of the ISP.

- Some ISPs assign you a user name, also called a screen name. Others let you choose your own. If you pick your own, remember that some ISPs assign it as part of your e-mail address. For privacy's sake, you may not want to use your full name.

- You may need a password to access your account, so try to think of one ahead of time. For help in choosing a password, see *Protect yourself with passwords* on page 252.

- Your ISP will probably assign you an e-mail address during the setup process.

Now that you know what to expect and how to prepare, you can set up your ISP connection whenever you're ready.

FYI ▶ If you're online with a dial-up connection, people who call you on the telephone will get a busy signal.

ISP or OSP: The choice is yours

When is an ISP more than just an ISP? When it's an OSP, an Online Service Provider. Prodigy, CompuServe, and America Online (AOL) are examples.

Both OSPs and ISPs can deliver Internet access, but OSPs also package content and services exclusively for their members. AOL members, for example, can read AOL's articles, download software from AOL sites, and chat electronically in AOL chat rooms — without actually surfing the Internet. Yet members can also visit the Internet to get to chat rooms, articles, and downloads outside AOL.

What if you chose an ISP but want OSP features? The Internet may have content or services similar to the ones offered by OSPs. Also, some ISPs publish their own content or provide extra services for free. Find out what your ISP offers. If it doesn't meet your needs, you may want to consider switching to an OSP.

Browsers: your path to the WWW

You may think a browser is someone who window-shops at the local mall. But in computer language, a browser is the software you use to view Web pages and to cruise from one Web page to the next. Web pages are stored on other computers, sometimes thousands of miles away. You can't delete or change the content of a Web page, but — thanks to your browser — you can see and hear what's there.

Microsoft Internet Explorer and Netscape Navigator are the most widely used browsers. They operate almost the same way, but the Web pages they bring up may look slightly different. Examples in this book will refer to Internet Explorer, but you'll find similar features in Netscape Navigator.

> **FYI ▶** Netscape Navigator is part of a package of software products called Netscape Communicator. You can get Navigator either by itself or as part of Netscape Communicator. When people refer to "Netscape," they probably mean the Internet browser, not the software package.

Like most software programs, browsers are constantly improving. Every now and then, a fresh version of a browser comes out. Each new version offers exciting just-added options as well as improvements on features you already like. Even better, they provide stronger protection from hackers than earlier versions did. For first-rate Web browsing and the most security, always choose the latest version of your browser whenever possible.

Internet Explorer 6.0 is used for examples in this book because it's the latest version at the time of this writing.

Finding a browser is simple and convenient — and won't cost you a cent. In fact, it may already be installed on your computer. The Windows operating system usually includes Internet Explorer. Check the Windows desktop. If you see a small "e" icon, Internet Explorer is installed and ready to go.

Here are two other ways to get a browser:

- **From your ISP.** Your ISP or OSP may provide Internet Explorer, Netscape Navigator, or its own browser. Some ISPs include a browser on their installation CD. Other ISPs may let you download a browser from their Web site. If your ISP's preferred browser isn't Internet Explorer or Netscape Navigator, don't worry. Some ISP browsers are just customized versions of Internet Explorer. If so, you'll still be able to do many of the same things Explorer does.

- **From the manufacturer.** If your ISP doesn't provide a browser, you can get one directly from the manufacturer. Either download a browser from the Web, or order it on CD. Try Internet Explorer at **www.microsoft.com/downloads/** or Netscape Navigator at **http://wp.netscape.com/download/**. To find out how to order an Internet Explorer installation CD from Microsoft, call 800-642-7676. To get an installation CD from Netscape, try **http://www.e-cdorder.com/index.html**. Downloading a browser is free but can take several hours through a dial-up connection. CDs may require a small fee to cover shipping and handling.

Play it safe ▶ If you check your e-mail by using a button or menu command in your ISP's custom browser, you may want to keep that browser. The button or menu command may be missing or different in the "generic" Internet Explorer or Netscape Navigator.

Once you've selected a browser and learned how to use it, you'll probably want to stick with what's familiar. But if it doesn't meet your needs, don't be afraid to try another. You can keep more than one browser on your computer and use whichever one you like.

Learn how to log on and off

Are you ready to surf the Web, e-mail your family, or instant message your friends? Or maybe you just want to read through some newsgroups or chat online. Learn how to get on the Internet — and get off again — and you'll be ready to go.

All you need to do is sail through three easy steps. First, type in an ID for your ISP. (By asking for a user name, password, or other ID, your ISP prevents strangers from using your Internet account.) Next, connect to the Internet with your modem. Finally, open whatever software you need to browse, e-mail, chat, or otherwise enjoy the Internet. Here are some hints to help you along the way.

Connect through your modem. When it comes to logging on with a dial-up connection, each ISP seems to have a different process. But don't worry, most ISPs supply helpful instructions to guide you. Just check your ISP's information to learn how to log on. Meanwhile, here's a sample of how log-on instructions for a dial-up connection might look.

1 Double-click on your ISP's icon on your desktop.

2 When a log-on dialog box appears, type your user name in the USER NAME box.

3 Press the TAB key to move to the PASSWORD box. Type in your ISP password. You'll probably see asterisks instead of letters as you type.

4 Click on OK or click on CONNECT, or press ENTER on your keyboard.

Logging on may trigger the connection process, so don't be startled if your modem screeches. It's just trying to connect with your ISP.

Launch your browser. Depending on your ISP's software, logging on may start up your browser automatically, or you may have to log on and then click a browser icon separately. If you have to start up Internet Explorer after you've logged on, just click the "e" icon (for Explorer) on your desktop.

Timesaver ▶ If you don't see a browser icon on your desktop, just click on the START menu button, then click on PROGRAMS. Your browser's name should be there. Click on it to open.

Close your browser. After you're through exploring the Internet or checking your e-mail, it's time to log off. Your ISP's log-off instructions may not actually close your browser, so you may need to close the browser separately. To quit Internet Explorer, click on FILE and click on CLOSE.

Quit your Internet connection. Logging off and disconnecting are not always the same thing, but some ISPs do both at once. Check your ISP documentation to find out how to log off and disconnect completely.

In some cases, you can log off and close your browser, but your dial-up modem stays connected. If your ISP plan has limited hours or per-hour rates, this can rack up huge bills. Check your System Tray for a tiny icon of two computers with a cord between them. If you see that icon, double-click on it and click on DISCONNECT in the dialog box. Although your ISP may disconnect automatically, take that extra moment to check for the icon — just to be sure.

Enjoy worry-free DSL and cable. If you have DSL or a cable modem, you probably don't have to worry about logging on or off the Internet. Your connection has an address that can act as your user name and password. In addition, DSL and cable connections are always on, so you connect to the Internet just by turning on your computer.

For these reasons, your ISP may not ask you to enter a user name and password to get online. Instead, you may skip the log-on and connecting process and simply start your browser or e-mail program. When you're through, you'll close them. You'll disconnect automatically when you turn off your computer.

Hang up on connection problems

Does your dial-up connection need help? Look on the next page to find the question that matches your trouble. You'll be on your way to solving your problem in no time.

Q **If I can't connect at all, how do I get online?**

A Check the modem connections to be sure nothing has wriggled free. If you have an external modem, check the power connection, too. Next, make sure the phone number is correct. If these don't work, try the suggestions from the modem story earlier in this chapter.

Q **What should I do when it won't accept my password?**

A Carefully type in the password again. Also, check whether your CAPS LOCK key should be on or off. If your password is case-sensitive, the capitalization (or lack of it) must be correct for each letter. So, if the password is PassWord, then password, PASSWORD, or even Password won't work.

Q **Why do I get a busy signal, and what can I do about it?**

A On evenings, holidays, and weekends, too many people may try to log on at the same times. Try again shortly or dial in at off-peak times. Also, see if your ISP has a new local access number for your area.

Q **Why was I disconnected, and how do I reconnect now?**

A If you logged in and connected successfully but the connection drops, redial to reconnect. You can often log back in without closing your browser or e-mail. If that fails, ask if anyone picked up the phone. Tell your family you need the phone before you reconnect. Also, if you have call waiting, incoming calls can kick you offline. To fix this, see the earlier story on temporarily disabling call waiting. Also, keep in mind that your ISP or modem may disconnect you automatically if your connection is idle for a long time.

Q **What should I do if a person answered instead of the modem?**

A Check the phone number. If it's correct, try dialing again.

Q **How do I handle error messages?**

A If your computer displays error messages when you try to connect, just try again. If the error repeats, write down the exact wording of the error message, check that your modem is plugged in, and call your ISP to check for technical problems on their end.

Q **What if I still have a problem?**

A For more dial-up troubleshooting tips, check the manuals or Web sites for your modem and for your ISP. Both may have troubleshooting or technical support sections to help you fix connection problems.

Take the 5-minute browser tour

Here are some screen elements you should be familiar with. They
will help you use your browser to navigate the World Wide Web.

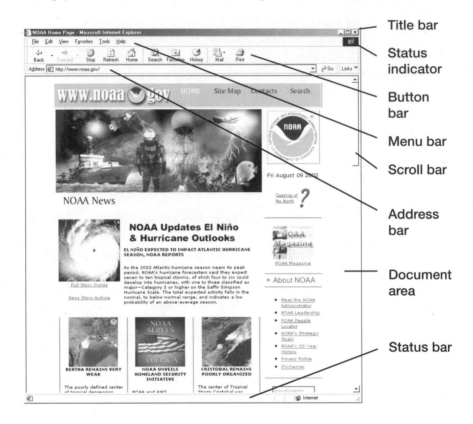

Title bar. Shows the title of the Web site you're viewing and the
browser name. The Minimize, Maximize, and Close buttons are
located on the right side.

Status indicator (access indicator). This browser logo spins
or moves while a Web page loads or while information is
being exchanged.

Button bar (Icon bar, Navigation bar, Standard toolbar). Row of
buttons that speeds up frequently used navigating or browsing

commands. BACK, FORWARD, and STOP are examples of Button-bar commands.

Menu bar. Displays menus of commands and options for browsing and navigating. In Internet Explorer, the Menu bar includes FILE, EDIT, VIEW, FAVORITES, TOOLS, and HELP.

Address bar. Displays the address of the Web page you're viewing. This is also the place to enter the address of any page you want to see.

Scroll bar. Use this to move up or down if a Web page doesn't fit in one screen. If the page is wide, you can also scroll from side to side.

Document area. This is where the Web pages show up.

Status bar. Shows status and progress messages while pages or files load. This bar may also display valuable security messages.

You can use the Menu bar to do useful tasks like these.

To do this	From the Menu bar
Print a Web page	Click on FILE then click on PRINT
Exit the browser	Click on FILE then click on CLOSE
Find a word in a long Web page	Click on EDIT then click on FIND (ON THIS PAGE)
Read instructions for using your browser	Click on HELP then click on CONTENTS AND INDEX
Learn which version of the browser you have	Click on HELP then click on ABOUT INTERNET EXPLORER

For more details on using your browser, go to the Menu bar and click on HELP. Click on CONTENTS AND INDEX, then click on CONTENTS. When the TABLE OF CONTENTS displays, click on any topic you want to know more about.

Now you're ready to learn how to surf the Web with your browser. Read on to open up a whole new world of information and fun.

Fast fix ▶ If you don't see the Button bar, or if the Address bar is missing, you can fix that. Move your cursor to the Menu bar. Click on VIEW and then TOOLBARS. Finally, click on STANDARD BUTTONS or ADDRESS BAR, as needed. The missing bar should appear instantly.

Master the meaning of URLs

In order to surf the World Wide Web, you need to type in an address for each Web site you want to visit. Just as you have a street address, every page on the Web has a unique address called a URL or Uniform Resource Locator. To get to a particular site, a surfer can use its URL.

Learn what a URL looks like. Whenever you see a combination of letters, numbers, and symbols that don't seem to make sense, you're looking at a URL. Examples are **http://www.fca.com** or **http://www.ssa.gov/OACT/babynames/2001/top100_of_2001.html**.

Get familiar with the parts. The URL **http://www.fca.com** is the main page for a Web site. Main-page addresses are often shorter than the addresses for other pages on a site. Long URLs can look confusing, but they actually supply useful information. Consider the second example above. If you take it apart, here's what it means.

URL part	Meaning
http://www	The first part stands for Hypertext Transfer Protocol and the second for World Wide Web. It shows that the address will direct you to a Web page.
.ssa	This is the domain name — often the name of the organization that owns or maintains the site. Here, it refers to the Social Security Administration.
.gov	The suffix shows either what type of organization owns the site or the country where the site's files are stored. Here, it means the site belongs to a government.
/OACT/ babynames/ 2001/ top100_of_2 001.html	This mixture of letters, numbers, and symbols tells where the Web page's file is stored on the Web site's computer. Each one is different so it's important to copy it exactly.

Two-letter suffixes such as **.us** (United States) or **.au** (Australia) specify which country the site is located in. For a list of these country codes, see **http://rsd.gsfc.nasa.gov/goes/text/web_country_codes .html**. Three-letter domain suffixes hint at what kind of organization owns a Web site. Suffixes for organization type include:

- **com** (commercial)
- **edu** (educational institution)
- **gov** (government)
- **int** (international)
- **mil** (military)
- **net** (network)
- **org** (organization)

If you're not sure of a Web site's exact URL, you sometimes can make a fairly accurate guess if you know the type of organization you're looking for.

Follow four easy steps. When you find a URL you want to use, here's what to do.

1 Start your browser.

2 Find the Address bar near the top of your browser. In Internet Explorer, ADDRESS is on one side of the bar and the GO button is on the other.

3 Click on the Address bar and type (or copy and paste) a URL. For example, you could type **http://www.fca.com.**

4 Either click on the GO button or press ENTER on your keyboard.

Your current page will vanish, and the status indicator will spin as the new page loads. (While a Web page's contents are being sent to your computer, that Web page is "loading.") When the status indicator stops spinning, you will see the complete Web page.

Shorten your workload. You usually can take a shortcut when typing a URL and simply type **www** without the **http.** That's because your eager-to-please browser helps you out. For any address that starts with **http://www**, you can skip the **http://** part. The browser still acts as if you typed it and fills it in by itself.

Tech term ▶ Splash page – a Web site's preliminary or introductory page that usually features graphics, animation, or important information. Not all Web sites have splash pages.

Beware of typos. What if you type in a URL and it doesn't take you where you want to go? First, confirm that no typing errors or blank spaces sneaked in. Make sure the typed URL has forward slashes (/) and correct punctuation, and check that periods, capital letters, and numbers are in the right places. Some URLs don't have **www** in them. Others may not start with **http.** Be careful to exactly match the URL you are typing from. And beware of the period that follows a URL at the end of a sentence. That should not be typed as part of the adresss.

Expect surprises. Sometimes when you start typing a URL a completed URL — or list of URLs — will pop up out of nowhere. That's the browser's AutoComplete feature. Here's how it works. Browsers can keep track of Web pages you've surfed recently. When you start typing, the browser checks your typing against its list of recently visited URLs. If you are typing a URL the browser recognizes, it tries to finish that URL for you.

Don't worry if that's not the URL you want. Just keep typing. Either the browser will offer the right URL or you'll finish typing the URL you need.

Speed up your surfing

URLs can be confusing, but luckily you won't have to type one every time you go to a different Web site. You can use hyperlinks and the Button bar to save time and speed up your surfing.

Take advantage of links. A hyperlink — or link for short — is a connection from one Web page to another. When you see a link on a Web page, you can click on it with your mouse. Your browser reads the invisible URL hidden in the link and zooms to that Web page.

The standard hyperlink is underlined text, usually colored blue. The link's text describes what you'll find on the connected page. For example, a link labeled HOME or MAIN could take you to the main page of the current Web site, whereas a link labeled MORE INFORMATION might send you to a different Web site. These handy text links even offer an extra bonus. If you're revisiting a list of links and want to know which ones you've already surfed, notice the colors. The links that have changed to a new color are the ones you have tried before.

229

Links aren't always underlined text. They can be pictures, icons, arrows, buttons, and nearly any kind of text you can dream up. So how do you tell when you're looking at a link? Slide your cursor over the item slowly. If the item is a link, the cursor changes to a hand with a pointing finger. You may also spot the link's URL in the browser's status bar.

Tech term ▶ Image map – a single picture on a Web page that is split into sections so each section is a clickable link. For example, a U.S. map might have 50 links, one for each state shown.

Use buttons for shortcuts. Remember the browser's Button bar? That's where you'll find five powerful buttons to supercharge your surfing.

Browser Button bar

- **BACK button.** The BACK button returns you to the Web page you just came from. You don't have to remember a URL or even type it in. Your browser keeps track of where you've been and keeps copies of those pages. Each time you click the BACK button, you'll go back one page further in your surfing history. When the button is dimmed, you'll have gone back as far as you can.

- **FORWARD button.** The sole purpose of the FORWARD button is to return you from wherever the BACK button took you. In fact, your browser opens with the FORWARD button dimmed, as shown in the illustration. Once you click on the BACK button, the FORWARD button brightens so you can use it.

- **STOP button.** This button cancels the loading of a Web page. But it cannot unload the images that have already appeared on the screen. To clean up your screen, simply go to another page. Here are some reasons you may want to click on the STOP button.

  - So you won't have to wait several minutes for a huge image or sound clip to load.

  - The page isn't what you expected or wanted.

  - You accidently clicked on this link instead of the one you meant to click on.

  - The page is taking too long to load, and you're tired of waiting.

- **REFRESH button.** Some Web pages take a while to load. To save time, browsers keep copies of pages you've visited. When you revisit a page, your browser whips out the copy from your hard drive so you don't have to wait for the page to reload. But if you're checking stock quotes or trying to get the latest news, you want the newest version of a Web page. That's when you click on REFRESH to load the most current version of the page, fresh from the Web.

HOME button. When you first open your browser, the same Web page always appears. This is your start page, sometimes called the home page. No matter where or how long you surf, you can always click on the HOME button to return to your start page.

5 ways to beat browser errors

You may have come across messages on the Web that block the pages you're trying to find. These are browser error messages. Like TV and radio stations, Web sites sometimes experience technical difficulties. Fortunately, you may be able to sidestep these snarls by using one of these five error-eliminating solutions.

- Click on the REFRESH button.

- Check the URL carefully to be sure it is correct. If you find an error, fix it and click the GO button.

- Move your cursor to the end of the URL and click after the last letter. Delete backwards until your cursor is next to a slash. Press ENTER to see if you can find a page with a link to the URL you want.

- Go to the site's main page (the part that ends in **.com**, **.org**, **.net**, etc.) and try to navigate to the page from there.

- If all else fails, try again in a few minutes or a few hours. Any technical difficulties may have cleared up by then.

Error messages can be frustrating, but everyone encounters them at one time or another. Understanding what they mean will help make them a little less scary. Here are some of the most common error messages you will find while surfing the World Wide Web. If these specific solutions don't help, try one of the five error eliminators.

401 — Unauthorized

403 — Forbidden

Connection refused by host

These messages mean you have entered a restricted or members-only site. If you have entered a password to the site, check it carefully and try again.

404 — Not found

The page you're looking for could not be located. Look for a message that says the site has moved. If you find it, look for a nearby link to the new location. Even better, you may see a message that asks you to wait while you're automatically transported to the new location.

If the site hasn't moved, the page may have shifted to a new spot within the site. Check for a link or a site search engine that can direct you to the page.

Host unknown

Unable to locate host

Unable to locate server

If you see one of these messages, check your Internet connection. If you are not connected, log back in. If you are connected, try each of the five error-eliminating solutions.

400 — Bad request

500 — Server error

503 — Service unavailable

Failed DNS lookup

File contains no data

Host unavailable

These error messages usually mean something is wrong with the URL address, the Web page, or the server. These errors may be fixed by applying the five suggested solutions.

Bookmark a trail to great Web pages

Found a great Web site? Want to go back to it without remembering all the links that got you there? Step into the hassle-free world of electronic bookmarks.

Like paper bookmarks, electronic bookmarks are placeholders. When you "bookmark" a particular Web page, you create a handy way to zip back to it — by linking to the site. To return to the site, you just open a menu and click on the link you want. In Internet Explorer, the menu is named FAVORITES, and each link inside that menu is a Favorite.

Browsers usually come with their own list of ready-to-use Favorites. You can add to this list as you please.

Bookmark a Favorite. Try the following steps to bookmark a site in Internet Explorer.

1 Go to a site you think you'll visit often.

2 On the browser's Menu bar, click on FAVORITES, then click on ADD TO FAVORITES.

3 When the ADD FAVORITE dialog box appears, check the name that will appear in your list of Favorites. Change it if you want. Click on OK.

Come back for a visit. So how do you go back to a site you've book-marked? Follow these steps to find any of your Favorites.

1 On your browser's Button bar, click on the FAVORITES button. The FAVORITES bar shows up on the left side of your browser window. It's the same list you saw in the FAVORITES menu, but this list is even more mouse-friendly.

Internet Explorer Favorites bar

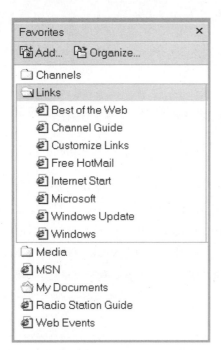

This mouse-friendly bar appears when you press the FAVORITES button.

2 Some Favorites in folders are temporarily hidden. To see a Favorite that's inside a folder, click on the folder icon.

3 When you find the Favorite you want, click on it. The site should start loading immediately.

4 To close the FAVORITES bar, click on the X on the top right side of the list.

Organize your sites. After a while, your list of Favorites may grow so long that it's hard to find what you need. That's why browsers have an ORGANIZE option. This option lets you file Favorites by moving them to folders, and create new folders whenever you want to add a category.

To create a new folder in Internet Explorer's FAVORITES:

1 On the FAVORITES menu, click on ORGANIZE FAVORITES.

235

2 Click on the CREATE FOLDER button.

3 Type a name for the folder, then press ENTER and CLOSE.

To move a Favorite to an existing FAVORITES folder in
Internet Explorer:

1 On the Button bar, click on the FAVORITES button.

2 Drag the Favorite (or a folder) to the appropriate folder.

Wouldn't it be great to add a Favorite and assign it to a FAVORITES
folder at the same time? You can. When you're bookmarking a site,
watch for the ADD FAVORITE dialog box. When you see it, click on
the CREATE IN button. Click on the folder where the Favorite should
go, and then click on OK. For more ways to organize Favorites,
check your browser's HELP menu.

Quick tip ▶ If you want to move your Favorites from Explorer to Navigator, or vice versa, look for the IMPORT option on both browsers. Check
your browser's HELP for instructions on using the IMPORT feature.

Surfing tricks and troubleshooting

If you want to know how to get more out of your browser, you've
come to the right place. You'll even find a few answers to those
"How do I fix it?" questions. Check out these surfing tricks and
troubleshooting tips. You'll be glad you did.

Q I'm on my ISP's limited hours plan. Reading a long set of Web
pages really eats up the minutes. Do you have any suggestions?

A Would printing the pages take less time than reading them? If so, print
the pages and save them to read after you log off. For quick printing,
just click on the PRINT button on your browser's Button bar. Another

option is to save the Web pages and read them offline. See your browser's HELP menu for instructions on how to do this.

Q **How can I print just one page of a long Web document? I can't tell where one page ends and the next begins.**

A With Internet Explorer, you can select the section you want to print. Simply highlight it, then go to your browser's Menu bar. Click on FILE and then PRINT. When the dialog box opens, look for PRINT RANGE, and click on SELECTION. Then click on OK.

Q **I don't like the home page that shows up each time I open my browser. Can I change it?**

A Your home page was probably set by your ISP, but you can select any Web page you want. Here's how to do it in Internet Explorer.

1 Go to the page you want as your new home page.

2 Click on TOOLS in the Menu bar, and then click on INTERNET OPTIONS.

3 Click on the GENERAL tab. In the HOME PAGE section, click on the USE CURRENT button.

4 Click on OK.

Q **I've been surfing a lot lately, and now my computer seems to be running more slowly. Is there anything I can do?**

A In Computer housekeeping, you learned how to clean up temporary files to free up extra disk space and improve your computer's performance. Your browser stores copies of all the Web pages you've surfed, which can also be considered as "temporary Internet files." If you still need more space, you can clean out these files. To do this with Internet Explorer, use these steps.

1 Click on TOOLS, and then click on INTERNET OPTIONS.

2 When INTERNET OPTIONS appears, click on the GENERAL tab.

3 Look for TEMPORARY INTERNET FILES, and then click on DELETE FILES.

4 In the DELETE FILES dialog box, click on OK. The INTERNET OPTIONS box will reappear. Click on OK to close.

Q **I visited a site yesterday that I really liked, but I forgot to bookmark it. Is there an easy way to find it again?**

A That site is not lost forever. Instead, the site is part of history — literally. Your browser has a history feature to help you find sites you've surfed recently. If you're using Internet Explorer, click on the HISTORY button. This displays a list of sites you've visited in recent days or weeks. Click on the folder for the day or week when you visited the site to find the Web page you need.

Q **Sometimes, when I click on a link, the new site opens in just a small part of the window I'm in. How can I make it bigger?**

A In Internet Explorer, you can position your cursor in the area you want to see and right-click. When the menu appears, click on OPEN FRAME IN NEW WINDOW. Now you can see the site better.

Q **Why do all those extra windows pop up when I open a Web page?**

A They're probably advertisements. Although some Web sites open a new window when you click on a link, many Web sites also open pop-up ad windows. If the ads are in your way, click on the CLOSE button. If you want to block ads from appearing, you can find software that will do the job for you. In fact, the EarthLink ISP has recently started offering its users free software to do this.

Q **I've been surfing for a while, but on some pages, my BACK button is dimmed. Why would that happen, and how do I fix it?**

A Sometimes, when you click on a link, the site opens a new browser window to display the linked page. When you finish reading it, simply minimize or close the window. You should see the previous page in the "old" window — and the BACK button won't be dimmed in that window.

Q **The words on my Web page are so small I can hardly read them. Is there a way to make them bigger?**

A If the print on a Web page is too small to read easily, you can make it larger. In Internet Explorer, click on VIEW on the Menu bar. Click on TEXT SIZE. Pick the size you want, and you'll be reading clearly in no time.

Q **I found a picture on the Web that I just love. How can I put it on my desktop?**

A If you find a picture online, and you'd like to make it the background on your desktop, place your cursor over it and right-click. When the browser menu appears, just click on SET AS WALLPAPER.

Plug in some browser fun

Your browser glides along the information superhighway as well as any race car at the Indianapolis 500. But wouldn't it be great if it had some car-like accessories — perhaps a music player or even a video player? That's where plug-ins come in. Plug-ins are small software programs that "plug in" to your browser to give it extra abilities.

Want your browser to play music, multimedia shows, or videos? Plug-ins like RealPlayer, Shockwave, or QuickTime can help it do that. Would you like to see documents your browser couldn't show you before? Acrobat Reader can help you out.

Plug-ins can do all kinds of things — and they're usually free. Just be careful to select a version that is designed for your browser. Get plug-ins from major download sites like Microsoft, Macromedia, or Apple. Or download and install a new plug-in when you surf to a site that requires it.

Start up your (search) engine

Sam Spade and Philip Marlowe may have been excellent private detectives — but the Internet puts them to shame. With the Internet, you can find anything you need — from great shopping deals to information on the most unusual subject. You just have to know how to look.

That's where search engines come in. Think of search engines as super-fast private eyes. You tell them what you're looking for, and they work quickly to find it — often in just seconds.

To choose the best search engine, consider what you're looking for. Do you want a specific answer or general subject knowledge? Is your topic something most others might look for, or is it pretty out of the ordinary? With these things in mind, you can choose from three kinds of search engines — search indexes, search directories, and meta-searchers.

Seek specifics with search indexes. These search engines hunt for words or phrases you type into a search text box. That's why search indexes are great for finding specific details or unusual information.

A search index constantly sends out "bots" — programs that scour the Web for new or updated sites. The bots scurry back to deposit hot new finds in the search index's database. You search that database whenever you use the index.

FYI ▶ Bots are sometimes called spiders, and their information-hunting process is known as "crawling the Web."

Because bots update their databases so frequently, you'll always see the latest Web pages possible. You'll also get lots of results to choose from. Although some may not be helpful, others may be exactly what you need.

Suppose you want to know what the weather will be like during your upcoming trip to Miami. Here's how you can find out through an index search.

1 Start by surfing to a search index site. (Check the list later in this chapter for suggestions.) When you get there, you'll see a text box near a button labeled SEARCH, SUBMIT, or some similar term.

2 To start your search, think of words or phrases to describe what you want to find. Each word or phrase is called a key

word. In this case, you could use the words weather forecast and Miami.

3 Type your keywords in the text box. Type a space to separate each keyword from the next one. If your keywords are phrases, put quotation marks around each phrase. For example, you would type *"weather forecast" Miami.*

4 Start the search by clicking on the SEARCH button.

5 When the search is complete, a results page comes up. Near the top, you'll see the number of results found. Below that, the jackpot — a list of links with Web page titles and descriptions. Read these to decide which results match what you're looking for.

6 To try a promising result, click on the link to go to that Web page. If that page doesn't have your answer, just click on the BACK button to return to the results list.

7 If you don't find your answer on the first results page, you're not out of options. Look for links at the bottom of the page to take you to the next set of results.

Don't worry if your first few searches don't go well. Just read *Secrets of successful searchers* on page 244 for more helpful tips.

Play it safe ▶ Advertisers can pay to have their links displayed along with top search results. The FTC has warned it may take action against search engines that allow this. To avoid unwanted advertising, use Google, which labels advertiser links clearly. Ixquick or Yahoo! may also be safe bets.

Now that you know how to search, you need to know where to search. Some of the most popular search indexes include Excite, AOL, or MSN — all great home pages, too. Following is an alphabetical list of some top Web sites for starting your search.

All The Web	www.alltheweb.com
Ask Jeeves	www.askjeeves.com
AOL Search	http://search.aol.com
Excite	www.excite.com
Google	www.google.com
HotBot	www.hotbot.lycos.com
Lycos	www.lycos.com
MSN Search	http://search.msn.com
Netscape Search	http://search.netscape.com
Northern Light	www.northernlight.com
Overture	www.overture.com
Teoma (formerly Direct Hit)	www.teoma.com
Wisenut	www.wisenut.com
Yahoo!	www.yahoo.com

Search directories for subject info. If you want an introduction to a topic — or just general information about it — the search directory is the engine for you. It sorts information into categories. Many search indexes also include categories so you can broaden your search. Yahoo! is one example of both an index and a directory. Here's how you would use the Yahoo! search directory to learn more about collecting stamps or coins.

1 On the search directory's main page, look through the list of subject area links. In this case, you'll click on RECREATION AND SPORTS.

2 The recreation page that appears lists types of recreation. Click on HOBBIES.

3 When the list of hobbies appears, click on COLLECTING.

4 You'll now see a list of COLLECTING subcategories. Click on STAMPS or COINS AND CURRENCY.

Directories are the "made by hand" search engine. People actually review the Web sites and classify them into categories and subcategories. That's why you'll often get better matches than you would from search indexes. On the other hand, you may get fewer links, and they're not as up to date.

Here are some popular directories to try.

LookSmart	www.looksmart.com
Yahoo!	www.yahoo.com
Open Directory Project	www.dmoz.org
About	www.about.com
Librarian's Index to the Internet	www.lii.org
The WWW Virtual Library	www.vlib.org

Send out a meta-search party. If you can't find something with one search engine, why not try a whole group of them at once? Meta-searches run several search engines at the same time. Results are usually separated by search engine so you can see which one found what. Here are some you can try for yourself.

Ixquick	www.ixquick.com
MetaCrawler	www.metacrawler.com
Dogpile	www.dogpile.com
Mamma	www.mamma.com
MetaGopher	www.metagopher.com

Hunt for news, bargains, and more. Some search engines specialize in finding you specific links. Want a shopping search engine where you can compare prices? Try **www.mysimon.com**. Looking for news stories, sound files, images, or extra shopping bargains? Find those unique search engines at **www.searchenginewatch.com/links** or **www.searchengineguide.com**.

How to deal with wacky results

Got results that don't seem to match your search at all? First, check for typing errors in your search text box. If your spelling is fine, but you don't see the keyword on the page, check to see if it's buried somewhere in the document.

To find it, click on the EDIT menu, and then click on FIND (ON THIS PAGE). Type the keyword in the FIND box. Check the settings in the dialog box. Change them, if needed, and then click on FIND NEXT.

If your keyword is there, you'll find it, and if you're lucky, the information will be helpful after all.

Secrets of successful searchers

Experienced searchers have learned tricks that help them get better results. You, too, can master the art of searching by following these handy tips.

Be specific. If you're looking for tulips, don't type *flowers* — type *tulips*. Being as specific as possible will help the search engine produce more focused results. Remember, computers aren't human. They don't know what you mean unless you tell them exactly.

Refine your search. One way to be more specific is to use symbols to narrow your search's focus. Most search engines recognize math symbols like "+" and "-." These let you add or subtract terms from your search. If you want information on both Fred Astaire and Ginger Rogers, you can type *Astaire + Rogers*. On the other hand, if you want information about saints, but not the New Orleans Saints, type *saints – New Orleans*.

You can also use Boolean terms, like *AND* or *NOT,* to do the same thing. You can even use *OR* whenever you want a search engine to find either one keyword or the other. For example, if you were looking for information on Christmas tunes, you could type *Christmas carols OR Christmas songs.*

Put phrases in quotations. If you're looking for a particular phrase — such as *The African Queen* — type the whole phrase in quotation marks. That way, you'll get only results pertaining to the 1951 movie starring Humphrey Bogart and Katharine Hepburn and not random information about ancient African rulers.

Group words in parentheses. To pinpoint exactly what you're hunting for, use parentheses to group words. For example, in searching for recycling information, you could type *(Paper OR Plastic) AND Recycling.*

Use a wildcard. Type an asterisk (*), known as a wildcard character, to find more than one form of a word. For example, *skat** instructs a search engine to look for skate, skates, skated, skater, and skating.

Look for synonyms. Don't give up if your search yields few results. Try again using a synonym for your original search term. Even if you were successful the first time, searching again with a synonym gives you even more options. Search for *dogs,* and then search for *canines.* You'll be surprised how different the results might be.

Include several keywords. You may end up with some strange results if you use just one search term. If you're looking for information about Queen Victoria, entering *Victoria* as a keyword may lead you to sites about the former British queen — and to the Victoria Square shopping mall. You'll get better results when you type several terms to describe what you're looking for.

Play the field. Don't feel married to just one search engine. They each work differently, so the same keyword will not produce the exact same results from one to the next. Explore, and see which ones work best for you.

Quick tip ▶ Select a few favorite search engines and bookmark them.

Get help. Most search engines feature a section called HELPFUL HINTS or HELP or ADVANCED SEARCH. They'll give you pointers about how to use that particular search engine. You'll save a lot of time if you learn the basics of each search engine you try.

For more searching secrets, try the following sites:

- http://searchenginewatch.com/facts/index.html
- http://www.searchengineguide.com/howtosearch.html

Find old friends fast

Looking for someone? Perhaps you lost touch with an old friend. Maybe you lost your Aunt Esther's phone number. Or maybe you need a way to contact a business. Don't hire a private detective. Just log on to the Internet. Several search directories exist just for this type of situation.

One of the best is Switchboard.com. At **www.switchboard.com**, you can track down a person or a business with equal ease. Just type in the name, city, and state — or as much as you know — and it will find matches. You can also search by business category, such as attorneys or restaurants. Other features include an e-mail directory and a reverse look-up, which lets you type in a phone number and see what person or business it belongs to. Here are some examples of other great directories with similar features.

AnyWho	www.anywho.com
411 Locate	www.411locate.com
Hoover's Online	www.hoovers.com
White Pages	www.whitepages.com
WhoWhere?	www.whowhere.lycos.com
Yellow Pages	www.yellowpages.com
The Ultimates	www.theultimates.com
Bigfoot	www.bigfoot.com
World Email Directory	www.worldemail.com
PhoneNumbers.net	www.phonenumbers.net
Yahoo! People Search	www.people.yahoo.com
BigBook	www.bigbook.com

You can also use a meta-search engine that searches several people-finding directories at once. You'll find it at **http://peoplesearch.net/peoplesearch/peoplesearch_classic.html.**

Try this URL to locate people in more than 170 countries: **http://teldir.com.**

Just as with search engines, not all directories produce the same results. Keep searching until you find your man (or woman).

Get the lowdown on downloading

Everyone you talk to recommends a certain software, but you don't have time to shop for it. No problem. You can pick out software online and have it sent directly to your computer without ever leaving your chair. You can even get software for free. How? Just find the software on the Internet and download it.

What exactly is downloading? When you request a file from the

Internet and then copy it to your computer's hard drive, you have downloaded a file. In other words, downloading is just passing files from the Internet "down" to your computer.

Here are some types of software programs you can download for free.

Freeware	A software program that you never have to pay for.
Shareware	A software program that is available for a free trial. If you decide to use the shareware program after the trial period, you have to pay a fee.
Demoware	A software program, usually from a major company, that you can try for a period of time before you must pay for it. When the payment deadline arrives, the software may stop working. Some demoware lacks the software's full range of abilities, but you can get the full-featured package once you pay for it.
Upgrade	A new version of a software program intended to replace an older version currently being used.
Patch	A small piece of software that is a temporary addition to a software product. Patches often fix one or more problems with the software or repair a security weakness that could be exploited by hackers.
Plug-ins	Small software programs that plug into your browser to give it extra abilities.

In addition to software programs, you can download sound files, video files, images, and documents — all at zero cost. Some files, of course, are not free. You can easily find name-brand software for sale on the Web. Just expect to pay with a credit card before you can download those files.

Play it safe ▶ Some freeware or shareware may not work well. A few may even cause computer glitches. Check software reviews at download sites like www.cnet.com or www.zdnet.com to make sure you get software that's problem-free.

Warm up for a download. For smoother downloading, try these tips before the download begins.

- Make sure your computer has an anti-virus program installed to stop any hidden viruses cold. Find out how to get and use an anti-virus program in *Keep viruses from bugging you* on page 255.

- Confirm that your anti-virus program is active (enabled) and set to check all incoming files. See your anti-virus program's online HELP for details.

- Check that you have enough free disk space to download this file.

- Find the folder called DOWNLOADS or MY DOWNLOADS. If it doesn't exist, create it. Save all downloads in that folder so they will always be easy to find.

- Before you download a software program, upgrade, or patch, create a new folder for it inside the DOWNLOADS folder. Plan to save just this download in the new folder, and don't delete it. If software trouble ever happens, the saved download can substitute for installation disks.

- Be prepared to supply personal information or technical details about your computer. Some sites require you to register before you can download a software file.

- Keep an eye out for instructions on how to install the software after you download it. Sometimes the software's installation instructions are only posted on the download site. Look for links to this information, and print it if you find it.

Get downloads down pat. Keep these ideas in mind as you download.

- Some sites ask you to pick the area you want to download your file from. Choose the location closest to you.

- After you click to download the file, always choose SAVE FILE TO DISK. Be sure to note the disk and directory where you save it. You'll need that information to use the file.

Once the download starts, you may see a dialog box counting how much time is left until the download finishes. Download times can range from a few seconds for a small file to hours for a jumbo-sized file. The speed of the download also depends on your modem speed, Internet traffic levels, and the speed of the computer sending the download.

Waiting for large software programs to download can be frustrating. Fortunately, technology has found a way to make things easier. Special software can compress the files to make them smaller — without losing a bit of essential information. It's like a technological trash compactor, except the files can be returned to their original shape. The compressed file — called a zip file — uses the same special software to get decompressed — or "unzipped."

Play it safe ▶ If the software has a license agreement, read all of it. Some license agreements state the software will monitor your activities or gather information about you for advertising purposes. Protect yourself by knowing what is in the license agreement before you agree to it.

You can choose either PKzip or Winzip software to handle this task. Check your PROGRAMS menu to see if one of these is already on your computer. If you don't see it, use the Windows FIND utility to track down PKzip or Winzip files. Get easy instructions for the FIND utility from *Find files and folders fast* on page 181.

If neither program is on your computer, pick one to download. You can get Winzip from **http://www.winzip.com** or PKzip from **http:/ /www.pkzip.com**. Each program offers a demoware version, so you can use it for free during the trial period. You don't even need to worry about how to unzip the PKzip or Winzip file after you download it. The installation process will do that for you.

Go from download to install. After you download the software, you still have to install it on your computer. Wrap up with these tips for safe installation.

- Scan your downloaded file or decompressed files with your anti-virus program if you haven't already.

- If your entire download is just a single file and that file has an .EXE or .COM extension, check for installation instructions on the download site. If you don't find any, double-clicking on this file may start an installation Wizard to help you install the software.

If decompressing or downloading a software program left you with a pile of files, follow the installation instructions. If you don't have instructions, see If one of your downloaded files has README, MANUAL, DOC, or DOCUMENTATION in its name. These are common names for helpful files. If no instruction files turn up, and you can't find any help on the download site, hunt for files with words like INSTALL or SETUP in their names. Clicking on one of these may trigger an installation Wizard.

Quick tip ▶ To easily download a picture from the Web, just position your cursor over the picture and right-click. When a menu pops up, click on SAVE PICTURE AS or SAVE TO DISK. Then choose where you want to save the picture and what you want to name it. Click on SAVE.

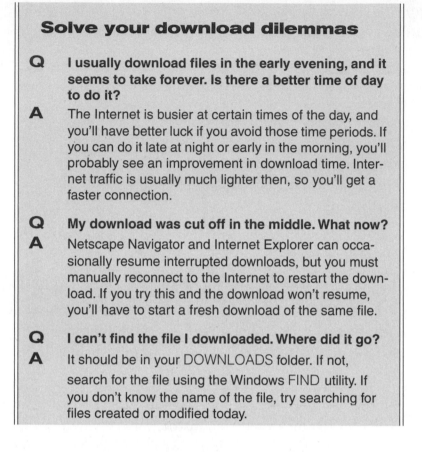

Solve your download dilemmas

Q **I usually download files in the early evening, and it seems to take forever. Is there a better time of day to do it?**

A The Internet is busier at certain times of the day, and you'll have better luck if you avoid those time periods. If you can do it late at night or early in the morning, you'll probably see an improvement in download time. Internet traffic is usually much lighter then, so you'll get a faster connection.

Q **My download was cut off in the middle. What now?**

A Netscape Navigator and Internet Explorer can occasionally resume interrupted downloads, but you must manually reconnect to the Internet to restart the download. If you try this and the download won't resume, you'll have to start a fresh download of the same file.

Q **I can't find the file I downloaded. Where did it go?**

A It should be in your DOWNLOADS folder. If not, search for the file using the Windows FIND utility. If you don't know the name of the file, try searching for files created or modified today.

Protect yourself with passwords

Think of a computer password as a kind of door key. Just as you can't get into your home without the key, you can't get into some files or computers without the password.

Passwords and door keys have something else in common. If the wrong person picked up the key to your home, that person could steal your credit cards as well as other important personal information. Computer criminals can do these things even more easily if they get hold of your password. That's why it's so important to choose one that is difficult to figure out and to keep it safe.

Computer passwords can guard all kinds of things. Here are some places you may need them.

- ISP account

- Shopping account with an online store

- Online banking account

- Settings or preferences for online services or subscriptions

- File, software program, or computer

- E-mail account

- Computer network

Using passwords is one of the best ways to preserve your privacy and protect yourself from computer crime. Here are the ins and outs of smart password protection.

Strive for security. The best passwords are a secret series of letter and number characters — and sometimes symbols, too. A secure password should not be a word because words are too easy for password-cracking software to guess. Any time you need to whip up a password, use these do's and don'ts to create one that's tough for hackers to crack.

- DO choose something easy for you to remember but difficult for anyone else to guess.

- DO make your password at least six characters long. A longer password is harder to guess.

- DO create a password that contains both letters and numbers. If the password can be case sensitive, mix uppercase and lowercase letters.

- DON'T pick a word from an English dictionary or any foreign language dictionary. Computer criminals use special software to guess a password. This software may try every word in English dictionaries and foreign language dictionaries.

- DON'T put your name or user name in your password. Don't even use part of your name or user name.

- DON'T include information easily obtained about you. For example, avoid using a pet's name, family member's name, phone number, birthday, or license plate number.

- DON'T tell anyone your password.

- DON'T display your password where anyone can see it. That means no taping a reminder note to your computer or desk.

- DON'T use the same password for everything. Use one password for online banking and another different password for shopping at your favorite online store.

Create a puzzling pattern. It can be difficult to come up with a unique password each time you need one. Follow these steps to form a password that's easy to remember but hard to guess.

1 Think of a sentence, a saying, or a title that would be simple for you to recall — but also isn't very well known. Choose a line at least five words long, and be sure it isn't something people normally associate with you. For example, you could choose "I wish I could walk on the moon."

2 Write down the first letter of each word in your sentence, saying, or title. In this case, the first letters would be *iwicwotm*.

3 Next, put a number somewhere in the middle of the letters. If you're allowed to use symbols, add a number or a symbol. For this example, if you dropped a nine in the middle, you'd have *iwic9wotm*. That's a secure password.

Enter your secret code. Now that you have created your password, here's how to use it. Whenever you need a password to enter a file, a dialog box or Web page will ask for it. As you type your secret code into the PASSWORD box, asterisks or dots appear in place of the letters and numbers. That prevents anyone from stealing your password by watching what you type.

If you see a second PASSWORD box, type the password there, too. The computer uses that to check whether the password in the first box is correct. This often occurs the first time you log on to a secure site. If the contents of the boxes don't match exactly, you'll be asked to type the password in both boxes again — just to be sure. Once your password is accepted, you'll have full access to what you need.

Since you should not use the same password for all your log ins, you may want to keep a list of your passwords in a safe place off the computer. If you want to be especially careful, you can put the list in a sealed envelope and hide it where you can find it. If the envelope turns up unsealed, you'll know someone has your passwords and you can change them before trouble starts.

Keep viruses from bugging you

A computer virus can make your computer sick, just as a real virus can make you sick. Get wise about viruses and keep your computer infection free.

Recognize the symptoms. The effect of a virus on your computer can be as mild as a case of hiccups or as hazardous as pneumonia. Some viruses are relatively harmless and may only display words or an image on your screen. The more serious viruses can change, delete, or damage files in your computer. A few can even keep your computer from working at all.

The symptoms of a hardware or software glitch can be similar to virus symptoms. So how do you know whether your computer is infected? Besides looking for obvious symptoms like jumbled words or disappearing files, keep an eye out for problems like your system slowing down or not responding, or your program or memory changing size. If you suspect a virus, you need to run an anti-virus program immediately. Just follow the tips given later in this story.

FYI ▶ Dormant viruses may hide on a computer, doing nothing until a special date or a particular event triggers the virus.

Avoid contagious files. Knowing how a virus spreads can help you shield your computer. These are some common ways your computer can catch a virus.

- Someone sends you an infected e-mail attachment or an infected e-mail. To learn more about this problem, see *Form healthy e-mail attachments* on page 289.

- You download a file from the Internet without realizing the file has a virus.

- You get an infected disk or CD.

- A software program has an infected macro. A macro is just a little file that automatically runs several commands back to back. Macros can be added to many commonly used software programs, such as Microsoft Word or Excel.

Viruses also spread across networks. Both home networks and business networks can be affected.

Get a virus shot. The best way to protect your information and your investment is to head off viruses before they hit. A few ounces of prevention can help repel viruses and keep your computer in tip-top health.

- Get and install anti-virus software. Both Norton Antivirus at **www.symantec.com** and McAfee's VirusScan at **www.mcafee.com** are good anti-virus programs. Either one can be downloaded on a trial basis. Scan your whole hard disk right after you install the software.

- Keep your anti-virus software enabled (active) and running all the time. Never disable the software unless specifically instructed to do so.

- Make an emergency disk immediately if your anti-virus installation instructions encourage you to do so. If you are ever infected with a virus, removing the bug can be much easier if this disk is ready.

- Schedule and run automatic or manual scans every week.

- Obtain virus updates several times each month. New viruses break out constantly, so don't just assume your computer is protected. Some anti-virus programs can be set to automatically download and install these updates. You can also do it yourself by going to the manufacturer's Web site. Updating can take as little as a minute, but it can save you hours or days of work if a bug gets into your system.

Tech term ▶ Worm – a harmful computer program that makes copies of itself and causes computer problems, sometimes by overwhelming the computer to force it to shut down. Worms are often built to spread to as many computers as possible.

- Set your anti-virus program to check all incoming files, downloaded files, e-mails, and e-mail attachments. This can save you a lot of grief up front. For example, if Norton Antivirus 2002 detects a virus in an incoming e-mail attachment, it displays a VIRUS FOUND message.

- Download only from reputable sites to avoid Trojan horses and other threats. Trojan horses masquerade as helpful programs, but they deliver viruses or other trouble-making software.

- Manually scan any newly obtained floppy disks, zip disks, or other removable disks.

- Scan compressed files both before and after unzipping.

- Back up your data files. If a virus ever damages your computer, you won't lose your valuable data.

Ask a specialist. For more information on how to handle a possible virus, check your anti-virus software manuals as well as the manufacturer's Web site. It's a good idea to be familiar with the process before a problem comes up. To learn about a particular virus or about the latest virus threats, try these sites.

- http://www.symantec.com/avcenter/

- http://www.wildlist.org

- http://www.mcafee.com/anti-virus/default.asp?

Safeguard your online security

"Don't talk to strangers" is good advice for kids, and it might be good advice for your computer, too. After all, nobody wants a hacker — or anyone else — to steal personal information or credit card numbers. You can make online choices that keep personal information "for your eyes only." Protect your privacy and make your computer secure with these tips.

Don't leave a paper trail. Filling out registration and other types of forms is often requested — or even required — for online shopping and services. Here are some things to try if you don't want to give out this information.

- Check whether registration is required. If registration is optional, don't feel obligated to do it.

- Search the Web to find out if you can get a similar product or service elsewhere. Perhaps another site can give you the same benefits without the hassle of registering.

- Hunt for a link to the Web site's privacy policy. It should explain what kind of information the site collects about you and what the site's owners do with that information. It will also tell you if it provides a way to keep your personal information private. Look for a check box that allows you to opt out of e-mail announcements or sharing data with other parties.

- If the privacy policy does not offer enough protection to satisfy you, focus on the fields in the form. Are many of the fields optional? Are the required fields enough to get you the correct product or service? If so, consider filling out just the required fields.

- As a last resort, you can always pass up the product or service to keep your private information "off the record."

Patch things up. From time to time, check to see whether new security patches are available for the software on your computer. Patches are usually free from the software maker's Web site. Snatch the latest patch to prevent hackers from taking advantage of new security holes in browsers and other software.

Tech term ▶ HTML – a code that tells a browser how to display text and images on the World Wide Web.

Beware of spyware. Spyware, also known as stealthware or adware, is a software with a secret mission. It gathers information about all your computer activities, then sends it back to its home company. The company uses this information to match advertisements to your unique interests. Each spyware program has a particular freeware or shareware program it uses as a cover. When you download that program, the spyware automatically runs as well.

Although spyware appears to be top secret, it really isn't. The license agreement of spyware-infested software tells you that you will be monitored when you use the software. By agreeing to the license agreement, you agree to this condition. If you want to stop spyware from spying on you, consider these options.

- Read license agreements from beginning to end. If you spot statements that say your activities will be monitored or that information about you will be shared with a company, you've probably got spyware. If you suspect the software, don't install it. If you've already installed it, uninstall it and delete its files.

- You can get software that removes spyware from the freeware or shareware program that hides it. Ad-aware from Lavasoft can do this for you, but you have no guarantee the freeware or shareware will still work after the spyware is pulled out. For information, go to **www.lavasoft.nu/downloads.html**.

- You can also check free software programs for spyware before you download them. Go to **www.spychecker.com**, and do a search on the software you're interested in.

- A firewall will block spyware from sending information out of your computer. Consider getting one, even if you have a dial-up connection. If you'd like to try a firewall for free, get ZoneAlarm from **www.zonelabs.com**.

Talk to your children. Teach children to follow the same guidelines you use to protect your privacy online. Make sure they know they should never give out contact information, credit card numbers, social security numbers, passwords, or any other personal information. For more information on Internet privacy, see **www.ftc.gov/bcp/conline/pubs/online/sitesee.**html.

Erase your browser profile. For your convenience, your browser probably stores your name and contact information so you can give it out to Web sites easily. But you can block this information so it won't be available to anyone. Here's how to do this in Internet Explorer.

1 Click on the TOOLS menu and then click on INTERNET OPTIONS.

2 Click on the CONTENT tab. In the PERSONAL INFORMATION area, click on the MY PROFILE button.

3 You will see all the tabs for your profile. Click on the NAME tab to see the profile fields for your name and e-mail address.

4 Type in dummy information for your display name. Make all other fields blank.

5 Click on the other tabs and make all the fields blank for each one. If you prefer, you can type in dummy information instead.

6 Click on OK, then click on OK again to leave the INTERNET OPTIONS dialog box.

Play it safe ▶ Don't publish your e-mail address or contact information on a Web site, newsgroup, chat room, or public forum.

Become invisible. Don't register with online people directories such as Switchboard or Bigfoot. If you have already registered, check the directory's site to find out how you can remove yourself from the list.

Expand your knowledge. Your computer can't be fully protected until you know about viruses, online communication, cookies, online shopping, and passwords. Be sure to read the vital information in the following stories.

Get the facts about cookies

If you're like most people, you think of cookies as a sweet treat. But Web cookies are something entirely different. In fact, one of the Internet's longest-running debates is about cookies. Are cookies the key to more convenient shopping and special Web site features — or are they an invasion of privacy? Perhaps the answers to some frequently asked questions about cookies can help you decide.

Q What are cookies?

A A cookie is a tiny text file that a Web site places on your hard drive to send information back to that Web site.

Q What are cookies used for?

A Some companies use the information from cookies to personalize your Web pages or match Web page ads to the things you like. If you check the local news, weather, and stock quotes each day, cookies will bring you back to the right pages. Cookies can also keep your shopping account information up to date and keep track of the options you set for services, accounts, or Web sites.

Q Then what is so bad about them?

A Some sites use cookies to find out where you surf — and particularly where you shop — on the Web. Marketers develop advertisements and marketing campaigns based on this information. When these cookies are added without your knowledge or consent, this may be an invasion of privacy. In fact, it's easy for people to accumulate cookies without knowing it. If your browser was set to accept cookies when you began using it, you may have many cookies that you have never known about.

Q How can I find out which sites ask for cookies?

A You can set your browser to prompt you every time a site tries to set a cookie. This means you decide which cookies to accept or reject on a case-by-case basis. Here's how to do this in Internet Explorer.

1 Click on the TOOLS menu, and then click on INTERNET OPTIONS.

2 Click on the SECURITY tab, and then click on the CUSTOM LEVEL button.

3 Scroll down to the COOKIES section.

4 Click on PROMPT under the message ALLOW COOKIES THAT ARE STORED ON YOUR COMPUTER.

5 Click on PROMPT under the message ALLOW PER-SESSION COOKIES (NOT STORED).

6 Click on OK, then click on OK to leave the INTERNET OPTIONS dialog box.

Q How can I control what cookies are allowed on my computer?

A You can choose how you want to control cookies. Internet Explorer includes options to prompt for cookies, to reject or accept all cookies, or even to block or accept just one type of cookie.

Q What types of cookies can I choose to accept or reject, and how do I do this?

A A Web site can create both a persistent cookie and a temporary cookie. The temporary cookie is deleted as soon as you leave the Web site, but the persistent cookie remains stored on your computer — even after you shut down your browser. To accept or reject cookies by type in Internet Explorer, follow the steps listed above and click on either ENABLE or DISABLE instead of PROMPT.

Q What about the cookies I already have? Can I get rid of them?

A You can delete all your cookies, but you may regret it. If you have personalized a Web site such as your home page, or if you have created other settings and preferences, you'll have to reset everything the next time you go to that site. Consider deleting your cookies one at a time. Here's how to do it in Internet Explorer.

1   Click on the TOOLS menu, and then click on
    INTERNET OPTIONS.

2   Click on the GENERAL tab.

3   In the TEMPORARY INTERNET FILES section, click on the SET-
    TINGS button.

4   Click on the VIEW FILES button. When the listing appears,
    look for the file names that begin with COOKIE. These are
    your cookie files.

5   As you read across the columns for each cookie entry, you'll
    probably be able to tell which cookies you want to keep. If
    you're not sure, look for a familiar URL or site name in one
    of the columns.

6   Highlight the cookies you want to erase, go to the FILE menu
    on the Toolbar, and click on DELETE.

FYI ▶ Temporary cookies may also be called session cookies.

Weed out offensive Web pages

You can find almost anything you want on the Internet, including
some things you'd probably rather not see. The good news is you do
have options to help you dodge offensive Web sites. You just have to
decide what's right for you.

Filter your searches. One easy way to bypass unwelcome Web pages
is to stick with search sites that block offensive results. Several major
search engines can be set to screen out harmful content. To sample
one of these, try Alltheweb, Alta Vista, Google, Lycos or Wisenut.
Most let you choose when to turn on the filter, and you may even be
able to tailor the settings the filter uses. If you're ready to try out a

filter, just scan your favorite main search page for a filter-is-on message or a link to the filter settings. Examples of common link names may be PREFERENCES, CUSTOMIZE, ADVANCED SEARCH, PARENTAL CONTROLS, or FAMILY FILTER. Click on the link, choose your filter settings, and start enjoying squirm-free searching.

If one of your favorite search sites doesn't have a filter yet, don't worry. Search engines add new features all the time. Just keep checking the search main page or the PREFERENCES page from time to time. You may be pleasantly surprised.

Hunt with kid-safe search engines. Some search engines only deliver search results that are appropriate for children. Even the advertising on most of these sites may stick to child-friendly material. If you'd like a kid-safe search engine for your children or grandchildren, start with Ask Jeeves for Kids or Yahooligans. For the latest list of kid-safe search engine choices, surf to **www.safekids.com/search.htm.**

Hire a content advisor. Just as movies are rated for their content, Web sites can be rated for content, too. Some Web sites rate themselves, but often, specialty companies or nonprofit organizations review Web sites. You can take advantage of these ratings with the Internet Explorer's CONTENT ADVISOR feature.

Here's how CONTENT ADVISOR works. First, you set the maximum rating to accept for each of four categories — language, nudity, sex, and violence. When you surf, Explorer checks each site's ratings before displaying the site. If a site's ratings are outside your rating limits, Explorer simply blocks the site. You can also use CONTENT ADVISOR to perform these useful tasks.

- Block or allow the viewing of sites that have not been rated.

- Adjust the type of content other people can view.

- Set up a list of Web sites that other people can never view, regardless of how site contents are rated.

- Set up a list of Web sites that other people can always view, regardless of how site contents are rated.

- Control access to settings with a supervisor password.

CONTENT ADVISOR does its best work with sites that are rated accurately. If a site has lied about its content, CONTENT ADVISOR may fail to block that site — even if it's harmful. What's more, many sites are not rated because raters can't keep up with the flood of new Web pages.

You can set CONTENT ADVISOR to exclude all unrated Web sites, but you'll probably keep out many useful sites as well. Yet if you allow unrated sites, you're sure to have offensive Web pages slip through. That's why *Consumer Reports* recommends using some other form of content blocking along with CONTENT ADVISOR.

For detailed instructions on using CONTENT ADVISOR, see Internet Explorer's HELP menu.

Investigate your ISP options. Check with your ISP to find out what content control products or services may be available through your membership. Be sure to ask about prices. Your ISP may offer content control at a discount or, if you're lucky, include it for free.

Quick tip ▶ AOL's Parental Controls can help you restrict activities and/or block content based on your child's age group. You can click to pick a package of pre-set options for KIDS ONLY, YOUNG TEEN, MATURE TEEN, or 18+.

Clean up with a content filter. Content-filtering software checks incoming Internet data and blocks unwanted content. Depending

on the software you select, the following features may also
be available.

- Blocks image files as well as text.

- Blocks or monitors newsgroups, chat rooms, or e-mail.

- Limits when or how long surfing can occur.

- Offers a way for a parent to set different levels of blocking based
  on the person who is surfing.

- Gives a parent the ability to decide which categories of content
  to block.

Because Web sites are added to the Web daily, you can subscribe to
software updates to lock out any new sites that aren't family-friendly.
Depending on which product you use, a subscription may or may
not cost extra.

If you want the inside scoop on how content-filtering software
decides to accept or reject a Web page, here it is. Most products
depend on one or more of the following techniques.

- The software compares each Web site to a list of those com
  piled by the company's reviewers. Some products work from
  a list of safe sites while others measure against a list of sites to
  be blocked.

- The software checks a Web site against a list of words and
  phrases common in objectionable material. Part or all of the
  Web page is blocked if those words are found.

- The software checks site ratings the same way CONTENT ADVI-
  SOR does.

Examples of popular filtering software include CyberPatrol at
www.cyberpatrol.com, CyberSitter at **www.solidoak.com**, and Net
Nanny at **www.netnanny.com**.

How effective is content filtering software? Ideally, it should block every unwanted site and display all other sites. When *Consumer Reports* tested several popular content filters, 20 percent of harmful sites slipped past popular filtering software packages. What's more, the test showed content filters can screen out harmless sites you may want to see. For example, an encyclopedia article about breast cancer may be blocked because it contains a word the content filter is supposed to keep out.

To learn more about content-filtering software as well as the features and options that accompany each package, go to the Web sites **www.getnetwise.org** and **www.safekids.com**.

Supervise your youngsters. Software and technical tools are not the only way to protect children and grandchildren who surf. Parents can help kids by teaching them about appropriate online behavior and how to deal with online advertising. It's even a good idea to spend time surfing with younger kids. For detailed information on guiding and protecting children on the Internet, try the sites below.

- **www.ed.gov/pubs/parents/internet/tips.html**

- **www.ftc.gov/bcp/conline/edcams/kidzprivacy/index.html**

- **www.getnetwise.org**

- **www.safekids.com**

After you feel comfortable surfing the Web, you will be ready to take advantage of one of the greatest features of the Internet — communicating with friends and loved ones. Read on to discover the thrill of keeping in touch online.

Keep in touch online

You've got mail — and more

If you are new to Web communications, you'll be thrilled with how just the click of a button puts you in touch with loved ones all over the world. You can e-mail your son in Sarasota and send birthday greetings to your sister in Des Moines. Send an instant message to a former co-worker. Express your opinions in an online newsgroup, and perhaps trade sewing tips in a senior citizens' chat room. You can even make phone calls from your computer, and — with your new video setup — check how much your grandchildren in Tampa have grown.

Best of all, you don't need postage, and even the phone calls can be free.

Tech term ▶ E-mail (electronic mail) – messages sent from one computer to another. Both sender and receiver must have an e-mail address and a connection to the Internet.

In this chapter, you'll learn about all kinds of online communication, but e-mail is by far the most popular. It is gradually replacing the postal service's "snail-mail," and here are some good reasons why.

E-mail is free. Once you get connected to the Internet, send as many e-mails as you'd like. It won't cost a thing, no matter where in the world you send them.

Messages move fast. Don't wait days for the post office — or hours for Federal Express — to deliver your letters. E-mail can get to the other side of the globe in minutes.

Convenience is a plus. You can send and receive e-mail at all hours of the day or night, even on holidays. And you don't have to stand in line for postage or lick any stamps.

Unlike the telephone, e-mail never interrupts what you are doing. If you are busy, it waits for you. And when you type, your e-mail program may even check your message for spelling errors.

Attachments make it versatile. You can send photos, artwork, and lots of other things by attaching them to your e-mail letter. About the only thing you can't do with e-mail is send a box of cookies to your best friend. You can, however, send the recipe, and, for good measure, throw in a picture of the goodies or even a video on how to make them. And it will get there — with no special crush-proof packaging — in time for her to bake a batch tonight.

You'll learn a lot about e-mail in this chapter, but, chances are, you'll be hungry for more. So check out these Web sites as well.

Everything E-mail	www.everythingemail.net
The Computer Lady	http://askTCL.com
About.com	http://email.about.com
Free E-mail Address Directory	www.emailaddresses.com

And don't forget the help section of your Internet Service Provider's Web site. It has a ton of information that will help you understand all the wonderful ways you can communicate online.

Explore your e-mail options

Your Internet Service Provider (ISP) probably offered you an e-mail account when you first connected to the Internet. You may not have considered any other options at the time, but if you aren't happy with that account, you're not stuck with it.

Some people use a free Web-based account like Excite, Hotmail, or Yahoo instead of — or in addition to — the one the ISP gave them. At one time it was the best way to check messages when away from home without making long-distance phone calls. While you can now do that with many ISP-based accounts as well, there are other reasons to consider using free Web-based e-mail.

Pick a permanent address. If you decide to change your ISP — perhaps because it's too slow or the service isn't good — you can no longer use the e-mail address it provided. So you must go to the trouble of notifying all your friends and family of the change. On the other hand, you can probably keep your Web-based e-mail address for life.

Get free e-mail without owning a computer. You can open an online account even if you only use a computer at the library or a friend's house. Some of the free services, however, are only available as a second account, so you may have to try a few before you find one that doesn't require a primary e-mail address.

Quick tip ▶ If you haven't upgraded your ISP-based e-mail in the last year or more, you may be missing out on some new features. Go to your ISP's Web site for the latest version.

Junk unwanted mail. You may be happy with your e-mail account but would like to cut down on unwanted mail from advertisers. The people who flood your box with those messages often get your address when you browse the Internet. Just open a second account, and give that address when you are online. You can empty the mail occasionally without having to read it. The mail you want to see will still come to your main account.

Keep personal messages private. If you only use e-mail at work, having a second address helps keep business and personal messages separate. And if you change jobs, you don't have to send a new e-mail address to family and friends. It's easy to set up a free account. Just type the URL into the address line of your browser, and follow the prompts. Here are some of the most popular free services.

Excite	www.excite.com
Hotmail	www.hotmail.com
Mail.com	www.mail.com
NetscapeWebMail	http://webmail.netscape.com
NetZero	www.netzero.net
Yahoo!Mail	www.mail.yahoo.com

Making an online account your main one does have a few drawbacks. Although it's free, you have to put up with the advertisements that pay the bill. The storage space for incoming messages and saved mail may be too small for your needs. Plus, it may not filter junk mail as well as your ISP-based account. (Read more about filters in *Top 10 ways to shrink spam* on page 298.) So weigh the pros and cons before deciding whether a free e-mail account is right for you.

Take a tour of your virtual post office

Having e-mail is like having your own post office sitting on your desk. With a click of your mouse, you can open your mailbox to see if you have letters. With another click, you can send out one you wrote. No waiting for a parking space — even the week before Christmas — or standing in line for service.

Open your e-mail program, and look at some of the rooms of your post office. Here's what you'll see if you use the Outlook Express program, which comes free with Internet Explorer. Although each program is different, most will be similar to this one. To open it, click on the Windows START button, select PROGRAMS from the menu, and choose OUTLOOK EXPRESS.

Outlook Express opening window

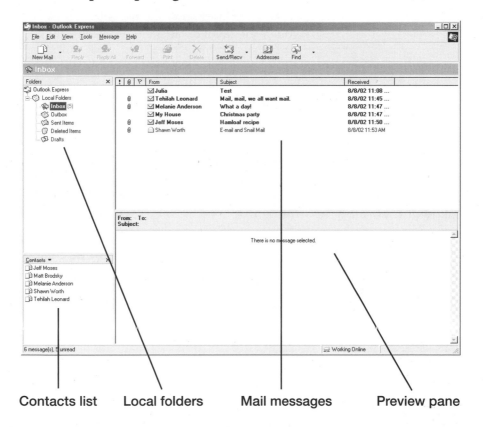

Contacts list   Local folders   Mail messages   Preview pane

If your opening window in Outlook Express doesn't look like this, go to TOOLS, select OPTIONS, click on GENERAL, and check WHEN STARTING GO DIRECTLY TO MY INBOX FOLDER.

The opening window is divided into four panes: local folders, contacts list, mail messages, and preview pane.

Local folders. E-mail messages are stored in these folders:

INBOX	Holds incoming messages until you move or delete them
OUTBOX	Temporarily stores messages you wrote while they wait to go out
SENT ITEMS	Saves copies of messages you have sent until you delete them or file them elsewhere
DELETED ITEMS	Holds messages you delete until you empty trash automatically or manually
DRAFTS	Keeps partial or completed messages until you are ready to send them

Contacts list. Although this space is probably empty right now, you'll soon learn how to add e-mail addresses to your address book. They will then show up on this list.

Mail messages. When the INBOX is selected, this pane holds a list of messages you have received. You'll see the subject of the message and who sent it. You may also see the date and time it was sent.

When you select a different folder, the contents of this window will change. If you select SENT ITEMS, for example, you'll see to whom you sent each message and the subject.

Preview pane. Click once on an item in the message list, and you can read it here without opening it. When none is chosen, the preview pane is empty except for a line saying, *There is no message selected.*

You are now familiar with the rooms of your cyber post office. Next you will learn how to send and receive mail.

How to become an e-mail expert

E-mail is like regular mail — you write a letter, address it, and mail it. You receive a letter, open it, and read it. You do it differently with a computer, of course. But once you get the hang of it, you'll be sending and receiving e-mail as easily as snail mail — more easily, in fact.

A good way to begin is to enlist the help of a friend who uses e-mail. Ask for her e-mail address, and tell her you'd like to send a practice message. Request a quick reply so you'll know right away if it's working. Keep practicing, and you'll soon become an e-mail expert.

Send a message. We'll use Outlook Express to show you how, but if you use a different e-mail program, it should work pretty much the same way.

1 Open Outlook Express and click on the NEW MAIL button on the Toolbar. An empty message window like the one below will appear.

New Message window

2 Click inside the lower pane, and write your message.

3 Type your friend's e-mail address in the TO space. (Soon you will be able to just click on a name in your contacts list, and the address will appear automatically.)

4 To show what your message is about, type *E-mail practice* in the subject line. The subject will now replace the words *New Message* on the title bar.

5 Click on the SEND button. If a number (1) appears in parentheses after the OUTBOX file in your folders list, it means it hasn't yet left your computer. Your program may be set to send outgoing mail periodically — at 5-minute intervals, for example. To send it without waiting, click on the SEND/ RECV button.

6 Click on the X in the top right-hand corner to close the window. Your message will be stored in the SENT MAIL folder until you delete or file it.

Fast fix ▶ You can change your setting so that mail is always sent as soon as you click on SEND. Go to TOOLS, select OPTIONS, and then choose SEND. Place a check in the box in front of SEND MESSAGE IMMEDIATELY, and click on the OK button.

Read your mail. When your friend replies to the practice message you sent, you'll find it in your INBOX. You'll see her name and the subject, which, unless she changed it, will read *Re: E-mail practice.*

It will be in bold print, and you'll see a closed-envelope icon to the left. Double-click on the message to open it in a window. (The entry on the message list will now appear in regular print with an open-envelope icon.)

Send a reply. To thank your friend for her help, click on REPLY. Her message will reappear in a new window. Write a response above her message, and click on SEND.

If you were replying to a message that had been sent not only to you but to others as well, you could click on REPLY ALL to send your response to all of them.

Quick tip ▶ You can store a message in the DRAFTS folder until you are ready to send it. Go to the FILE menu and select SAVE. When the SAVED MESSAGE dialog box opens, click on OK. To retrieve it later, open the DRAFTS folder and double-click on the message. It will open in a window where, if you wish, you can change the message before sending.

Forward a message. Imagine that your friend's message also included information about a book you're interested in reading. Since a mutual friend also wants to know about the book, this is a good time to practice forwarding a message.

With the message selected, click on the FORWARD button. A new message window containing the original will appear. Delete any part you don't want to forward, and add your own message if you wish. Fill in the second friend's e-mail address in the TO space, and click on SEND. If you want to forward this message to more than one person, separate the e-mail addresses with commas.

Timesaver ▶ If you are browsing the Web using Internet Explorer and you want to send a message, you don't have to open Outlook Express. Just click on the MAIL button on the Toolbar and choose NEW MAIL.

As you get more familiar with your e-mail program, you may want to change some of your settings. Go to TOOLS and then OPTIONS. Click on the different tabs to see all the things you can control.

Sign off in style

You may receive an e-mail with a saying or slogan at the end, like *Let a smile be your umbrella* or *Save the whales.* These are called signatures and are a good way to add a little personality to your messages.

Signatures can also be practical. You might create one to save time if you have to type the same contact information — your address, phone and fax number, for instance — into your messages again and again.

You can automatically add the same signature to every message. Or you can create several and choose the one you want each time you send an e-mail. Here's how to do it using Outlook Express.

Signature Options dialog box

1　Click on TOOLS, open the OPTIONS dialog box, and click on the SIGNATURES tab.

2　Click on the NEW button and type your quote or other message into the text box. Keep it brief, two or three lines at most.

3　Click on APPLY. The first one will be listed as Signature I in the upper text box. The second will be Signature II, and so forth. You can change the name by clicking on RENAME and typing the new name in.

4　If you wish, you can check the box next to ADD SIGNA-TURES TO ALL OUTGOING MESSAGES. The one shown as the default signature will be sent automatically. If you want to change the default, select the one you prefer, and click on SET AS DEFAULT.

5　When you have finished adding signatures and making any changes, click on OK.

If you want to manually add a signature to an e-mail, go to INSERT on the Toolbar, and select SIGNATURE. Click on the one you want, and it will automatically appear in your e-mail message.

Keep friends at your fingertips

It may be time to toss your old-fashioned address book in the trash. A modern electronic version will keep all the old information — plus your new e-mail addresses — in order.

By putting your friends' addresses in your new electronic book, they will be available instantly. You can send a message to a friend, or a group of friends, with just the click of your mouse. You can even speed up your regular mail — Christmas cards, for example — by quickly printing mailing labels for them from your new address book. See *A lesson in creating labels* on page 127 to learn how.

Set up your address book. It's easier to add an e-mail address directly from a message, but sometimes you'll need to type addresses in. Here's how to do both in Outlook Express.

To add addresses from e-mails you receive:

1 Select the message, and right-click on the sender's name.

2 Choose ADD TO ADDRESS BOOK. The name should now appear in your contacts list.

To manually insert an address and other information:

1 Click on the ADDRESS BOOK button.

2 Inside the ADDRESS BOOK dialog box, click on NEW, and select NEW CONTACT from the drop-down list. A PROPER-TIES dialog box will open with the NAME tab selected.

3 Fill in at least the first and last name and the e-mail address. Click on ADD.

4 Double-check to be sure the address is correct. Edit if necessary, and then click on OK.

5 To enter additional information, like telephone numbers and regular mailing addresses, click on other tabs — BUSINESS, HOME, PERSONAL, and OTHER — and fill in whatever you wish.

Fast fix ▶ If your list of contacts suddenly disappears from the Outlook Express window, it probably means you accidentally clicked on the X and closed it. Go to VIEW and then to LAYOUT. Place a check in the box in front of CONTACTS. Click on OK, and the names should reappear.

Select names from the address book. Simply double-click on a name in your contacts list, and a NEW MESSAGE window with the TO address filled in will open. Just write your message, click SEND, and it's on its way.

Take a shortcut to an e-pal

If you e-mail one special friend a lot, here's how to save time with a shortcut to her address.

1 Right-click on your desktop, and select NEW from the drop-down menu.

2 Select SHORTCUT.

3 Type in *mailto:* followed by the friend's e-mail address. Leave no spaces. *(mailto:friend@provider.com)*

4 Click on NEXT.

5 In the text box SELECT A NAME FOR THE SHORTCUT, type in the friend's name or nickname.

6 Click on FINISH. An icon for the shortcut with the name below it will appear on your desktop.

When you want to e-mail that friend, just click on the icon. A NEW MESSAGE window will open, already addressed to your friend.

Create mailing groups. If you frequently send one message to the same group of people, you can save time by creating an address group that contains all their names. Then, with just a click you can address it to all of them at once.

Here's how:

Group Properties dialog box

1 Open ADDRESS BOOK.

2 Click on NEW and select NEW GROUP. A PROPERTIES dialog box will open. (See illustration above.) Type in a name for the new group, like *Family* or *Golfing buddies.*

3 Click on the SELECT MEMBERS button, and a new dialog box will appear. You will see a list of your contacts in a pane on the left-hand side.

4 Scroll through your contacts list and choose the first name you want to add by clicking on it once. Click on the SELECT button. The name will then appear in the members list on the right.

5 Repeat with each name you want to put in your new group.

6 When all are selected, click on OK.

7 To add a name not already in your main address book, click on NEW CONTACT, type in the name and e-mail address, and click on OK.

When you want to send a message to a group, just click the group's name in your contacts list.

Make messages quick and clear

E-mail operates at a fast pace, and sometimes, in the rush, it seems that anything goes. But if you stick to the following practices, you'll make a better impression, and your reader will look forward to opening your messages.

Get the reader's attention. A good friend will be delighted to open a note from you with a simple *Hello* in the subject line. But most busy people are likely to bypass messages with unclear subjects and move on to those that appear more important.

Make it easy on the eyes. Words are harder to read on a screen than on paper, so choose a reasonably large font. Also, keep your paragraphs short, and use a blank line between them.

Be brief and friendly. Some people will scan, at best, a long e-mail, so make it short. And use a conversational tone to make it more appealing.

Please your English teacher. Correct spelling, punctuation, and grammar show your ideas in their best light and help prevent misunderstandings. On the other hand, sentence fragments and one-word responses can be appropriate — and efficient — if the message is clear.

Reply promptly. If you can't respond right away to an important e-mail, send a quick note saying it's going to be a while before you can give a full reply.

FYI ▶ You may get a message that was intended for someone else, probably a person with an e-mail address similar to yours. Send a quick note to let the sender know the wrong person received it. He can then correct his address book and send the message to the person who was supposed to get it.

Respond clearly. When you answer an e-mail, you'll save confusion by using the reply form instead of starting a new message. That way your response will contain a copy of the original, making it clear to the reader what you are responding to. To make it even simpler, you can delete everything except the part related to your reply.

Write above, not below, the message you received. Some people place parts of their reply within the original e-mail, but that can get confusing, and the reader may overlook some of it.

Review your message. Always read each e-mail carefully before you send it to make sure it is clear, and the tone matches your intent. If something could be taken two ways, reword it to remove any doubt.

If you wrote in anger, give yourself an overnight cooling-off period, and then review it before sending it. Once you click on

SEND, it's too late to change your mind.

Sign your name. Unless your user name leaves no doubt the message is from you, put your name at the end of your message. And, if appropriate, give your phone and fax numbers as optional ways for the reader to respond.

Quick tip ▶ Mark an e-mail HIGH PRIORITY if you want the reader to look at it right away. But make sure it truly is important. A busy person may resent being interrupted if the message could have waited.

Don't rely on delivery receipts. You may sometimes need to find out right away if your e-mail reached the intended person. If so, ask him in the message to let you know he got it. You could request an automatic delivery receipt, but not all mail programs provide that function. And some people find them annoying and set their preferences to ignore them.

Mind your on-line Ps and Qs

Most e-mail is informal — kind of like passing notes to friends in school. But even these casual communications require certain courtesies, known as "netiquette." As your mailbox begins to get busy, you'll understand why they matter.

Follow these tips to avoid making some of the mistakes newbies — newcomers to e-mail — often make.

Start with brief greetings. Your excitement over sending and receiving e-mail can tempt you to go overboard in the beginning. Thinking you can catch up with everyone you've ever known, you search for their addresses and plan long, newsy letters.

But go slow. Short notes at first will seem less pushy to busy people, and correspondence can develop naturally with those who have the time and interest.

Share with consideration. You may be delighted with the jokes and heart-warming stories you receive by e-mail. But they may have lost their charm for those who have seen the same stories circulating for years.

Don't assume everyone in your address book shares your sense of humor. Consider, especially, who might be bothered by offensive language or questionable subject matter. If you wouldn't tell a particular joke to someone face to face, think twice about e-mailing it to her.

Tech term ▶ Flame – a mean, hostile e-mail (or the act of sending one) usually expressing a difference of opinion over a controversial topic. If two people flame each other back and forth, it's called a flame war.

Choose your recipients carefully. When answering an e-mail, ask yourself if every person who received the original message really needs to see your response. If not, don't hit the REPLY ALL button. Be especially careful about subjecting other people to on-going debates over pet issues.

Respect the privacy of others. Don't forward a personal message without the OK of the writer. And when sending the same message to several people, remember that some may prefer to keep their e-mail address, like their telephone number, private. Put your own address in the TO space and all others in the BCC (blind carbon copy) space. That way, those who receive the e-mail will see only your address.

Be patient about replies. Don't expect an immediate response to every message. Some people check their e-mail only once each day, others, even less often. Need a quick response? It's probably best to pick up the phone.

Learn the lingo. You may wonder about those mysterious capital letters — LOL, KIT, BFN — you sometimes find in messages you receive. These acronyms are a kind of shorthand that frequent e-mailers use to save time.

Acronyms are especially helpful in chat rooms where conversations move rapidly. But think twice about using them in e-mail. You may confuse and frustrate your reader, who may not be familiar with the ones you use.

Here are some examples of acronyms you may run into.

Acronym	Stands for
AFAIK	As far as I know
BFN, B4N	Bye for now
BTDT	Been there, done that
CYAL8R	See you later
FWIW	For what it's worth
FYI	For your information
HHOK	Ha ha, only kidding
JMO	Just my opinion
KIT	Keep in touch
LOL	Laughing out loud
SYS	See you soon
TA	Thanks again

For more acronyms, go to the Internet Acronyms Dictionary at **www.gaarde.org/acronyms**. To search for the meaning of one you don't understand, try The Acronym Database at **www.ucc.ie/acronyms**.

Say it with a smile. Others can tell how you feel during a conversation by the look on your face or sound of your voice. You can show your emotions when sending e-mail, too. Just use keystrokes to make sideways smiley faces and other images called "emoticons," short for emotion icons.

Check out the emoticons below. Tilt your head to the left, and you'll get the picture.

Image	Meaning
:-)	happy
:-(	sad
:-D	laughing
;-)	winking, joking
:-o	surprised, shocked
:-&	tongue-tied
:'-(	crying
>:-<	mad
:-@	screaming
( ), [ ], or { } with your name inside	hugging you

To see more emoticons, check out the ComputerUser High-Tech Dictionary at **http://www.computeruser.com/resources/dictionary /emoticons.html**. Just be careful not to over-do them, or you may get a few screams (:-@) in reply!

Form healthy e-mail attachments

Attaching something to your e-mail makes it more fun. You can send an article about a favorite vacation spot to a friend and receive digital pictures — or even a video — from the grandkids. And your formal letters and important documents look more impressive if you send them as attachments rather than as part of your e-mail.

On the other hand, attachments can contain destructive viruses that make your computer "sick." So you should never open one unless you know who sent it and what's in it. You'll read more about avoiding viruses later in this story, but first, here are the basics of sending and receiving attachments.

Open an attachment. In Outlook Express, you'll know an e-mail has an attachment when you see a paper clip icon to its left on the list of incoming messages. Here's how to view it.

1 Select the message with the attachment. In the preview box, you will see a large paper clip icon in the top right-hand corner.

Preview pane with attachment

From: Shawn Worth To: Julia Walker
Subject: E-mail and Snail Mail

Julia:

According to a local radio report, the amount of snail mail is decreasing as the amount of e-mail increases.

-Shawn

2 Double-click on the paper clip icon. A dialog box will open that warns you about viruses and gives you the options of opening an attachment or saving it to a disk.

Open Attachment Warning dialog box

3 Let's assume you know the sender and were expecting this one, so you feel sure it's safe to open. Select OPEN IT and click on OK. The attachment will then open, and you can view it and decide if you want to save or delete it.

Sometimes, an attachment won't open. This is probably because your computer doesn't have the software that created it. If the file isn't too long, the easiest thing to do is to ask the sender to cut and paste it into an e-mail and send it again.

Send a photo or document. A friend is planning to take the same cruise you took last year, and you want to send her some information about the ship, which you saved in your MY DOCUMENTS folder. Here's how to use Outlook Express to attach and send the file.

1 Open a NEW MESSAGE window. Fill in the address and subject, and write any note you wish to send.

2 Click on the ATTACH button on the Toolbar, and an INSERT ATTACHMENT dialog box will appear.

3 Use the LOOK IN drop-down list to select MY DOCUMENTS.

4 Click on the file you want to send and then click on ATTACH. The dialog box will disappear, and you can see the attachment listed below the subject of your e-mail.

5 Click on SEND, and the attachment will be on its way.

Break up a large file. If the cruise ship file is large, it can take a long time to send and receive. If your friend pays by the minute for Internet service — and especially if she has a slow modem — it may be more expensive than it's worth. Try to keep attachments under 50KB. To check a file's size, right-click on the file's icon and choose PROPERTIES.

One way to handle a big document is to break it down into several smaller ones. Outlook Express can do this for you.

1 Go to the TOOLS menu and select ACCOUNTS.

2 Click on the MAIL tab and then PROPERTIES.

3 Click on the ADVANCED tab.

4 Check the box in front of BREAK APART MESSAGES LARGER THAN … KB.

5 Select a suitable number, perhaps 100, and click on OK.

You can also zip files to make them smaller. See *Get the lowdown on downloading* on page 247. Or, if you send a lot of large attachments, consider signing up for Whale mail at **www.whalemail.com**.

Pass on a Web page. While browsing the Internet, you find another cruise article you want to share with your friend. Here's how to quickly attach it to an e-mail using Internet Explorer.

1 From the FILE menu, choose SEND, then PAGE BY E-MAIL.

2 A NEW MESSAGE window containing the attachment will

open. Enter your friend's address, write a message if you wish, and click on SEND.

If it's a long article, you may prefer to send a Web link instead. Simply go to the FILE menu, choose SEND, and then select LINK BY E-MAIL. The URL will appear in the body of the e-mail, and your friend need only click on it to open the page.

Don't play host to a virus. You learned in the previous chapter about the dangers of downloading a virus from the Internet. But 62 percent of all computer viruses arrive via e-mail, according to a recent study by *Consumer Reports.* And it's not just the attachments you have to worry about, but the e-mail itself.

The surest way to prevent damage is to use an anti-virus program that scans all e-mail automatically before it reaches your mailbox. Save each attachment you receive to a disk and run it through this program before you open it. See *Keep viruses from bugging you* on page 255 for more information about anti-virus software.

Here are some other ways to safeguard your computer, along with those you e-mail.

- Never open an attachment unless you know what it is and who sent it. Be especially suspicious if the file name ends with .VBS, .SCR, or .EXE.

- Watch for anything else that looks odd — maybe peculiar wording in a message from someone you know. A virus can get into a computer and send itself to people in the address book. If it seems at all suspicious, e-mail the sender and ask if he intended to send an attachment. If not, delete the message right away.

- Disable your e-mail program's preview pane, since some viruses can be triggered there. In Outlook Express, go to VIEW and then LAYOUT. Uncheck SHOW PREVIEW PANE.

- Always put your name at the end of your e-mails and ask others to do the same. A virus can find a message you received and send a reply. But it probably won't include your name in the body of the e-mail. To be on the safe side, if a message isn't "signed," e-mail the person and ask if he really sent it.

- Don't write in RTF (Rich Text Format) or HTML (HyperText Markup Language) if your e-mail program has those. Your messages may not look as fancy, but viruses are less likely to travel in those written in plain text.

- Don't fall for virus hoaxes — they can be almost as bad as the real thing. If you receive a virus warning in an e-mail, check the Web sites below to learn if it's a real threat before you pass it on.

F-Secure Computer Virus Info Center	www.F-Secure.com
McAfee Virus Information Library	http://vil.mcafee.com
Symantec AntiVirus Research Center	www.symantec.com

When it comes to viruses, slower is better. With a 56k dial-up connection you are less likely to fall victim to a virus than if you have a faster connection. But that doesn't mean you absolutely won't get one, so don't ignore all these suggestions.

Manage your mail with ease

Most computer newbies print copies of all the e-mail messages they want to save. Even if you have passed that stage, you may still have a problem with disorganized mail. It just clutters your computer now instead of your desk.

When your mailbox overflows, it is not only hard to find what you need, it also takes longer to receive mail. But with these tips, you can keep your files under control and speed up mail delivery, too.

Deal promptly with incoming mail. You can probably delete much of the old mail that is sitting in your INBOX. And you should do the same with most new messages as soon as you read and reply to them.

Some mail, however, you'll need to keep — at least temporarily. For example, perhaps you get a lot of mail as chairperson of your garden club's community project. Here's how to create a folder, using Outlook Express, for those messages you need to save until the project is over.

Create Folder dialog box

1 Go to the LOCAL FOLDERS pane, and click on INBOX.

2 Under FILE, select FOLDER, then NEW. A CREATE FOLDER dialog box will open (see above illustration).

3 Type in a name for the folder. Make it something easy to recognize — like *Garden Club.*

4 Click on OK. You'll now see your new folder listed under
your INBOX folder.

Inbox Folders

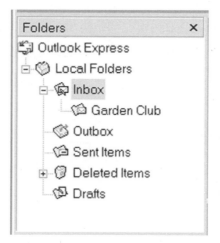

```
Folders                            ×
Outlook Express
Local Folders
    Inbox
        Garden Club
    Outbox
    Sent Items
    Deleted Items
    Drafts
```

When you want to save an e-mail about the garden club project, just
drag it to this folder. Or you can right-click on the message and
choose either MOVE TO FOLDER or COPY TO FOLDER, and follow
the prompts.

Sort your mail before reading it. If it takes too long to move all
those garden club e-mails — and messages from your grandkids get
buried in their midst — it's time to take a second step. You can send
the club mail straight to the new folder, where it will wait until you
are ready to read it. Then you can quickly select other messages
without a lot of scrolling and searching.

1 Under TOOLS, select MESSAGE RULES and then MAIL. A
MESSAGE RULES dialog box will appear. Click on NEW, and
the following dialog box will appear, with instructions on
how to set your e-mail program rules.

New Mail Rule dialog box

```
New Mail Rule                                          ? X

Select your Conditions and Actions first, then specify the values in the Description.

1. Select the Conditions for your rule:
  ☐ Where the From line contains people          ▲
  ☐ Where the Subject line contains specific words
  ☐ Where the message body contains specific words
  ☐ Where the To line contains people
  ☐ Where the CC line contains people            ▼

2. Select the Actions for your rule:
  ☐ Move it to the specified folder              ▲
  ☐ Copy it to the specified folder
  ☐ Delete it
  ☐ Forward it to people
  ☐ Highlight it with color                      ▼

3. Rule Description (click on an underlined value to edit it):
  Apply this rule after the message arrives


4. Name of the rule:
  New Mail Rule #1

                              OK            Cancel
```

2 Inside the SELECT THE CONDITIONS FOR YOUR RULE pane, choose WHERE THE MESSAGE BODY CONTAINS SPECIFIC WORDS.

3 Go to the third pane, RULE DESCRIPTION, and click on the underlined words CONTAINS SPECIFIC WORD.

4 Another dialog box will open. Type in the word *garden*, and click on the ADD button. You could add other words as well, but in this case most of the messages should be caught by this one word.

5 Click on OK.

6 The NEW MAIL RULE dialog box will reappear. This time go to the second item, SELECT THE ACTIONS FOR YOUR RULE. Choose MOVE IT TO THE SPECIFIED FOLDER.

7 Again, in the rule description pane, click on the underlined word SPECIFIED. Another dialog box will open with a list of folders you have created. Select the garden club folder, and click on OK.

8 Again, a MESSAGE RULES dialog box will open, allowing you to edit, remove, or create another rule. When you are through, click on OK.

With this rule in place, every e-mail you get that has the word *garden* in the body will be sent to your garden club folder. This system isn't foolproof, of course. Some e-mails from the garden club may not contain the word *garden*, and some that do may not be from club members. So you may have to move some messages in or out of the folder manually, but the message rules should catch most.

Create folders for long-term storage. When the Garden Club project is over, you'll probably want to delete most of these files. But you may need to save some for future reference. Create a new folder on your hard drive or a disk, and save them as text files, which use less space than e-mail files.

When you have moved or deleted all the files, highlight the folder name on the LOCAL FOLDERS list and click on DELETE. Also click on TOOLS, then MESSAGE RULES and MAIL, and remove the rules connected to this folder.

Timesaver ▶ The quickest way to print an e-mail is to right-click on the message and select PRINT.

Delete copies of out-going mail. You probably leave your program set to open to the INBOX folder since you check it frequently for new messages. On the other hand, you may seldom think to look inside your SENT ITEMS folder.

You have good reasons to set your preferences to automatically keep a copy of every e-mail you send. If, for example, an address is wrong and the message bounces, you can simply correct the address and send it again. And if the reply doesn't contain a copy of what you wrote, you may need to refer to it. But this folder can fill up fast, so make it a habit to empty it regularly. Delete those you don't need, and move those that need to be kept long-term to a more permanent folder.

Empty the trash often. It's a good idea to set your preferences to empty the deleted files folder each time you exit the program. Just be careful not to delete a file until you are sure you won't need it again.

Soon you'll be in the habit of dealing with mail promptly and cleaning out your folders regularly. Then you can pat yourself on the back for your neater — and faster — e-mail system.

Top 10 ways to shrink spam

Remember how, in the beginning, every e-mail message you received was a treasure? It's disappointing to find that now much of your mail is unpleasant, irritating — even offensive. While there's no simple solution for dealing with junk mail, or spam, the following suggestions should help reduce the amount of unwanted mail flooding your INBOX.

Never respond to a spam offer. Those fantastic deals for high-paying stay-at-home jobs or miracle health supplements can be tempting. But they definitely are too good to be true, and responding will just bring a new flood of mail to your address.

Delete without reading. This is the easiest way to remove an unwanted message. Unfortunately, it takes time to delete each one, and it doesn't help slow the flow of spam.

Tech term ▶ Spam – unsolicited e-mail sent to multiple addresses at one time. Also called junk e-mail.

Enroll with caution. Before you register for anything online, always read the privacy policy. If you decide it's a dependable organization — they won't share your address or they'll let you say no to future mailings — go ahead and sign up. Just be sure to scroll to the bottom of the page to find the place where you can opt out. You may be surprised to find their list of mail topics already have checkmarks. That means you will automatically receive all of those mailings. Click in the boxes to unselect any you don't want to receive.

Unsubscribe to e-mail lists. Maybe you enjoy getting the joke-of-the-day e-mails you requested. And you welcome the alerts when your favorite online bookseller is having a sale. But now you get lots of other mail you never bargained for.

If you are reasonably sure it's from a reputable source, use the address given at the bottom of most e-mails to unsubscribe. It seems to work better, if given the option, to go to the Web site to do this rather than sending an e-mail. Let the Federal Trade Commission (FTC) know if a "remove me" link doesn't work or a mailer doesn't honor the request. Fill out an online complaint at **www.ftc.gov**, or call 877-382-4357 toll free.

If you don't think the source of the unwanted mail is trustworthy — especially if it contains pornography or other offensive material — don't respond at all. A request to remove your name only serves to let these spammers know yours is an active address, which just leads to more trash in your mailbox.

Use a filter. Your Internet Service Provider (ISP) may filter out a lot of junk e-mail before it gets to you. Some also provide their users with an optional free program, like Earthlink's Spaminator or AT&T Worldnet's Email Screener.

In addition, most mail programs will let you block a specific sender or use other filtering processes. You learned earlier to use Outlook Express's Message Rules to manage mail files. With this same option, you can create rules to handle unwanted mail, too. Whatever mail program you use, check the HELP menu for information about how to use junk mail filters.

You may also buy software programs like those listed below to help get rid of spam.

Postal Inspector	www.giantcompany.com
Spam Arrest	http://spamarrest.com
Spam Killer	www.spamkiller.com

But don't sign up with a service that says it can remove your name from spam lists. The honest ones don't work well, and others are actually scams — a way spammers get more addresses.

Send junk mail to a separate address. Set up a second e-mail account to use when you need to give an address online. See *Explore your e-mail options* on page 270 for help. Any junk mail it generates will go to that box, which you can ignore, except to empty it occasionally.

Select a unique user name. Unless yours is an unusual name, use number and letter combinations in your user name to foil a "dictionary attack." Some spammers create alphabetical lists of probable addresses, using common names. When they send e-mail, for example, to johnanderson@everymajorISP.com, they are sure to hit some real addresses.

Keep your address under cover. You can use a remailer to keep your real address secret and to help track where your spam comes from. The next story, *Send your secrets with care* on page 302, will tell you where to find one. And you can buy software, such as Spam Motel at **www.spammotel.com**, that hides your address when you send a message.

Don't give your real e-mail address when posting messages to a discussion board either. Some companies that send out junk e-mail in bulk scan newsgroups to get addresses.

Complain to both ISPs. Your service provider can do a better job of filtering mail if you report to it any spam you receive. Most have an address just for this purpose, like abuse@provider.com. Try to notify the spammer's ISP as well, since most have policies against using their service for spam.

The e-mail header — the details of the path the e-mail took from the originator's computer to yours — will provide the most useful information. Unfortunately, junk mailers often are able to hide their identity. The e-mail return address, for example, is easy to fake, so it may not be helpful.

Speak up. Ask your congressional representative to support laws against spamming. To learn about current legislation, go to the CAUCE (Coalition Against Unsolicited Commercial Email) Web site. It's listed along with other sites devoted to fighting spam.

Now that you have some strategies for fighting spam, you can look forward once again to hearing the words, "You've got mail."

Spam-fighting site	Web address
CAUCE	www.cauce.org
Elsop's Anti-Spam Page	www.elsop.com
Fight Spam on the Internet!	http://spam.abuse.net
Junkbusters	www.junkbusters.com
Network Abuse Clearinghouse	www.abuse.net
SpamCop	www.spamcop.net

Send your secrets with care

When you seal a letter to a friend, you feel pretty sure no one else will read it. You may feel the same confidence as you sit at your computer typing an e-mail. But that would be a mistake. Whether your e-mail is friendly chit-chat or highly classified information, don't count on it being private. Here are some ways other people may view your personal messages.

- **Forwarding without permission.** You may discuss a personal matter in your e-mail, but your friend may not consider it confidential. It's easy for her to hit the forward button — maybe without thinking — to share your message with someone else. Even if your friend regrets it immediately, with most programs it's too late to call it back.

- **Unsecure routes.** Your message goes through a number of computers before it arrives at its intended address. At any point along the way, someone else could read it. This may be unlikely, but it's not impossible.

- **Pesky viruses.** Certain types of viruses or worms can pick up random messages from your computer, even those you thought were deleted, and send them to others.

Although you can't guarantee no one will ever see your e-mail without your permission, here are some things you can do to make it less likely.

Hide the key to your mailbox. Your password is like the key to your post office box. If you want privacy, don't share it with anyone else. And always "lock up" by signing out when you close your e-mail connection. If more than one person uses your computer, you can set up a separate e-mail account for each. Some Internet Service Providers offer more than one, and free Web-based accounts are another option. In fact, you might consider HushMail at **www.hushmail.com**. Security is their specialty.

Take the slow route to security. You may complain about how slow dial-up access is with your 56K modem. But it has an advantage — it's more secure than faster DSL and cable connections.

Go offline more often. The more time you spend online the more access others have to what you are doing. Disconnect after you open your mail program. You can read and compose e-mail offline, and then reconnect when you are ready to send your messages.

Keep confidential communications secure. It doesn't take a shrewd hacker to find information on your computer. If you want to save copies of personal e-mails, put them on a floppy disk or CD, and store them in a private place.

Scramble for safety. If security is that important to you, check out your mail program's encryption option. It scrambles messages between your computer and that of the recipient, so no one in between can read them. Encryption programs require a digital ID, which costs about $15 per year from VeriSign, the source recommended by Microsoft. Go to **www.verisign.com** to sign up for a free 60-day trial.

Hide your identity. If you don't want your recipient to know who you are, you can use an anonymous remailer. Sneakemail, at **http:// sneakemail.com**, provides free "disposable" e-mail addresses to keep your real one — and your identity — a secret. Remailers are also helpful if you want to avoid spam or find out who is sending it. But no program exists that absolutely cannot be traced, so don't be tempted to use a remailer to harass someone.

To prevent a possible financial disaster, never e-mail your social security number or a credit card number to anyone. In fact, to be on the safe side, think twice before you send anything in an e-mail that you wouldn't post on a bulletin board.

Ignore the lure of e-mail riches

You signed up for e-mail to get friendly notes, not threats of bad fortune. Yet that's what you see every time you open a chain letter. The truth is, your luck could get worse — you could lose all your friends — if you hound them with those warnings.

While most chain letters are simply a nuisance, those that offer get-rich-quick schemes are a more serious matter. That's because it's against the law to start or forward a chain letter that promises a big return on money or any item of value.

Learn how chain letters work. The letter asks you to send money — perhaps $5 — to the name at the top of a list. Then you are to remove that name, add yours to the bottom of the list, and send copies of the chain letter to a certain number of other people, asking them to do the same. When your name makes it to the top, many new people will be involved, so you should receive a huge amount of money. One recent chain letter, for example, promised $50,000 or more in 90 days.

It is not worth your time and money to fool with these get-rich-quick schemes. They are generally rigged so the people who start them get most of the money. Sometimes they list fake names and addresses that lead all the money back to them. Also, some people forward chain letters without sending any money at all.

Nobody down the line ever got rich from chain letters, and most who have gotten involved have lost money. You can read more about how illegal chain letters work at **http://www.usps.com/postal inspectors/chainlet.htm.**

Deal with unlawful chains. Some letters may say they are legal because they are selling something or they're endorsed by the U.S. government. Don't believe it. Here's what to do when you get one.

- Don't forward the e-mail or send anything to the name at the top of the list.

- Notify the person who sent the letter to you that it is an illegal scheme and should not be forwarded.

- Alert the FTC by forwarding the e-mail to uce@ftc.gov, and let your Internet Service Provider know about it, too.

Not all chain letters are illegal. Those that aren't may even end up being fun. Perhaps you get one requesting a favorite recipe. Over time, your mailbox may, indeed, fill up with tempting new recipes. If not, you've lost nothing more than a few minutes of your time. It's up to you to decide if it's worth it.

Tech term ▶ Mail bombing – when someone, usually as part of a flame war, overloads someone else's mailbox with so much junk mail it causes the e-mail program to crash.

FTC's top spam scams

Once it was door-to-door salesmen, and then along came telemarketers. Now the Federal Trade Commission (FTC) warns you about e-mail solicitors who tempt you with offers too good to be true. This is their current list of the most popular scams.

Chain letters. Usually just a nuisance, these are illegal if they involve money or valuable items. You will break the law if you start or forward one.

Work-at-home schemes. Stop fighting rush hour traffic, they say, and make lots of money. In truth, the up-front costs — often including large fees for their training — bring little or no return on your dollar.

Weight-loss claims. The testimonials are impressive, but save your money. For real, long-lasting results, exercise and diet are still your best bets.

Credit repair offers. Who wouldn't want to get bad debts off their credit record? But there is no legal way to do what they promise.

Advance-fee loan scams. These financial traps, aimed at people with bad credit, are not from legitimate banks. See a consumer credit counselor for useful advice.

Adult entertainment. Alluring offers of "free" viewing turn into expensive phone bills, at $2 to $7 a minute.

Give hoaxes the axe

You may pride yourself on using common sense while surfing the Internet — questioning everything you read and checking information carefully. But you may not realize you have to be just as careful with e-mail. How many times have you forwarded a heart-wrenching story or dire warning without knowing it was a hoax?

Unfortunately, it's not always easy to tell which disturbing e-mails are true. Some are obvious jokes — like the warning that you may catch a computer virus from an infected mouse. Others are not so clearcut.

At their worst, hoaxes can cause people to waste money or do something dangerous. You certainly don't want that to happen to you or anyone else. Here are some hints to help you avoid becoming a victim.

Learn to recognize a hoax. Most hoaxes contain three parts:

- the bait — perhaps something shocking — to make you read it

- a threat that something bad will happen if you don't pay attention to it

- an urgent request to spread the word to others

Let these be the red flags that warn you to investigate before you send it to others or take any other action.

Watch out for common deceptions. These are some of the most popular kinds of hoaxes. If you haven't yet seen these or similar stories in your mailbox, just wait. You will.

- **Computer viruses.** Will opening the *Life is Beautiful* e-mail really erase your hard drive? No. But there are enough real virus threats around without spreading false rumors of more. Don't pass this one on.

- **Sympathy hoaxes.** It's hard to resist a message from a little girl with cancer — especially when the American Cancer Society will donate three cents toward her treatment every time the e-mail is forwarded. Unfortunately, it's not true.

- **Jokes.** Maybe the FBI really does have a file on you, complete with a picture of your driver's license. It can't hurt to find out, right? You'll just feel foolish when you follow the instructions, only to end up looking at a picture of a monkey.

- **False medical information.** One hoax suggests you can survive a heart attack by coughing vigorously. Experts, however, say quickly dialing 911 is a better use of your time.

- **Phony legislation.** Don't get hot under the collar over the warning that e-mail will now require postage. No such law has been passed, nor is a bill like that under consideration by Congress.

- **Money or free merchandise cons.** Neither Bill Gates nor anybody at Victoria's Secret or the Gap will give you money or anything else for forwarding e-mails. Even if they wanted to, there's no reliable way to track the number of times an e-mail is forwarded.

- **Urban legends.** It makes a good story, but Donald Trump didn't pay off the mortgage of someone who changed a flat tire on his limo. Widely circulated tales like these, based on hearsay or partial truth, are generally harmless.

If you aren't sure a sensational story or warning is true, check it out on one or more of these Web sites.

Web site	Type of hoax	Web address
Centers for Disease Control	Medical	www.cdc.gov/ hoax_rumors.htm
Hoaxbusters	Multiple types	http://hoaxbusters.ciac.org
McAfee	Computer	http://vil.nai.com/VIL/ hoaxes.asp
Scambusters	Multiple types	www.scambusters.org/ legends.html

Snopes	Urban legends	www.snopes.com
Symantec	Computer	www.symantec.com/avcenter/hoax.html
VMyths	Multiple types	http://Vmyths.com

If you have any doubt about the story, don't pass it on. For more information about hoaxes and things you can do to discourage them, go to Break the Chain at **www.breakthechain.org**.

Make free calls from your computer

Sending free messages by e-mail is great, but sometimes you really want to hear that special person's voice. How would you like to dial them right from your computer? With a headset or microphone, speakers, and the right software, you can place phone calls over the Internet. And the calls — to any place in the world — may even be free.

Make calls "on the house." PhoneFree.com (**www.phonefree.com**) will let you download the software you need to make free calls from your computer to another computer. The only catch is that the computer at the other end must have the same software installed. The other person must also be online to talk, but if they aren't, you can leave voice mail. PhoneFree allows you to make conference calls, too, and even lets you block calls.

Dial up a low-cost conversation. You can also use your computer to reach people on their regular telephones. While the calls aren't free, you can get some good deals compared to regular telephone charges.

- DialPad (**www.dialpad.com**) is a good choice if you do a lot of calling within the United States. The rate is based on the number of calls you make but may be as low as 1.7 cents per minute. International rates per minute from the U.S. include London for 2.9 cents, Tokyo for 4.5 cents, and Mexico City for 4.9 cents.

- Net2phone (**www.net2phone.com**) offers calls within the U.S. at 2 cents per minute and international calls as low as 3 cents per minute.

- iConnectHere (**www.iconnecthere.com**) has similar rates. But currently, if you want to receive calls, your computer must have the Windows 2000 or Windows XP operating system.

Talk face-to-face with a video call. Not only can you hear the people you contact over your computer, you can also see them in living color. Video cameras connected to both computers make this two-way viewing possible. Even if you don't have a video camera, you can still see your grandson, for example, as long as he has one hooked up to his computer. He just won't be able to see you.

Use PhoneFree.com, mentioned earlier, to make free video calls. Visitalk (**www.visitalk.com**) also offers audio and video telephone service for $19.95 a year. Check their Web sites for the hardware and software requirements.

Say it with an electronic greeting card

Your sister's birthday is tomorrow, and you forgot to send her a card. No worry — you have plenty of time to "shop" at a variety of electronic greeting card Web sites. Your selection will reach her in Albuquerque today, and to make it even better, you don't have to spend a dime.

With hundreds of choices — far more than you'd find at the mall — you'll enjoy selecting a card that's just right. Perhaps your sister would enjoy an animated cartoon, or maybe something beautiful and sentimental. You can select music to go with the card and add your personal message. Then you simply address it and send it.

These Web sites aren't limited to birthday greetings, either. You'll find cards for Christmas, Hanukkah, and anniversaries — even Groundhog Day! You can also select a no-particular-occasion greeting card or postcard when you just want to get in touch with a little more pizazz than you can with regular e-mail.

If you want to send more than just a greeting, check out Hallmark's site at **www.hallmark.com**. You can attach a gift certificate to your card that can be redeemed at any of more than 300 online merchants. And when the occasion calls for flowers, how about an electronic bouquet? Go to VirtualFlowers at **www.virtualflowers.com**, and click on the SEND A FREE VIRTUAL BOUQUET button. The flowers are beautiful, and they won't ever fade or need water.

Blue Mountain, at **www.bluemountain.com**, was one of the first companies to offer free greeting cards on the Internet. Now this site lets you send free cards for one month. After that you have to pay. But at other online companies, some, if not all, of the cards are still free with no time limit. Check out these popular Web sites.

CardMaster.com	www.cardmaster.com
Egreetings.com	www.egreetings.com
Greeting-cards.com	www.greeting-cards.com
MyPostCards.com	www.mypostcards.net
Ohmygoodness.com	www.ohmygoodness.com

IM — making contact quickly

E-mail is much faster that snail mail — but if it's still not quick enough, you're ready for instant messaging (IM). This increasingly popular way of communicating lets two people — sometimes more — send brief messages back and forth immediately. It's like a telephone call, but you have time as you type to think about what you want to say.

Select your software. Check with those you want to instant message with to see what client, or application, they already use. You'll need the same software as theirs on your computer. Chances are they'll say MSN Messenger or AOL Messenger (AIM). But ICQ and Yahoo!Messenger are growing fast in popularity as well.

If you are the first in your circle of friends to IM, you'll need to lead the way by choosing the client. All four mentioned above are free. They offer similar basics, like a split screen where one part shows the conversation and the other allows you to type your message. They all let you alert your contacts you are online and show what your availability status is — using terms like "busy," "on the phone," or "be right back."

Tech term ▶ Post – to enter a message into a newsgroup, chat room, or instant message exchange. Also, the message itself.

Here are some ways the main clients differ from each other.

- AOL Instant Messenger (AIM) is available even if you don't use AOL as your Internet Service Provider. It is easy to use but doesn't have as many features as the others. For example, it doesn't let you know your buddy is typing a response. It lets you use a voice but not a video connection. AIM, however, takes your privacy seriously. It allows you not only to block messages but also to place a public warning that someone's posts are objectionable. To download the software, go to **www.aim.com**.

- ICQ, which got its name from the chat room acronym for "I seek you," has the most "bells and whistles." It lets you play games with a buddy and allows you to leave voice mail — even call a contact's pager or cell phone. But it's more complicated than the others to set up and use. Get the ICQ software at **www.icq.com**.

- MSN Messenger comes installed with Windows, but you have to get a .NET passport to use it. That's easy to do — just launch the program and follow the prompts. MSN allows more than two people to IM together without opening a chat room. The Windows XP version has some additional advanced features. If you don't already have it, you can get MSN Messenger at **http://messenger.msn.com**.

- Yahoo!Messenger is the newest and most fun. While the others provide you with a list of emoticons to quickly show emotions without words, Yahoo offers creative IMVironments — backgrounds with animated characters, like Dilbert — to liven things up. This client lets you invite others into a conference or open a private or public chat. It offers other extras, including privacy options, and is easy to use. Download the software at **http://messenger.yahoo.com**.

Since they are free, why not try them all and see which you like best? If your friends use different ones, you might need to sign on with more than one anyway.

Chat with your buddies. Each time you log on to the Internet, the client automatically connects you with your IM account. Once you have created a list of contacts, you'll see their names and which friends are currently online. They can see that you, too, are available.

With the fast pace of instant messaging, courtesy may be even more important than with e-mail. These practices will help keep good relations with your contacts.

- **Treat buddies with respect.** For example, always ask if your friend has time for a chat. If he says no, accept it graciously.

- **Show your status.** If you are online, but not available to IM, be sure to set an "away" message. But don't get angry if someone else forgets to do so.

- **Be brief.** Long stories are best saved for telephone or e-mail. Some clients set a limit for one message — with AOL it's 79 words. If your buddy agrees to read a long post, and if the client supports it, at least break it into multiple messages. And occasionally ask *Are you still with me?* to acknowledge your friend's patience.

- **Keep IM conversations light.** More serious discussions are best held in person or on the phone. Use emoticons and acronyms for speed, efficiency, and fun when you IM with your hip friends and grandchildren. But don't confuse a newbie with too many of those.

Look over the rules of e-mail netiquette found in the story *Mind your on-line Ps and Qs* on page 285. Most apply to instant messaging as well.

Play it safe. When you set up the software, be careful about what personal information you provide, since others, not just your IM buddies, may see it. Read the privacy statement, and answer only the required questions.

Because instant messaging is so popular, it is a major target for those who create viruses. A firewall will help protect against those invasions. Go to your IM client's HELP or FAQs link to learn how to configure your software to work with it. Also keep your anti-virus software updated, and use it to scan any files you download using IM software. See *Keep viruses from bugging you* on page 255 and *Safeguard your online security* on page 258.

Be suspicious if you receive an instant message that warns you of a virus and tells you to go to a specific Web site to download a program to fix it. It could be a trick by the virus creator to guarantee you get the virus. It might be a good idea to review the information about viruses in *Form healthy e-mail attachments* on page 289.

Online sites for meeting and greeting

Do you wish you had a group of neighbors who shared your enthusiasm for *Gone With the Wind* trivia, Saint Bernard dogs, or the poems of Emily Dickinson? You can find a community like that on the Internet — and you don't even have to clean the house before you invite them in.

Getting in touch with others online — through chat rooms, newsgroups, bulletin boards, discussion forums, and the like — is growing in popularity with seniors. It's a good way to meet people and make new friends, especially for those who don't get out as much as they once did.

These groups are a valuable source of information, too. No matter what your question, you are sure to find someone who has the answer — or at least can suggest where to find it. Sometimes you can even communicate directly with experts and specialists you could never reach by telephone.

Post messages at your leisure. If you are new to Internet exchanges of this kind, you may prefer to start with bulletin boards, newsgroups, and discussion forums. They are less intimidating than the fast-paced chat rooms.

In boards, groups, and forums, someone starts a message "thread" by asking a question or bringing up a topic for discussion. Then others add their posts — or articles, as they are also called — in response. While it looks a lot like an e-mail between two people, anyone with Internet access can see and respond to it.

Sometimes a moderator looks at the posts and decides if they are appropriate to the discussion and fit certain guidelines. So it can take a while for the post to appear where people can view it. And when you read what others have written on a topic, you can take time to think about it, even leave and return later to add a response.

Any time you browse the Internet you will run across a number of interactive groups and boards. You are sure to find some that interest you on one or more of these Web sites. Just go to the site, and click on the location mentioned below.

Site	Web address	Location
AARP	www.aarp.org	Online community
Excite	www.excite.com	Connect, Boards
ICQ	http://web.icq.com	Boards
MSN	www.msn.com	People & Chat
Oprah	www.oprah.com	Message boards
SeniorNet	www.seniornet.org	Discussions & Chat
Yahoo	www.yahoo.com	Connect, Groups

Your ISP also provides a news server — software that connects you to Usenet, a source of thousands of newsgroups. To make the connection using Outlook Express, go to the main window. If you have the program set to open to the INBOX, as suggested earlier, click on the OUTLOOK EXPRESS icon above the list of local folders. Under NEWSGROUPS, select SET UP A NEWS GROUP ACCOUNT, and follow the prompts. You may have to check with your ISP for the name of the NNTP (Network News Transport Protocol) server it provides.

Once the setup is complete, you can view the list of available news-groups. Since the list is long, you need to understand the prefixes for the categories so you can locate those that interest you more quickly. Here are some you'll see.

Prefix	Category
biz	business
comp	computers
news	Usenet/newsgroups (not current events)
rec	recreation, games, hobbies, sports
sci	science
soc	social issues, culture
talk	politics, religion, and other hot topics

You also have the option of searching on key words — Saint Bernard, for example — to find groups related to that topic.

Browse through the list of newsgroups and read a few posts to get a feel for any you'd like to subscribe to. Return to the list, highlight the name, and click on SUBSCRIBE. That newsgroup will appear in a folder below LOCAL FOLDERS in the Outlook Express window.

Rap in real time. Chat room exchanges are a lot like instant messaging (IM). As soon as someone posts a message, others see it and can respond immediately. You can hold a private chat with friends or enter public chats with strangers. When you IM with a buddy, you probably talk about whatever comes up. In a chat room, most people focus on one particular topic.

Because chat room conversations move so quickly, newcomers may find them a little overwhelming. Before you jump in, read the group's rules and frequently asked questions (FAQs). And it's a good idea to lurk, or hang around and observe, before you start posting.

Respect the rules of chat room netiquette when you join in. Only post if you have something important to say, use appropriate language, stick to the topic, and never try to sell anything. And, as an added courtesy, always say hello and goodbye when you enter and leave the chat room.

FYI ▶ If you'd like to know what people have said about a topic over the years, check out Google's archive of Usenet postings at http://groups. google.com.

You can choose between two kinds of chat rooms:

- **Web-based.** These chat rooms are probably the best way to start, since you can find them everywhere, and they are easy to use. America Online makes chatting simple for its members and AIM users. Just go to **www.aol.com**, and click on the PEOPLE button. Most of the Web sites in the first table in this story also have chat rooms, and ChatMag lists a lot more at **www.chatmag.com**. Or you can use a search engine and type *chat AND baseball*, for example, to find a discussion of your favorite sport.

- **Internet Relay Chat (IRC).** This kind is a little more complicated to use, but it tends to be faster and has features you aren't likely to find with Web-based chat. It requires software you get with a client program — mIRC (**www.mirc.com**) for Windows or Ircle (**www.ircle.com**) for MacIntosh are good choices. You can learn more about IRC at the ChatMag Web site.

Tech term ▶ Whisper – to send a chat room message to just one person without others seeing it.

Be careful what you reveal online. You may think you are immune to the dangers younger people face on the Internet. But whether you are 7 or 70, you should never give your real name, address, or other personal information in a chat room. Even if you don't intentionally reveal yourself, you would be surprised at the clues you can innocently drop into a conversation — where you live, if you live alone, when you plan to be away from home, even your financial status.

The problem is, people can pretend to be anyone they choose online, so that friendly grandmother you share family stories with could really be a 30-year-old male con artist. But that shouldn't keep you from enjoying online connections. Just don't be too trusting.

The chances are greater that you'll run into someone who is obnoxious. Since chatting is anonymous, it sometimes brings out the worst in people. If the language is offensive, for example, you may prefer to choose another chat room. Or use the IGNORE option most programs provide for screening messages from a particular source.

Look, too, for newsgroups and chat rooms that have a moderator to make sure articles are proper and focused on the topic. These groups may be more enjoyable and less chaotic than some of the unmonitored ones.

Get the news by mail

Mailing lists are much like newsgroups. But rather than going to the newsgroup to read the articles, you — and everyone else who subscribes to the list — get a copy of each message by e-mail. You might want to receive these mailings at a separate account to keep them from cluttering your regular e-mail inbox. Look for a directory of mailing lists at **www.listtool.com**.

Quick fixes for e-mail irritations

Your e-mail goes like clockwork most of the time. But problems can pop up. Here are some common complaints and a few suggestions for fixing them.

Q **Why didn't my friend get my e-mail?**

A E-mail can fail to reach its destination for a variety of reasons. Perhaps you made a mistake in the address. Check to see if you can find something obvious like a misspelling, a comma instead of a period, or a space. Correct it and send it again. If it's in your address book, be sure to change it there, too. Also, your friend could have changed e-mail addresses and neglected to tell you. Or her mailbox could be full. This can cause the message to bounce back to you.

Q **None of these seem to be the problem. What else could it be?**

A If you never got a message saying it wasn't deliverable, the e-mail may have gone to the wrong person. You wouldn't know unless the person e-mailed you back and told you. It's also possible you didn't actually send the e-mail. If you lost your Internet connection while writing, when you clicked on SEND, it went to your OUT box. If you haven't reconnected since, it's probably still waiting to go. You can check the OUT box or the SENT ITEMS box to see if it went out.

Q **What can I do when I receive an e-mail that's unreadable — just a hodge-podge of random words and symbols?**

A You may be looking at a long record of the path the message took to get to you. When an e-mail has been forwarded many times, this first part can look scrambled. Keep scrolling down, and see if a clear message appears. Since e-mail can originate anywhere in the world, it's also possible it was written in Chinese, Japanese, or in some other language with a script your computer can't handle. If you can't find a reason for the garbled message, try using a software program to decode it. For a free download of one called Fastcode, go to http://tools.jproof.com.

Q **How did all those people get into my address book? I don't even recognize some of the names listed there.**

A If you have people in your address book you don't recall adding, your preferences may be set to add addresses from incoming e-mails. In Outlook Express, this is how to change that setting.

1 Under TOOLS, select OPTIONS.

2 When the dialog box opens, click on the SEND tab.

3 Uncheck AUTOMATICALLY PUT PEOPLE I REPLY TO IN MY ADDRESS BOOK.

4 Click on OK.

5 To remove names, go to the Toolbar and click on ADDRESSES. When the list comes up, delete each one you don't want.

Q **I've heard it's a good idea to send blind carbon copies when you e-mail a large group of friends. But all I see is TO and CC in my NEW MESSAGE window. Where do I find BCC?**

A In Outlook Express, go to VIEW and select ALL HEADERS. The BCC option will be added to the window.

Q **Why does my e-mail program say it needs my password when I have asked it to save it?**

A This can happen if your computer decides too quickly after you dial up that the server isn't answering. Here's how, using Outlook Express, to increase the time it waits.

1 Go to TOOLS and click on ACCOUNTS.

2 Select the account that has the problem, and click on PROPERTIES.

3 Click on the ADVANCED tab and move the SERVER TIMEOUT slider toward LONG. Three minutes should do it.

Q **Why doesn't my password work?**

A Is it possible you have gotten your passwords mixed up? That's easy to do if you, like most people, have more than one for different uses. Carefully type the password exactly like you did when you set up your account. If your password is snoopy, it won't accept Snoopy or SNOOPY. You can't see the letters or numbers you've entered, so it's not easy to recognize what you may have done wrong. Check your keyboard to be sure the CAPS LOCK key light isn't on by accident.

Q   **I've been trying passwords with no luck. Now my e-mail program won't even let me do that.**

A   If you keep trying passwords that don't work, you may get frozen out of your account temporarily. This measure is intended to keep a hacker from breaking in. If you figure out what the password is, wait a while — it may take as long as half an hour — and try again. If you have truly forgotten your password, check with your ISP to find out what to do about it.

Quick tip ▶ If you send an e-mail to a group of people, and you get an unable-to-deliver message, check to see who, specifically, didn't get it. They are the only ones you'll need to include when you resend it.

Explore the e-Universe

New ways to shop for new cars

When it's time for a new car, don't tromp from lot to lot listening to slick car dealers — find bargain prices from the comfort of your own home.

Eliminate the "middle man" and "hard-sell" pitches. Here's how to buy your next automobile — hassle free — at the price you want to pay.

Shop around. Like dealers, Internet automobile sites offer varying prices. Check a few sources for the best deal. This might mean working with a dealer — but on completely different terms than a high-pressure sales pitch on his own turf.

Many sites provide general price quotes, then give you the option of getting the best deal. You provide contact information — either a phone number or e-mail address — and within 24 to 48 hours, a dealer or representative will contact you with his best price. Remember, you're under no obligation to buy. But it might be a good way to get a feel for prices.

A good starting point is Edmunds at **www.edmunds.com**. Here, you can find out what the dealers are paying for the car. Check all the options you want — air conditioning, automatic transmission, etc. — to get the most accurate price. At the very least, this gives you a basis for negotiating with a dealer if you choose to shop for cars the traditional way.

This site also gives you the Trade Market Value, a range of what you should expect to pay for the car you select. Then, if you wish, a dealer will contact you with the best available price. A sampling of other sites that work in a similar manner include:

AutoVantage	www.autovantage.com
Autoweb	www.autoweb.com
AutoNation	www.autonation.com
CarPrice	www.carprice.com
NADA Guides	www.nadaguides.com

Go direct. Perhaps your best option is CarsDirect at **www.cars direct.com**. This growing company recently bought out some of its competition, including Greenlight, another fast-growing Internet auto site. Choose your desired make, model, options, and color, and get a guaranteed low price — usually several thousand dollars below the manufacturer's suggested retail price.

If you wish, go ahead and buy the car through them. Place your order, and either deal with one of the company's vehicle specialists or a local dealer. You can even handle the financing over the phone if you want. Either way, you'll soon be able to pick up your car at a nearby dealership. The company claims one-third of its customers get their car within 24 hours and 75 percent get it in two days or less after talking with a vehicle specialist.

Another quick, easy way to buy a new car online is through Car-Max at **www.carmax.com**. However, the service is limited to certain areas. Check out the site and see if there's a CarMax location near you.

Both CarsDirect and CarMax also include a used car service, which provide actual listings of available used cars in your area. For more on buying a used car, see *Lemon aid for used cars* later in this chapter.

Thanks to these and other Internet automobile sites, you have a brand new way to shop for cars.

Lemon aid for used cars

If you're buying a used car, use the Internet to outsmart any would-be hucksters. Check out the car's value and run a lemon check online before you make a decision.

Find out what it's worth. Do a little homework, and you'll have a better idea what you should pay for your car. Armed with a fair price, you'll be able to negotiate better with a dealer or private seller. Here are some good Web sites for pricing used cars.

- **Edmunds.** This site at **www.edmunds.com** gives you the Trade Market Value (TMV) for each model. The TMV is an estimate of the average national selling price. Enter the make, model, and other features, and find out roughly what you should expect to pay. Edmunds also provides ratings, so you know whether it's even worth buying a particular car.

- **Kelley Blue Book.** You'll find all sorts of useful car-related information at **www.kbb.com**, including articles, advice, trade-in values, and pricing for used cars. Specify the condition of the car, mileage, features, and the state you're in to get the most accurate results.

- **Consumer Reports.** Browse ratings for new and used cars at **www.consumerreports.com**. You can see which models are good bets — and which are reliability risks. If you subscribe to the site, you can get more detailed ratings. For $10, you'll receive a used car report, complete with ratings, value, and reliability history, as well as current price ranges.

- **IMotors.** Search for used cars in your area and get an idea of the prices local dealers are asking. Enter the desired make, model, mileage, and your ZIP code, and you'll get a list of available cars and prices. Find all this at **www.imotors.com**.

- **Autotrader.** Just enter the make of car and your ZIP code at **www.autotrader.com**, and it will show you what prices sellers — both dealers and private sellers — are asking. You can even enter the price you're willing to pay, and it will only show cars in that price range.

- **National Automobile Dealers Association (NADA) Guides.** At **www.nadaguides.com** you'll find average trade-in and retail values. This site also lets you compare and research various models. It's great for new cars, as well as other types of vehicles.

- **MSN's Carpoint.** Another all-around car site, **http://carpoint.msn.com** gives you reliability ratings, prices, and photos for a wide range of used cars.

Squeeze the lemons. Lemons, as you probably know, are cars that break down repeatedly for the same reason and cannot be fixed. If you're worried about buying a lemon — or afraid that you already did — you can find help at these sites.

- **CARFAX.** Check the history of any vehicle at **www.carfax.com**. Just enter the vehicle identification number (VIN) and your ZIP code, and you'll get results within seconds. It's a great way to discover any hidden problems. It will track the title and registration history and let you know if the car's been in an accident.

- **CAR Lemon.** Brush up on lemon laws for your state and get tips on how to protect yourself at **www.carlemon.com**.

- **Autopedia.** An encyclopedia-like collection of car information, this site provides great lemon law advice and links to almost everything you need, including dealer finders and crash test results. Visit them at **www.autopedia.com**.

Not every used-car salesman will try to rip you off. But by knowing the value and history of the car and your rights under your state's Lemon Law, you'll be ready just in case.

Find free stuff online

You can get things for free without ever leaving home — what could be better? Freebie sites on the Internet have thousands of interesting and valuable offers. Check out these top picks.

- **TheFreeSite.** You don't have to register to search the free offers on this site, but you can sign up for e-mail updates of free offers. Check it out at **www.thefreesite.com**.

- **Freeze.com.** This fun site at **www.freeze.com** contains an extensive directory of links that offer free stuff, as well as online coupons.

- **Free.com.** With over 9,000 links to free stuff, you're sure to find something you need at this mega-site. You have to register, so if you don't like getting a lot of junk e-mail, unclick the box that asks if you want to receive special offers. Visit them at **www.free.com**.

- **TotallyFreeStuff.** The content on this site — **www.totally freestuff.com** — changes daily, so you know the offers are up-to-date.

- **Free-n-Cool.** It's easy to navigate and contains free stuff, special offers, contests, and more. See it all at **www.free-n-cool.com**.

Dig up great gardening info

From bulbs to bougainvillea, caladiums to compost, weeds to water-melon — everything you need to green up your thumb is as close as the Internet. Whether you're an agricultural veteran or just beginning to play in the dirt, you can harvest a bumper crop of information with just a few keystrokes.

A good general place to start is a Web site like GardenNet at **www.gardennet.com**. This one has links, descriptions, and contact information for gardening companies, mail order catalogs, associations, services, products, and events.

Other sites you'll want to hit first are GardenWeb at **www.garden web.com**, and National Gardening at **www.garden.org**.

There's nothing wrong with wandering through some of these larger sites — you never know what might sprout. But if you're fairly confident in the kind of information you need, you can focus in on just a few sites.

Start with a plan. There's nothing like a little professional help when it comes to designing a landscape. There is, of course, software you can buy that lets you play around with different plantings in your virtual garden. Visit Amazon.com or your local computer store to browse through the options. You'll want to check out Garden Organizer, Custom LandDesigner 3D, and Sunset Home and Garden.

Or visit a Web site like Clearwater Landscape Design at **www.clear waterlandscapes.com** where you submit your ideas and specific landscaping needs, and professionals create finished plans, images, and specifications.

Pick the best plant. The glossy catalog pictures may make your mouth water. And the rows of little seedlings at the nursery may be tempting. But are you bringing home the very best plant for your soil type and climate zone? Getting it right can be a thorny task. Don't worry — there's advice by the wheelbarrow on the Internet.

Welcome to the Plants National Database at **http://plants.usda.gov**. This comprehensive government site includes names, checklists, automated tools, and information on identifying, choosing, and growing plants.

GardenGuides at **www.gardenguides.com** claims to be a growing resource for gardeners. In addition to just about everything else, this site has a very friendly drop-down list of plants that link you to background and growing information.

The HortiPlex plant database, **http://hortiplex.gardenweb.com/ plants**, is a bit simpler. And a site like Landscape USA at **www.land scapeusa.com/plantfinder.asp** lets you input specific information on the kind of plant you're looking for and offers suggestions.

Look it up. If you want still more reference information, try one of the plant encyclopedias online.

Botany.com	www.botany.com
My Deer Garden	www.mydeergarden.com

Ask the experts. Many names you're familiar with have Web sites packed with gardening information. Tapping into their expert advice is just a keystroke away.

Lowes	www.lowes.com
Better Homes and Gardens	www.bhg.com
Home & Garden Television	www.hgtv.com
The Farmer's Almanac	www.almanac.com

Order seeds and such. Founded in 1876, Burpee is one of the oldest and most well-known seed companies. Of course, today, they sell much more than seeds — everything from their special potting formula to cooking videos. While they offer all their products in six separate catalogs throughout the year, you can find almost everything online as well. Read about perennials, annuals, bulbs, and kitchen gardening in their online gardening guides. You can even sign up for a free gardening newsletter and get great deals only available through the Internet. Visit Burpee at **www.burpee.com**.

Here are a few other Web sites that offer seeds.

Park Seed	www.parkseed.com
Henry Field's Seed & Nursery	http://henryfields.com
Gurney's Seed & Nursery	http://gurneys.com
Seeds of Change (organic seeds)	www.seedsofchange.com
Virtual Seeds	www.virtualseeds.com
Seeds Unique	www.seedsonline.com

Buy some bulbs. If tulips and hyacinths are your thing, then you've got to shop for bulbs. Check out everything to do with bulbs at the International Flower Bulb Centre at **www.bulbsonline.org**. You'll learn when and how to plant plus find an extensive list of links to other sites that sell bulbs. These are the two most well-known suppliers of commercial bulbs.

Brecks	www.brecks.com
Michigan Bulb Company	www.michiganbulb.com

Learn all about veggies. Who doesn't love a tomato right off the vine or a handful of fresh strawberries? The Kitchen Garden at **www.kitchengardener.com** is a good place to read, learn, and chat with others.

Discover the world of herbs. Freeze them, dry them, cook and decorate with them. Herbs are useful plants that can even make you feel better when you're sick.

The Whole Herb at **www.wholeherb.com** has advice on how to grow them plus weekly gardening tips. Learn how to plant a windowsill herb garden and make herbal shampoo.

Get the bugs out. No matter how long you've been gardening, you still have to face aphids, slugs, and other pests. Here are several sites that help you deal with them.

Natural Insect Control	www.natural-insect-control.com
Ortho Online!	www.ortho.com
The Invisible Gardener	www.invisiblegardener.com

Join in. If you're attracted to the social side of gardening, find out about plant societies, clubs, and other gardening organizations. The Garden Web directory has a searchable database at **http://dir.garden web.com/directory/a-home.html**.

Get out and about. Plan your weekend getaway around the next flower show. Visit every botanical garden in your state. Want to know where the garden tours and butterfly shows are? What about seminars, plant swaps, festivals, and workshops? All this information is a mouse-click away at Internet sites like **www.gardencalendar.com**.

Don't forget the lawn. If you want nothing more than a lush carpet of green at your doorstep, then check out one of these grass sites.

Yardcare.com	www.yardcare.com
Lawngrasses.com	www.lawngrasses.com

And if outdoor power tools are your game, you'll want to visit CyberLawn at **http://.opei.mow.org** and What's the Best Lawnmower? at **www.whatsthebest-lawnmower.com**.

Plan on watering. A good lawn needs the right amount of water, and a built-in sprinkler system makes it worry-free. Find free irrigation information at **www.jessstryker.com** or **www.rainbird.com**. There's even an Irrigation Association Web site at **www.irrigation.org**.

Scout out these specialty sites. From bonsai to butterflies, everyone has his own special passion. And there's sure to be a Web site devoted to it. Here are just a few specialty sites you might want to explore.

EveryRose	www.everyrose.com
The Tropical Hibiscus	www.trop-hibiscus.com
All American Rose Selections	www.rose.org
The American Orchid Society	www.orchidweb.org
OrganicGardening.com	www.organicgardening.com
Home of Clematis	www.homeofclematis.com
The Perennial Gardener	www.pbs.org/perennialgardener

Get the forecast. Last but not least, don't let the weather catch you by surprise. Go online for the latest forecast. Some sites, like **www.weather.com/activities/homeandgarden** offer regional gardening reports and garden weather maps.

Trace your roots

The Internet is a great tool to help you research your family's history, putting a wealth of information at your fingertips.

Whether you want to write your autobiography, solve the mystery of an adoption, or find out your family's health history, the Internet offers free — and sometimes for-fee — help with your research.

Search engines specifically designed for genealogy make it easy. They'll guide you to databases — some containing millions of names and locations. You can read online newsletters, and "how to" articles. So start discovering the story of your heritage and learn how to keep it safe for your descendants. These Web sites are good places to start.

About Genealogy	www.genealogy.about.com
FamilyTree	www.familytree.com
GenealogyTODAY	www.genealogytoday.com

Build your family tree. You're going to have to deal with a lot of information as you search. Make organizing it all easier and more fun than you thought possible by downloading software — for free — at Family Tree House at **www.usaafter.com** or Ancestry Family Tree at **http://aft.ancestry.com**. Or purchase software at Family Tree Maker Online at **www.familytreemaker.com**.

And with sites like MyFamily at **www.myfamily.com** you can create a private Web site to share your history and keep in touch with family and friends.

Get the historical facts. No matter what your genealogy project, you're going to need names, dates, and places. You'll want to visit the National Archives at **www.nara.gov** to get a feel for what records the government has. But there are other places you can search for historical records like:

- Birth, baptism, marriage and death certificates at **www.vital rec.com**

- Historical newspapers

- Military service records at sites like **www.vetfriends.com**

- Social Security records

- Land deeds at sites like **www.glorecords.blm.gov**

- Tax records

- U.S. Census Records at **www.census.gov**

Access ever-growing pools of information like the Civil War Research Database. It currently contains records of over 2 million soldiers. At Third Age **www.thirdage.com/familytree** you're guided through the search process — whether you're looking by the name of a soldier, a particular regiment, or a hometown. In addition, you can view original documents and images of battle maps online.

There are literally hundreds of databases, from A (the Australian Convict Index) to Z (the Zanesville, Ohio Directory of 1890). You're sure to find one that fits your needs.

Go international. If your tree was planted in another country, there's help for you, too. One collection of Internet links is designed just to help you locate your immigrant ancestors, **www.genealogy. about.com/cs/immigrationhowto**. Here you can learn how to track down immigration and naturalization records, view passenger lists for all major American ports, and even identify your ancestor's original hometown.

The American Family Immigration History Center spearheaded an Ellis Island immigration database. Visit it at **www.ellisisland.org**. Through this comprehensive site, you can trace your family's journey to America.

Get specific. Find maps at **http://plasma.nationalgeographic.com/ mapmachine** of every place from 1757 New England to the Pacific railroad routes of 1855. They'll provide clues to where your ancestors may have lived and where to look for written records about them. Also search **www.census.gov/ftp/pub/geo/www.tiger/tiger map.html**.

Find cemeteries and look for your ancestors' tombstones at **www.genealogy.com/VG/vcem_search.html**. Even explore the Alaskan Valdez Gold Rush names database at **http://cedar.forest. net/thevaldez**. There are databases organized by different religions, providing information even when civil records didn't exist.

If you have questions no one else can seem to answer, try the National Genealogical Society at **www.ngsgenealogy.org**.

Connect with others. Visit a site like **www.OneGreatFamily.com** and you can chat with others on their own journey into the past. Post questions on message boards regarding specific areas of interest or ask for help when you hit a dead end. Share photographs online for free.

There are genealogical societies based on locations — like a state, city, or county — or a name — like Smith. For instance, Virginia has over two dozen historical societies, from Children of Shenandoah to the Jamestowne Society. Most are non-profit organizations founded to assist you in your genealogical research.

Learn more. At **www.genealogy.com** you can sign up for an online genealogy class. With their self-paced tutorials you'll explore various topics one lesson at a time. Their professional genealogists have put together everything for the beginner to the advanced. Their Beginning Internet Genealogy Lesson 1, for instance, explains and lists Usenet Newsgroups and Mailing Lists. At the end of each lesson is a review and links to other Internet sites that pertain to the lesson.

Get lots of free stuff. Either download or print right from your computer free genealogy forms. There's one for your every need, whether you want to create a time line, compose letters requesting records from various agencies, or record information from deeds and census records. Visit 1 Stop Free Shop at **www.1stopfreeshop.com/ genforms.htm**.

Subscribe to a free monthly e-newsletter at Treasure Maps at **www.amberskyline.com/treasuremaps** or find more free information at **www.genfree.com**. This site offers products to help you complete your family roots project. Receive a free trial copy of *Family Chronicle*, the magazine for families researching their roots.

Or perhaps you need help getting started. A free 24-page booklet from Family History Centers of the Church of Jesus Christ of Latter Day Saints contains charts and hints on finding and recording your information. Receive a free bi-monthly newspaper, the *Family Tree*. Browse through free catalogs of all kinds of forms, charts, research books, and CDs. And much, much more.

Just for fun. Now that you're beginning to think fondly of your relations, plan a family reunion with help at **www.family-reunion. com**. You'll find tips on organizing, selecting a theme, planning locations and activities, even recipe ideas and menu plans. What could be easier?

And if somehow the reality of your heritage doesn't quite live up to your expectations, browse the family tree of famous Americans at **www.genealogy.com/famousfolks/index.html**, a site sponsored by Biography.com, or study the European royal lines at **http:// ftp.cac.psu.edu/~saw/royal/royalgen.html**. Who knows — you might stumble upon a long-lost relative.

Here are some more general genealogy sites, some requiring a paid subscription. Many may seem overwhelming with the amount of information they offer. Just get organized before you start surfing and stay focused as you go through different links.

Ancestry.com	www.ancestry.com
Family Search	www.familysearch.org
RootsWeb.com	www.rootsweb.com

Cyndi's List of Genealogy Sites	www.cyndislist.com
The US GenWeb Project	www.usgenweb.org
FamilyHistory.com	www.familyhistory.com
The Genealogy Home Page	www.genhomepage.com

Make a date with your computer

If you can't remember things like you used to, let your computer come to the rescue. It can keep track of appointments, birthdays, and more.

Use your software. Some software programs come with a calendar function. For example, Entourage, which is part of the Microsoft Office package, has a calendar that allows you to record your entire schedule. You can even set it to make a notification sound at the appropriate time, and a box will pop up on your computer screen with the text of your reminder.

Set your Internet start page. Your ISP (Internet Service Provider) has a start page that pops up when you first log on to the Internet. This page probably has a reminder setting that allows you to add events. Web sites, such as **www.yahoo.com** and **www.excite.com** also offer start pages you can personalize with your own reminders.

Let the Web remember. If you don't have calendar software, use the Web to help jog your memory. Collabrio has a whole collection of programs to help you get organized. At **www.MyEvents.com** you can try them out free for 15 days. Then it's only $4 a month. Fill out their web calendar and they will remind you of events via e-mail. Of course, you must check your e-mail regularly for this option to work well.

Iping at **www.iping.com** is an Internet reminder and Wakeup Call service. Sign up and you can receive wakeup calls and other reminders on your telephone. There's even a "Dr. Dose" section that reminds you to take your medication. Iping is an ideal service for someone who doesn't necessarily spend a lot of time online. It does charge a fee, however. Subscription prices currently range from $4.95 a month to $14.95 a month.

Discover a wealth of health info

Benjamin Franklin would have loved the "Information Superhighway" because it has the potential to make you healthy, wealthy, and wise. The Internet is bursting with information that can make your life better. It can also help make you healthier by providing you with valuable medical advice.

But how do you know that the health information you find is reliable? One way is to look for the HON (Health on the Net Foundation) seal of approval. This nonprofit foundation provides a code of conduct to help regulate Internet sites that offer health information and advice.

Here are 11 essential medical Internet sites you must know about. They all subscribe to the HON code. It could save your health — or your life.

- **WebMD.** Get information on any illness at this superb site, where you can also search for health insurance or a doctor near you. Talk with others who want to share their experiences and information on the site's chat rooms or message boards. Just pay a visit to **www.webmd.com**.

- **Mayo Clinic.** Learn from one of the world's most respected clinics. In addition to information on health conditions, drugs, and first aid, this site also features programs to help you lose weight, become more physically fit, quit smoking, and cope with stress. Go to **www.mayoclinic.com**.

- **Discovery Health.** This Web site that accompanies the Discovery Health cable TV channel is packed with information about a wide range of diseases and conditions. Get information on drugs, dieting, and the latest health news. You can even submit a question to medical experts or join in conversations on various health topics. Tune in at **www.discoveryhealth.com**.

- **Achoo.** Billed as "The Gateway to Healthcare," this site offers so much health-related information that it can be overwhelming. Explore its links to organizations, resources, and sources of news. You can also look up any health topic through a few different search engines. Check it out at **www.achoo.com**.

- **HealthScout.** Read feature articles, take fun quizzes, browse the health library and drug index, and look for a doctor in your area. You can even subscribe to a weekly newsletter for the latest health information. Scout it for yourself at **www.health scout.com**.

- **HealthAtoZ.** If you register at this site, you get the benefit of an online health records organizer, an online calendar to keep track of appointments, prescription refills, or other important events, and e-mail reminders to make sure you keep your appointments. There's even a special section called 60-Something Plus for older adults. Go to **www.healthatoz.com**.

- **InteliHealth.** Get the benefit of an Ivy League education from this site, featuring information from Harvard Medical School. You'll also find interactive quizzes and helpful tools like the Symptom Scout, which asks you questions and lists common signs to pinpoint your condition. Be smart and learn at **www.intelihealth.com**.

- **Drug InfoNet.** Read all about prescription drugs at this useful site, which also provides information and links to other sites on a variety of topics. Disease information, government sites, hospitals, medical schools, health news — get it all at **www.drug infonet.com**.

- **Med Help International.** Search for health information on any condition in simple, non-technical language at this helpful site. You can also post questions on several specialized medical forums. Help yourself at **www.medhelp.org**.

- **MyPhysicians.** Go online and find a doctor "on call." You'll get information on almost any health concern. Ask a question of a primary care physician or a specialist and get a personalized answer within 72 hours. This e-mail service does cost money, but you can read archives of old questions and participate in forums for free once you register at **www.myphysicians.com**.

- **Hardin Meta Directory.** This service of the University of Iowa provides links to sites about every imaginable health condition. Be prepared to look through several lists of sites, but you'll definitely find the information you're seeking. Begin your search at **www.lib.uiowa.edu/hardin/md**.

Count on government sites for more reliable and conservative information. Try MEDLINEplus at **www.medlineplus.gov** for general information on almost any health topic you can imagine. Its extensive resources include the National Library of Medicine and the National Institutes of Health.

Or check out Healthfinder at **www.healthfinder.gov**. It contains an alphabetical index of links to reliable Web sites covering a wide variety of health topics, from abstinence to youth at risk.

You might not be wealthy — but after checking out these wonderful online health resources, you'll be healthy and wise.

Safe savings on prescription drugs

Going online beats waiting in line to fill a prescription. The prices at Internet pharmacies may be better, too, because they have lower overhead than walk-in drugstores. It's also easier to compare prices sitting at your computer than it would be to drive to several different stores, or to call and wait for a druggist to look up your prescription.

Although the savings can be substantial, be careful. Some online sites don't take the proper steps to protect your health. Get the wrong medication, or even a fake one, and you're at risk of losing more than your money.

The best way to choose a reliable Internet pharmacy is to see if the VIPPS (Verified Internet Pharmacy Practice Sites) seal is displayed on the Web site. This seal shows that a pharmacy is licensed by the states in which it operates and has passed the National Association of Boards of Pharmacy (NABP) requirements for quality and security.

If you click on the seal at a certified site, you will go directly to the NABP Web site. These online pharmacies have received VIPPS certification.

Accurate Pharmacy	www.accuratepharmacy.com
Caremark, Inc.	www.rxrequest.com
CIGNA Tel-Drug	www.teldrug.com
Clickpharmacy.com	www.clickpharmacy.com
CVS Washington, Inc.	www.cvs.com
Drugstore.com	www.drugstore.com
Eckerd Pharmacy Services	www.Eckerd.com
Familymeds.com	www.familymeds.com
Merck-Medco Managed Care, L.L.C.	www.merck-medco.com

NCS Healthcare Care For Life	www.careforlife.com
Savon Drugs	www.Savon.com
VitaRx.com	www.Vitarx.com
Walgreens	www.walgreens.com

To find out if others have been added to the VIPPS certified list, you can go directly to the NABP Web site at **www.nabp.net** or call 847-698-6227.

Many of these Web sites also offer free health and nutrition advice as well as information about the drugs you order. You can check for side effects and possible drug interactions. Phone numbers are available if you need to talk to a pharmacist.

Lose weight with help from the Web

Let's face it — losing weight is no fun. It's tough to stick to your diet and exercise schedule, especially when you don't see results right away. Sometimes you just feel like plopping on the couch, eating a pint of ice cream, and throwing in the towel.

Don't give up — boot up. Next time you start a weight loss program, start with the Internet. With a wealth of free information, advice, and diet aids, you can get the help you need to lose all the weight you want.

Here are just a few examples of helpful sites.

- **Diet-Links.com.** A good place to start, this site provides links to several weight-loss sites. Find general information, healthy recipes, magazines, free software, support, and more at **www.diet-links.com**.

- **DietPower.** Read all about the weight loss program that tailors itself to your individual needs. The DietPower software includes a food log, exercise log, recipes, and helpful graphs to track your progress. Sample it with a free 15-day trial at **www.dietpower.com.**

- **Dietsite.** This site provides information about diet and nutrition. It also analyzes your diet and tracks your progress for free. Go to **www.dietsite.com.**

- **Recipe Calc.** Download a free 20-day trial of this software, which lets you analyze your recipes, meals, or daily intake for nutritional value. It calculates calories, calories from fat, percentage of calories from fat, fat grams, saturated fat, cholesterol, carbohydrates, fiber, sodium, and protein. Give it a try at **www.recipecalc.com.**

- **HealthKeeper.** This company specializes in online dieting and dieting software. Get all sorts of free trials — including software, books, charts, and tips — at **www.healthkeeper.com.**

- **Calories Per Hour.** This fun site tracks how helpful your exercise program is. Just enter your weight, height, age, and sex. Then choose an activity — choices range from accordion playing to yoga — and fill in a length of time. Hit CALCULATE and you'll see how many calories you burned. You'll also see how many Big Macs that equals. Start calculating at **www.calories perhour.com.**

- **100 Weight Loss Tips.** This site has a vast collection of helpful tips and motivational thoughts to keep you on the path to success. Check it out at **www.100-weight-loss-tips.com.**

- **Diet Information.** Get sensible advice on diet, weight loss, and nutrition at **www.diet-i.com.**

Spot special health offers online

Go on the Internet and find plenty of information, advice, and cool offers for any health-related issue.

For example, you can protect your vision with free information from this eye-friendly site. AllAboutVision.com is packed with helpful articles on contacts, glasses, eye disease, and LASIK surgery. You can even find an eye doctor in your area, ask the site's experts a question, or download coupons for contact lenses and other eye products.

Sign up for a free e-mail newsletter to get updated information regularly, and you may even win free sunglasses. Look for it all at **www.allaboutvision.com**.

While you're looking for health information, check out our own FC&A Publishing Web site. You can browse our collection of health books that supply accurate medical information in clear, simple language. It's also a great source for consumer and craft books. You'll even get a free health and consumer secret of the week. Just go to **www.fca.com**.

How to find the best insurance buys

You need insurance, but you don't need to spend astronomical amounts on it. Use the Internet to find out if you are paying too much. These services compare insurance companies' rates according to your personal needs. And you won't have to listen to one sales pitch, either.

- **Quotesmith.com.** Check out the lowest prices from 300 leading insurance companies. This site lets you compare several types of insurance, including Auto, Dental, Medical, Long-term care, Travel, Life, and Homeowners. It also has a hotline you can call if you're having trouble. Start browsing at **www. quotesmith.com.**

- **Get-Insurance.net.** This service provides links to several other Web sites for fast, free insurance quotes. Get competitive quotes for Auto, Home/Renters, Business, Life, and Health insurance. Just go to **www.get-insurance.net.**

- **Insweb.com.** Register at this site, answer some questions, and get insurance quotes. Some are immediate, while others might take several days. Choose a quote you like, and purchase the insurance through the company. Check it out at **www.ins web.com.**

- **All Quotes Insurance.** Answer a few questions, fill out an application, and get quotes within 24 hours. Visit **www.all quotesinsurance.com.**

- **Quicken.com.** Compare quotes for Health, Term Life, Auto, and Homeowners/Renters insurance. You can also get advice. For example, if you answer a few questions, you can find out how much coverage you need. Go to **www.quicken.com/ insurance.**

- **Insure.com.** This great source of insurance information provides articles, tips, and links to instant quotes. Read all about it at **www.insure.com.**

- **YouDecide.** This site has sections that help you make decisions about coverage and calculate your coverage needs. Take some time to answer a few questions, and receive several quotes. It can take up to 48 hours, however. Decide for yourself at **www. youdecide.com.**

- **4Insurance.com.** This site claims you can save up to 35 percent on Auto, Home, Life, and Health insurance. Give it a try at **www.4insurance.com.**

If it's automobile insurance you want, two good places to go are

Progressive at **www.progressive.com** and Esurance at **www. esurance.com**. Progressive gives you instant quotes and lets you buy insurance online. It also compares quotes from other insurance companies so you always get the best deal. Esurance, meanwhile, promises its quote is "the fastest on the Web."

Before you start shopping for insurance, you might want to learn a little bit about it. Check out LIFE, a nonprofit organization designed to educate people about Life, Health, and Disability insurance. It explains everything very simply, in language everyone can understand. Go to **www.life-line.org** and become a wiser insurance consumer.

Get the verdict on free legal aid

Don't ever be intimidated by the legal world again. Whether it's confusing terms, complex paperwork, or outrageous fees, you can take back control — with the help of your computer and the Internet.

Begin by surfing around on a few general legal Web sites. Explore their glossaries and look through their archives. Then, when you feel a bit more comfortable, zero in on a site that can fulfill your specific legal needs.

- **NOLO.** *Newsweek* calls NOLO "The nation's premier publisher of do-it-yourself law." If you want to file it, fight it, plan it, patent it, authorize it, sell it, or settle it yourself — you've come to the right place. Here you can download software or complete electronic books full of self-help information and forms. Read legal guides on specific topics from Investing For Retirement to Resolving Your Travel Dispute. Download collections of electronic forms, complete with instructions, or select the single form you need, fill it out online, download, and print. There's usually a fee for these services, but many of the other options on this extensive Web site — like the Law Center — are free. NOLO at **www.nolo.com** truly does put the law into plain English.

- **USLaw.com.** Another good legal Web site offering a range of information and services is **www.uslaw.com**. Their free library contains over 2,000 easy-to-understand articles. Or use their Affiliate Network to find a lawyer near you. Note that several of their services, such as chatting with a lawyer or creating your own legal documents, require a fee.

- **FindLaw.** The Public channel at **www.findlaw.com** has even more free legal information in 10 major categories, including Personal Injury and Money.

Use your computer and the Internet for at least background research no matter what your legal dilemma.

Get free advice. You can learn a lot about your legal rights and get answers to some general legal questions right on the Internet — without giving personal information or paying a penny. For instance, what should you do if you slip and fall in a store? What can you do if you purchase a defective product? At FreeAdvice.com, **www.freeadvice.com**, you'll find basic information that will help you decide if you can and should take legal action.

Become savvy on senior law. The National Academy of Elder Law Attorneys, Inc. is a non-profit association really designed to help lawyers who deal with senior issues. However, one of their pages is called Questions & Answers When Looking For an Elder Law Attorney. Find it by clicking on their PUBLIC icon. This Q and A page has lots of good advice about how to find an attorney specializing in Elder Law, and then what questions to ask before you retain him. Be sure to visit this site at **www.naela.com**.

SeniorLaw at **www.seniorlaw.com** also has links to resources geared specifically for seniors, a searchable list of Elder Law Attorneys, and an archive of articles on the rights and issues of the elderly and disabled.

Find a lawyer. Don't pick an attorney at random. Lawyers.com is a free service offering profiles of over 400,000 attorneys and law firms worldwide. You can then link to the home page of one you're interested in and read about fees, areas of expertise, professional credentials, even directions. Plus there are tips on selecting a lawyer and 12 questions you must ask. If you want more, delve into their About the Law and Legal Resources sections. Under Law Talk you'll find message boards, discussions groups, and chat areas. You have to register to participate in these, and remember, you're not necessarily talking to experts. Visit this site at **www.lawyers.com**.

FindLaw.com, **www.lawoffice.com**, also has a legal directory of lawyers and law firms. Select your state, or browse through their list of close to 100 areas of specialized practice — from Adoption to Worker's Compensation. Based on your selections, you'll get a list of matches. Look up each attorney and make your choice.

If you don't mind giving some personal information upfront, you can register with a matching service called LegalMatch at **www.legal match.com**. The attorneys listed with LegalMatch pay a yearly membership fee, so it's free to you. However, you must give them your name and e-mail address, among other things. Then you anonymously post some specific information about your legal problem and you're matched with qualified attorneys.

Learn about legal documents. Let's say you need a copy of your credit report, or you decide it's time to make a Living Will. Go to a Web site like Legaldocs at **www.legaldocs.com** and you can do it for free in a matter of minutes. While many of their 80-plus documents require a fee, none is more than $30. Also try out USlegalforms.com at **www.uslegalforms.com**.

If you just want to read examples of various legal documents, go to **www.laweasy.com/ii.htm**. You'll get an idea of the kind of information needed for various legal issues and the questions you should ask a lawyer.

Nolo.com also has certain legal forms you can fill in on the Web, purchase, and print. It will cost you about $8 for a bill of sale for your car and close to $13 for a promissory note.

Load your own software. If you prefer to have everything on your own computer, you can purchase legal software from the general to the specific. Quicken Lawyer is perhaps the most well known. They have both business and personal versions, plus software devoted just to wills. You can purchase software like this online or at your local computer store.

Look for an alternative. If you find yourself in a legal dispute and want options on how to work things out, check out Martindale.com at **www.martindale.com**. Among other things, this Web site has an Alternative Dispute Resolution Services Locator. This means they'll help you find an individual or an organization that offers alternatives to going to court. You select the kind of help you need — say a consultant or a mediator — type in your city, and you'll get the name, address, and qualifications of any expert in your area.

Stay informed. Do you like keeping current on the latest cases and legal decisions? Then you'll want to visit **www.law.cornell.edu**, Cornell Law School's Legal Information Institute. The language can be a bit complex, but it makes interesting dinner conversation.

Emory University School of Law has a similar site at **www.law. emory.edu/FEDCTS**. Look up legal opinions from all federal appellate courts and the Supreme Court — for free.

Called the catalog of catalogs, CataLaw at **www.catalaw.com**

arranges all law and government into one giant index. Choose a topic, a region, or the type of information you need. You'll be directed to other Web sites that gradually narrow down to the exact information you're looking for.

If you are truly serious about law research, there is The Internet Law Library at **www.lawresearch.com**. A monthly subscription fee of $18.75 gives you access to what is claimed to be the largest law library on the Internet plus over a million legal resource links.

And, of course, the federal government has its own storehouse of legal information. Go to the National Criminal Justice Reference Service at **www.ncjrs.org** and click on WHAT IS NCJRS? Do research, ask questions, or check out their official publications.

Profit from money management

You can use your personal computer to do just about anything related to financial management. There is a wide variety of software from the simple to the complex. One is bound to fit your needs. With the right software and access to the Internet, you can:

- manage your checking account

- monitor your savings accounts

- receive and pay bills

- create a budget

- plan for retirement

- keep tax records and file with the IRS

- analyze and trade stocks

- track your portfolio

Pick your program. Intuit Quicken Deluxe is one of the most popular financial programs. With it you can track your spending and saving, organize your finances, manage your investments, prepare for filing taxes, and plan for the future.

While it can help you with money management on a daily basis, it can also guide you through the sometimes confusing world of investments.

To do your own research on this product, go to **www.intuit.com** and click on their product information pages.

Another top-selling money management program is Microsoft Money. Visit **www.microsoft.com** and browse through their products for a firsthand look at all it has to offer.

Go bigger if necessary. Have a home business? Let your computer be your secretary, accountant, and printer — all in one. You can find more sophisticated software that's better suited to home-based or small businesses, and for serious accounting needs. These programs can help you create invoices, track accounts payable, generate reports, and even simplify your taxes.

Don't forget the details. Find out which software will interact with your bank or credit union if you plan to use their online services. Just think — you'll never have to balance your checkbook again.

Once you decide which software you want to use, get the latest version. Of course, there will be changes to financial, tax, and banking laws over time, but you can update your version easily. Usually you can download any upgrade from the manufacturer.

Earn money with your computer

The computer age has made it possible for many people to earn money from the comfort of their own homes.

If you currently have a job, talk to your employer about telecommuting. More and more companies allow their employees to work from home this way. The Clean Air Campaign gives you advice on how to approach your boss about teleworking. Go to their Web site at **www.cleanaircampaign.com** and look under Commute Solutions. Or call 1-877-CLEANAIR.

Tap into your talents. Even if you're officially retired, you might want to make a little extra money, and your computer can help you do just that. Use skills you already have or learn new ones — there are many online or correspondence courses that can help. Edit term papers, sell your craft ware, or provide accounting or secretarial services to small local businesses. Become a proofreader, transcribe medical records, or work in sales or customer service.

Build a Web page. Another popular way to earn money with your computer is by creating and using your own Web site. If this is new territory for you, a good place to start is HTML Goodies at **www. htmlgoodies.com**. Their online tutorials will walk you through the entire Web page setup process. Then learn how to display advertising banners on your site and get paid for it.

Another option is through a company like the Six Figure Income Marketing Group (SFI) at **www.sfiaffiliate.com**. They offer free training in turning your computer into a moneymaking machine.

Let the Net lend a hand. Check out these Internet sites dedicated to helping you find work at home.

Homeworkers.com	www.homeworkers.com
2-work-at-home.com	www.2work-at-home.com
HomeBasedWork.com	www.homebasedwork.com
MoneyMakingMommy.com	www.moneymakingmommy.com
Work At Home Dot Com	http://work-at-home-dot.com
Work At Home Top Picks	www.work-at-home-toppicks.com
Work At Home Parents	http://work-at-home-parents.com
Work At Home Index	www.work-at-home-index.net
Home2Work.com	www.home2work.com
Home-Based Working Moms	www.hbwm.com

All these sites list home-based jobs, give advice on how to make this type of venture work, help you write a resume, offer free e-mail newsletters, and give tips on avoiding scams. You can even order books and other materials to help you start your own home-based business.

Steer clear of the suspicious. Not all work-at-home opportunities are legitimate and many require you to spend your own money. Remember, if it sounds too good to be true, it probably is. While you can earn money using your computer, few people become millionaires this way.

Check out any work-at-home opportunity with the Federal Trade Commission at **www.ftc.gov/bcp/conline/pubs/invest/home wrk.htm** and the Better Business Bureau at **www.bbbonline.org** or **www.bbb.org/library/workathome.asp**. These sites list scams, tell you how to avoid fraud, give the most common signs of an unscrupulous scheme, and tell you what to do if you are a victim of a work-at-home scam. Another way to stay safe is by looking for the BBB Online Seal. Then sit down and go to work. Your computer could pay for itself — and then some.

Expand your compact disc collection

If you're looking for compact discs, use the Internet to shop from the comfort of your own home.

A great starting place is the All Music Guide at **www.allmusicguide.com**. Just type in any artist's name, and you'll get a biography and a complete listing of albums, including compilations. Each album is rated on a five-star system and reviewed. The reviewers indicate which albums they recommend and which ones are currently in print.

You can even buy certain compact discs by clicking on a link to CDNOW, one of the Web's best sources for a wide range of CDs. You can also go directly to CDNOW at **www.cdnow.com**.

Other good sources for compact discs online include:

Amazon	www.amazon.com
Borders	www.borders.com
Barnes & Noble	www.barnesandnoble.com
CD Universe	www.cduniverse.com
Half.com	www.half.com
Tower Records	www.towerrecords.com
Wherehouse Music	www.wherehousemusic.com

Search these sites by artist or title. You'll see which songs are on the album, and maybe even listen to certain songs just by clicking on them. Ordering is a breeze, usually taking just a few clicks.

Name that tune — and find it online

Over the years, the way you listen to music has steadily changed.

From turntables to 8-tracks to cassettes to compact discs, music technology keeps improving.

Not surprisingly, the Internet has contributed even more changes. Now you can bring the world of music to your living room. Any style, any artist, any song can be found on the Internet and played on your computer.

Here's what you need to know about this latest musical breakthrough.

Know the basics. Music files come in two main forms, MP3 and RealAudio. The most popular format, MP3 is a compressed file, meaning it doesn't take up much disk space on your computer. It allows you to save and replay songs. The sound quality is great, but it might take a long time to download, or copy, this type of file to your computer.

RealAudio, on the other hand, is called a stream. This means you can click on a RealAudio file and hear it right away without having to download it to your computer first. This is the format usually used for online radio stations. One possible glitch — If a lot of people are using the Internet at the same time, your stream might be interrupted.

Now that you know the types of music files available, learn how to enjoy them on your computer.

Download free music. If you keep up with the news, you have probably heard of Napster, the first widespread way to download music. This popular free service used the concept of file sharing. In other words, people could go to the Napster Web site and download music files from any other Napster user currently online.

Users loved it, but Napster raised legal issues because none of the recording artists received royalties. After much legal pressure from the recording industry, Napster closed down.

In Napster's wake, several similar free services popped up. They're easy to use. Just go to the site, sign in, and follow the directions to download the application that lets you access the music. Check out the site's Help section if you're having trouble.

Then search for a song or artist you like. For example, type in *That's Amore* or *Dean Martin*. You'll get a list of available MP3 files. Simply click on what you want to download to your computer. It's a good idea to create a file on your hard drive just to store music.

Here's a short list of some of the more popular free sites. Remember, the legal issues that plagued Napster remain, so these sites might not be around (or free) forever.

Audiogalaxy	www.audiogalaxy.com
KaZaA	www.kazaa.com
KaZaALite	www.kazaalite.com
Gnutella	www.gnutella.com
WinMX	www.winmx.com
Zeropaid	www.zeropaid.com

This last site, Zeropaid, is a great source for the latest information about file sharing. It also provides recommendations and links for where to go for free downloads.

Play it safe. You can also find plenty of 100 percent legal sites supported by the record companies. Some of them charge a small monthly fee or even charge per song. Others are free, with a limited selection.

ArtistDirect	www.artistdirect.com
Rolling Stone	www.rollingstone.com
Listen.com	www.listen.com
Emusic	www.emusic.com
MP3.com	www.mp3.com
MP3GrandCentral	www.mp3grandcentral.com
MadeForMusic	www.madeformusic.com

You might be able to get a free trial of some of these services before signing up for the monthly rate. Check for these offers, and shop around.

Listen up. Now you have your music files — or at least you know how to get them — but you need to be able to hear them. This requires special software. Don't worry — it's free, and easy to download. Some kinds even come with your computer. For example, if your computer uses Windows 98 or higher, it probably comes with Windows Media Player.

If you don't have player software, you can download one from the following sites.

MusicMatch	www.musicmatch.com
RealJukebox	www.real.com
Windows Media Player	www.microsoft.com
Winamp	www.winamp.com

Once you have the right software on your computer, all you have to do is browse your personal musical library and click on the song you want to hear. You'll be able to enjoy your favorite tunes through your computer speakers.

If you prefer radio, you can find a wide range of stations online.

Tune in and hear music from all over the world. Go to one of these sites to search for stations.

Live Radio on the Internet	www.live-radio.net
Radio-Locator	www.radio-locator.com
Radio Tower	www.radiotower.com
Virtual Tuner	www.virtualtuner.com

Get high-tech. If you want to get really ambitious, you can even create (or "burn") your own compact discs. For this, you need a CD burner and blank CDs. You also have to convert, or decode, your MP3 files to a format called WAV. The CD-burning software, which comes with your CD burner, and certain player software, like MusicMatch, let you do this.

Simply pick what songs you want, and burn them onto your blank compact disc. It will cost about $150 to $350 to buy the CD burner, but in the end, it will be cheaper than buying a lot of compact discs.

You can do it all with your computer. Listen to samples or online radio stations, download and listen to songs, or turn those music files into your own personal compact discs. That should be music to your ears.

Digital photography: It's a snap

Picture this. You just returned from a wonderful vacation, and you're eager to see how your photos turned out. After all, you took several rolls of film. You don't want to pay the high fees at a one-hour photo shop, but the suspense is killing you.

Don't wait to see another photo — not even an hour! Shoot and print beautiful photos in minutes with your own digital camera, computer and printer.

With a digital camera, you don't have to fool with film. You can also review pictures as soon as you take them. When you snap the shot, it appears in a little monitor on the camera. If it's not the way you want, simply delete it and take another one.

After you've taken the photos you want, hook your camera up to your computer's USB or serial port and transfer the photos. Once the photos are saved on your computer, you can print them or even e-mail them to friends and family.

You can send and receive the latest pictures of your loved ones in minutes, and never have to miss a birthday celebration, graduation, or family reunion again. Share the memories as soon as they happen.

Read on to discover all you need to know about digital cameras — what to look for when you're buying one, and simple instructions on using it.

Consider these factors when shopping for a digital camera.

- **Resolution.** High resolution means a higher quality image. It also usually means a higher priced camera. If you want to take photos to view on your computer and send via e-mail, a lower resolution camera will work fine. If you plan on printing out your photos, buy a higher resolution camera — particularly if you plan to print out large photos. Resolution is measured in pixels or megapixels. The more pixels, usually the sharper the image.

- **Exposure.** With a conventional camera, you can buy different types of films for different lighting conditions. Since digital cameras don't use film, you don't have that option. Digital cameras have an "equivalent ISO number," which tells you how sensitive the camera is to light. In addition, a camera with a wide span of shutter speeds and apertures will also be more capable of taking photos in various light conditions.

- **Storage capacity.** Although you may take your digital camera on vacation, you might not take your computer. That means the number of photos your camera can store is important. Most cameras come with a memory card that you can swap out, making it possible to take more pictures. But extra cards can be expensive. Compare storage capacities before making a buying decision.

- **Features.** Digital cameras come with a variety of features, just like conventional cameras. What features you choose will depend on how you plan to use the camera, as well as how much money you're willing to spend. One feature that everyone should probably spend a little extra for is a zoom lens. Other features include automatic exposure control, auto focus, red-eye reduction, and automatic flash.

Leading brands include Kodak, Nikon, Olympus, and Sony. Prices vary, but here's a general guide to how much you'll pay for a digital camera.

Resolution	Price range
Less than 1 megapixel	Less than $100
1-megapixel	$150 to $500
2-megapixel	$250 to $700
3-megapixel	$400 to $1,000

You can find cameras with even higher resolutions — and higher price tags. But most people will get the best blend of quality and affordability from a 2-megapixel camera.

For more information and advice, check out some sites with reviews of digital cameras.

Digital Photography Review	www.dpreview.com
Digital Camera Resource Page	www.dcresource.com
Imaging Resource	www.imaging-resource.com

Now that you know what to look for in a digital camera, here are some tips on digital photography.

Point and shoot. Digital cameras operate pretty much like other cameras. You can buy one that lets you just point and shoot, or one that allows more manual control. Generally, the more bells and whistles a camera has, the more complicated it is to operate.

Keep batteries on hand. Digital cameras drain batteries rapidly, and you don't want to miss that once-in-a-lifetime photo opportunity. Always keep extra batteries in your camera bag.

Touch it up. Your digital camera will probably come with software that lets you crop, re-size, and touch up photos. Popular programs include Adobe PhotoDeluxe, MGI PhotoSuite, Microsoft Picture It, and Ulead PhotoImpact. With these programs, you can adjust the brightness and contrast, straighten tilted pictures, and eliminate red-eye. The result — perfect pictures.

Think small. If you're going to e-mail photos to your friends and family, remember that large images can take a long time to transmit. To avoid tying up their e-mail for an extended period, send smaller images, and consider sending just one or two photos at a time.

Quick tip ▶ Conserve disk space by saving photos in the JPEG file format, which is much more compressed than the TIFF format.

Develop a new strategy. Turn that box of old photos into a beautiful album — complete with labels showing exactly who or

what you're looking at. Interested? Check out DotPhoto at
www.dot photo.com.

This free service lets you make online photo albums. If you have a
digital camera or scanner, you can create your own digital photos
and upload them to the DotPhoto Web site. Or just send them a roll
of film, and DotPhoto will process and upload the pictures for you.
Then you can use their editing tools to crop your pictures or add
sound clips and captions. Friends and family can access your online
photo album with a secret password. Other Web sites have similar
photo-storage services.

Most developers will put the prints from your conventional film
onto a CD or floppy disk. Just ask when you drop off your film. It's
a good way to get your photos "digitized" without a digital camera
or scanner.

Uncover info fast online

Looking things up used to mean making a trip to the public library
and paging through stacks of reference books. Libraries are still great
resources, but now you can find much of the same information right
in your own home.

Thanks to the Internet, you can handle all your reference needs with
your computer. It's quick, easy, and convenient. And you don't have
to be quiet if you don't want to.

Define on your own terms. Tired of lugging a heavy dictionary
around? Get a definition in just a few keystrokes instead. With
online dictionaries, you simply type a word in the SEARCH field to
get a definition. Here are just a few dictionaries available online.

Merriam-Webster	www.merriam-webster.com
American Heritage Dictionary	www.bartleby.com/61
Cambridge Dictionaries Online	http://dictionary.cambridge.org

A quick way to browse several dictionaries at once is to go to OneLook Dictionaries at **www.onelook.com**. Type in a word or phrase, and you'll get a list of results.

Track down a turn of phrase. Who said that? Look up a famous quote at one of these online quotation dictionaries. Or just enjoy browsing through the indexes of authors, categories, or keywords. You're bound to find something worth repeating.

Bartlett's Familiar Quotations	www.bartleby.com/100
The Columbia World of Quotations	www.bartleby.com/66
Simpson's Contemporary Quotations	www.bartleby.com/63
Quoteland	www.quoteland.com
Quotation Central	www.quotations.com

Kick off your quest for knowledge. The late Washington Redskins owner Jack Kent Cooke began his business career selling encyclopedias door-to-door during the Great Depression. If someone tried this today, he'd probably have trouble earning the price of admission to a single football game. That's partly due to high ticket prices, but also because encyclopedias are so readily accessible online. Here are some of them.

Encyclopaedia Britannica	www.britannica.com
Encyclopedia.com	www.encyclopedia.com
Encarta Encyclopedia	www.encarta.msn.com/reference
Columbia Encyclopedia	www.bartleby.com/65

Explore other options. Sometimes your research requires more than just a dictionary or encyclopedia. These general reference sites can come in handy.

- **World Factbook.** Developed by the CIA, this site gives you detailed information about every country, including facts and stats on background, geography, population, economy, transportation, and military. Spy it for yourself at **www.cia.gov/cia/ publications/factbook.**

- **Refdesk.** A one-stop source for reference information, this site features links to dictionaries, encyclopedias, almanacs, newspapers, even national obituary archives. That's not all — there are also facts, search engines, other reference tools, and a section called JUST FOR FUN. Look it up at **www.refdesk.com**.

- **Internet FAQ Consortium.** Many Web sites feature a section called Frequently Asked Questions, or FAQ. Get your questions answered at this site which covers a wide range of topics: **www.faqs.org**.

- **WebRing.** A Web ring is a way of linking related Web sites so you can go from one to the other easily. These communities of Web sites exist for almost every topic. Find one that interests you at **www.webring.org**.

Elect to use government sites. It only makes sense that a government by the people and for the people would have Web sites that work well with people. For census statistics, legislative information, a virtual tour of the White House, and links to government information, visit these sites.

FirstGov	www.firstgov.gov
SearchGov	www.searchgov.com
FedWorld	www.fedworld.gov

U.S. Census Bureau	www.census.gov
THOMAS	http://thomas.loc.gov
The White House	www.whitehouse.gov

Find fun facts and places. Quick — what's the state bird of South Dakota? If you're stumped, check out 50states.com at **www.50 states.com**. This fun site includes all sorts of trivia about every state, as well as links to newspapers, libraries, and more. By the way, it's the ring-necked pheasant.

Whether it's driving directions, weird facts, or good old-fashioned wisdom, you can find it at these other neat sites.

Yahoo! Maps	http://maps.yahoo.com
MapQuest	www.mapquest.com
How Stuff Works	www.howstuffworks.com
Farmers Almanac	www.farmersalmanac.com

8 best sites for seniors

The Internet is growing so fast that no one even knows how many pages of information are out there — and more are being added every day.

How do you find your way through this maze of millions of sites? Trial and error will help you find the sites that you like best. When you do find them, make sure you bookmark them (add them to your "favorites") so you can find them again.

If you're over 50, here are eight sites that you'll probably want to include in your bookmarks.

- **ThirdAge.** This site doesn't bill itself as a site for seniors. It is aimed at those people who are in the "life stage following youth and young adulthood and preceding senior." Nevertheless, it contains a wealth of information that seniors will find useful. You can read articles, chat, post your opinion on a variety of topics on the discussion boards, play games, and participate in free online classes. There is even a section for personal ads. Check it out at **www.thirdage.com**.

- **AARP.** No longer called the Association of Retired Persons, this organization serves people age 50 and older. If you're not a member, you can join online and take advantage of hundreds of member benefits and discounts. However, even nonmembers can enjoy the site's excellent information, which is geared specifically toward people over 50. You can find it at **www.aarp.org**.

- **SeniorLaw.** This site provides legal information in plain language that anyone can understand. Features include basic explanations of Medicaid and Medicare, links to resources on elder abuse, and information about wills. You can also find attorneys in your area who specialize in elder law. Just go to **www.seniorlaw.com**.

- **ElderWeb.** A calendar on this site includes conventions and symposiums that deal with senior issues. Go to the Regional Information area of this site to find links to resources in your state, including legal matters, housing, insurance, education, and finance. It also includes regional information for Australia, Canada, New Zealand, the United Kingdom, and other countries. Explore for yourself at **www.elderweb.com**.

- **Elderhostel.** Elderhostel is the world's largest educational travel organization. If you'd like to learn "on the go," you have to check out this site. You can browse programs by location. For example, if you're interested in a trip to Wyoming, you might find a trip to the Black Hills, sponsored by the University of

Wyoming, which includes educational instruction about the native environment and history. Learn all about it at **www.elderhostel.org**.

- **SeniorSite.** Find a doctor, hospital, or health plan in Senior Site's Doctor Directory; read top news stories chosen for seniors; send questions to a panel of experts in different topics (one expert is Pat Boone!); and check out the nursing home report card. That's just a sampling of what this site has to offer seniors. Find out more at **www.seniorsite.com**.

- **Mature Connections.** If you want a portal to hundreds of other sites for seniors, surf here. In addition to articles of interest to seniors, it also has links to other sites, organized by topic. Check it out at **www.matureconnections.com**.

- **Social Security Administration.** This site is a must-see for seniors. It allows you to apply for benefits online, check the accuracy of your personal records, and request a replacement Medicare card. You'll also find many other helpful features, including easy-to-understand explanations of confusing Social Security rules and regulations. Go to **www.ssa.gov**.

Shop safely on the Net

Shopping on the Internet offers all sorts of benefits. You can shop anytime, 24 hours a day, seven days a week — even on holidays. You can often find greater selection and lower prices than you would in a regular store. And you can shop in your pajamas.

But, in order to take advantage of these conveniences, you must divulge some personal information. Companies routinely need your name, mailing address, and credit card number to complete a transaction.

Naturally, you want to know which companies you can trust. And you don't want your personal information shared with others. But what can you do to protect yourself from hackers and other criminals? And is it really safe to use a credit card on the Net?

You'll find answers to all these concerns soon enough, but first, learn how easy online shopping is. Look over this guide to the process — it's your first step to shopping safely.

1 Browse and select items just like you would in a catalog.

2 For each item you want to buy, click on ADD TO SHOPPING CART.

3 When you're through shopping, click on PROCEED TO CHECKOUT. You may have to create a user name and password for your account or log in to an existing account. This step should take you to a secure server.

Tech term ▶ Secure server – a Web server that codes and decodes messages to protect them against third party tampering.

---

4 Fill out a form with the required purchasing information. This includes your name, billing and shipping addresses, type of shipping, and payment information.

5 Review your list of items to purchase and confirm that it matches what you want to buy.

6 Click the final confirmation button to complete the purchase.

7 You may also receive an e-mail confirmation of your order.

Fortunately, protecting yourself from fraud can be as easy as shopping online. Just follow these guidelines.

Stick to familiar companies. The same big names you know from catalogs and stores are probably the most reliable. One famous online merchant is Amazon. Avoid companies that do not have a phone number, street address, or other contact information readily available.

Check with the BBB. Find out more about the company before ordering. Visit the Better Business Bureau's Web site at **www.bbb. org**. If you're tempted to buy from an online company you're not sure of, check it out on this consumer protection site first.

Look for a secure server. You can tell if a Web site is secure by the unbroken padlock or key symbol in the browser corner. You might get a SECURITY NOTICE dialog box that says you are entering a secure page. Or you may see **https** in the address line. Also make sure the site uses encryption, or a secret code, to store your information.

Get the details. Study the terms, conditions, and costs involved in the sale. This includes shipping charges, delivery time, and the return policy. Look for the site's privacy policy and read it.

Be choosy with your info. Fill out only the "required" fields on the site's registration form, if you must register with the site before making a purchase. Don't give out any more information than you have to, and never give out your Social Security number. No shopping site should need it. Only do business with sites that won't share your personal information with other businesses — or at least give you the chance to "opt out" of such an arrangement.

Pay with a credit card. Under the Fair Credit Billing Act, this limits your losses to $50 in case of fraud. It's a safer option than a debit card, check, or money order. Check your credit card statements to make sure the charges match what you meant to buy.

Provide your credit card number only over a secure server. Never try to e-mail your credit card number to the shopping site since e-mail is easily intercepted. When you enter your credit card number in a secure order form, it is not being e-mailed.

Don't leave out the middleman. Insist on an escrow service for expensive purchases. This means a middleman makes sure both the goods and the money are sent.

Get a record of your transaction. Print your order confirmation page to keep as a receipt. Also print the page describing the company's return policy in case it changes after you place your order.

Play it safe ▶ For more information about safe online shopping and avoiding online scams, check out the Federal Trade Commission's Web site dedicated to E-commerce and the Internet at www.ftc.gov/bcp/menu-internet.htm.

While you're surfing the Internet for deals, bargains, or sales, here's one more way to find out which stores offer the best and safest shopping experience.

BizRate.com's Customer Ratings of Stores rates shopping sites based on what their customers have to say. It's updated weekly and uses a neat, smiley face method for ranking sites in a variety of categories, including delivery and customer support. You can even give your own feedback. See what people have to say at **www.bizrate.com/ratings_guide/guide**.

Grab good buys with expert advice

The more choices you have, the harder it can be to make a decision. You know that's true every time you step inside an ice cream shop, or walk up and down the cereal aisle. If only you had a place to go for expert advice the next time you need to make a purchase — a place listing the best buys in home computers, which appliances last longest, or which laundry detergents clean best. Such places exist on the Internet.

- **Consumer Reports.** Perhaps the most popular organization to help you find the best product at the best price is Consumer Reports. The online version has some of the same information. You'll need to subscribe — for a fee — in order to view all their articles, but there's still plenty of good, free advice at **www.consumerreports.org**.

- **Consumer World.** At **www.consumerworld.org** you'll find a catalog of over 2,000 consumer resources. There are links to places like America's Test Kitchen, where experts rate everything from waffle irons to corkscrews. Or jump to their Shopping Roadmap and study product test results, reviews, or features. Compare prices or check out store reputations. You can even link up to state and federal consumer agencies.

- **ConsumerReview.com.** Stop off here if you're in the market for electronics. There are product reviews, classifieds, hints and tips, and hot deals. Log on to this site at **www.consumer review.com**.

- **Clark Howard.** This consumer guru has his own radio show, newspaper column, and now Web site at **www.clarkhoward. com**. It's packed with hints, tips, late-breaking news, and hundreds of ways for you to become a more informed consumer.

- **Appliance.com.** If you're looking for any home appliance, from dishwashers to vacuums, check out the information source at **www.appliance.com**. Browse through product overviews, check out a list of manufacturers and brands, or study a buyer's guide on each appliance. And there's even an official industry Web site called the Association of Home Appliance

Manufacturers at **www.aham.org**. They've got a section chock-full of buying information, consumer bulletins, tips for using and caring for appliances, and help for when things go wrong.

- **ConsumerSearch, Inc.** They claim to be the best product review site on the Internet. They're certainly one of the largest. Browse through the many categories at **www.productopia.com** to see what expert reviewers have to say about each product.

- **CNET Networks.** If you need buying information on computers, technology, or consumer electronics, you'll find it at **http:// shopper.cnet.com**. Get up-to-date reviews and price comparisons as well as information on trends and top picks.

- **Epinions.** Sometimes you just want to know what other consumers are saying about a product. Try **www.epinions.com**. They claim to be a source of personal recommendations and comparative shopping. They cover over 2 million products in more than 30 different categories. With a free membership, you can get personalized recommendations on almost any product or sign up for an e-mail alert when a product you want becomes available at your target price.

Many of these other Web sites will help you make a good buying decision and some will simply help you save money when you decide to buy.

BargainDog	www.bargaindog.com
BizRate	www.bizrate.com
DealTime	www.dealtime.com
Esmarts	www.esmarts.com
MySimon	www.mysimon.com
PriceGrabber.com	www.bottomdollar.com

PriceSCAN.com	www.pricescan.com
SalesCircular.com	www.salescircular.com
SalesHound.com	www.saleshound.com

Buy and sell with online auctions

Make money by selling everything from that horrible wedding gift from Aunt Emma to those old 45s gathering dust in the attic. It's easier than ever to turn your trash into another man's treasure — with Internet auctions.

Whether you're an individual or a business, you can put things up for bid. If you like, you can set the lowest price you'll accept for an item. Then, pick a specific time for the bidding to close. At that time, the high bidder wins. The seller and buyer usually communicate by e-mail to arrange payment and shipping.

There's a variety of ways to pay — credit card, debit card, personal check, cashier's check, money order, cash on delivery, and an escrow service. This last option is most popular since it adds a safety net to the whole process. An escrow service works as a middleman between the buyer and seller. When the service receives payment from the buyer, it notifies the sender to ship the item. When the buyer receives the item, the escrow service gives the money to the seller. This protects both parties.

The most well-known auction Web site is eBay at **www.ebay.com**. Others are Yahoo!Auctions at **www.auctions.yahoo.com** and Amazon's auctions at **www.auctions.amazon.com**.

Here are some tips if you plan on buying through an online auction.

- **Investigate the seller.** Some sites allow you to check a seller's feedback rating — to find out how satisfied most people are with the merchandise from that particular individual. If you're dealing with a company, check with the Better Business Bureau at **www.bbbonline.org** to see if any complaints have been filed against it.

- **Set a limit and stick to it.** Just like with real-world auctions, it's easy to get carried away and bid more than an item is worth. Before you begin bidding, decide how much you're willing to pay and don't go higher.

- **Pay with a credit card.** If the site offers an escrow service, you're fairly well protected. However, if you pay with a credit card, it's much easier to dispute charges if a problem does occur.

And these are tips if you want to sell an item online.

- **Know the value.** Check the value of any prized collectible before you offer it for purchase. Visit sites like **www.appraiseit net.com** or **www.hiddenfortune.com**.

- **Describe your product accurately.** Don't try to make your item sound better than it is. And make it clear what the terms of the sale are — for instance, who will pay shipping costs.

- **Answer questions.** If a buyer or potential buyer has questions, make sure you answer them promptly and courteously.

- **Act quickly.** As soon as the auction is over, contact the winning bidder to confirm the sale. Then ship the item as soon as you receive payment.

AuctionBeagle	www.auctionbeagle.com	allows you to search several auction sites at once
BidXS	www.biddersedge.com	an auction search engine
Auction Patrol	www.auctionpatrol.com	everything on auction
Ubid.com	www.ubid.com	an auction supersite

Escrow.ca	www.i-escrow.com	an online escrow service
PBS Antiques Roadshow	www.pbs.org/wgbh/pages/roadshow	for the antiques junkie
Icollector.com	www.icollector.com	a connection to auction houses around the world
Collector Online	www.collectoronline.com	a worldwide marketplace for antiques, collectibles, crafts, and fine arts
the-forum	www.the-forum.com	an online art gallery and antiques mall
tias.com	www.tias.com	offers fine antiques and collectibles

If you have a special interest, there are Internet sites to help you buy, sell, and collect wisely. CoinClub.com at **www.coinclub.com** is sponsored by Independent Coin Grading (ICG) and can tell you everything you need to know about buying and selling coins. Other coin-collecting sites are Coin-Universe at **www.coin-universe.com** and The Coin Library at **www.coinlibrary.com**.

Every stamp collector should check out About Stamps and Coins at **www.collectstamps.about.com.** and philately.com at **www. philately.com.**

Discover a coupon clipper's paradise

If you've always been a coupon clipper, you can put that thrifty habit to work on the Web as well. Many sites have virtual coupons you can use when you shop online. Even better, some sites let you print money-saving coupons you can use in real stores.

- **H.O.T!Coupons.** Find hundreds of useful real-world coupons at **www.hotcoupons.com**. You can search by your ZIP code or city to find coupons to use in your neighborhood. They are categorized efficiently, so you can quickly find the ones you want. For example, the food category in your area might include Asian food, bagels, bakery, fast food, pizza, and more. You only print the ones you want. Then go shopping.

- **CoolSavings.** Register at **www.coolsavings.com** and you can save big with coupons, discounts, free samples, rebates, and special offers, for both online and real-world stores.

- **myClipper.** Search **www.myclipper.com** by state or ZIP code for the best local coupons, or browse offers that are good nationwide.

- **DailyEDeals.** This site contains links to coupons and discount deals at various online stores, such as Amazon.com. Visit them at **www.dailyedeals.com**.

- **Valpack.** Go to **www.valpak.com**, enter your location, and you can print coupons that are specific to your area.

Hang up on hefty phone bills

If all your loved ones live in the same area code, you're lucky — and highly unusual. Most families today are spread out all over the country — even the world. This can create some sky-high phone bills. Luckily, your computer can help you stay in touch and whittle those bills down to size.

E-mail is great, but most people will never completely give up using the phone. If you still want and need traditional long-distance telephone service, let your computer help you choose the cheapest. Go to one of these Web sites and, for free, you can compare rates from various providers.

SmartPrice.com	www.smartprice.com
SaveOnPhone.com	www.saveonphone.com
Attitude Long Distance	www.attitude-long-distance.com
Cognigen Networks, Inc.	www.page-fx.com
Calling-Plans.com	www.calling-plans.com

You usually have to type in just part of your telephone number and then select the type of long-distance usage you prefer. The Web site may come back with several recommendations. Be sure you check out the company you want to switch to. There are many consumer protection organizations that will help you make a safe choice.

Remember, Internet services come and go. If these Web addresses don't take you to good information, use your favorite search engine to find others. Type in key words like *long distance*, *phone service*, and *compare*.

Tour the Internet for great travel deals

As a senior, you may have more time than ever to travel, but who wants to spend a fortune doing it? Luckily, you can save money — and time — online.

It's like going around the world in 80 seconds. Here's how the Internet can take you places you've never dreamed of — at prices you won't believe.

Some of the best buys on airline tickets are last-minute bargains. If you're retired and able to travel on short notice, you could get a great deal. Visit the Web sites of individual airlines and sign up for e-mail notices. AirTran at **www.airtran.com**, for example, has a Net Escapes e-mail service that sends you weekly notices of its special fares.

If you can't travel spur-of-the-moment, you can still take advantage of the Internet to search for the cheapest airfares, car rental, hotel rooms, and entertainment.

- **BestFares.** Seniors can get special rates on a variety of goods and services if they just ask. Many airlines, hotel chains, restaurants, and entertainment outlets give senior discounts. Learn to ask before you buy, and check out **www.bestfares.com**. In addition to a Quickfare Finder and lots of helpful links and travel articles, it offers a section devoted to senior specials.

- **Priceline.** If you're willing to be flexible in your travel plans, and take a gamble, you could get an impressive deal on air travel and more at **www.priceline.com**. For flights, you name the price you're willing to pay for a particular date and destination and provide a credit card number. If an airline accepts your offer, Priceline immediately buys the ticket and charges your credit card. It's non-refundable, so you can't change your mind once you've made an offer. And while you choose the days of travel, the airline chooses the time — you might fly at noon, or you might fly at 2 a.m. In addition, you're not guaranteed a nonstop flight. Priceline has similar services for hotel rooms, rental cars, vacation packages, long distance phone service, home financing, and new cars.

- **Hotwire.** This site allows you to search for the lowest prices on airline tickets, car rentals, and hotel accommodations. Once you have the quote, you have one hour to complete the transaction and take advantage of that price. Sales are non-refundable, and you won't know the airline or specific flight times until after the sale is finalized. Check it out at **www.hotwire.com**.

Here are some more Web sites that let you be your own travel agent. Comparison shop without making dozens of calls. Make no-hassle travel arrangements — and find the best deals around.

Travelocity	www.travelocity.com
Expedia	www.expedia.com
Cheap Tickets	www.cheaptickets.com
Orbitz	www.orbitz.com

Become a computer know-it-all

Are you ready for hands-on instruction that goes beyond what you can learn from a book or manual? If so, join the flocks of seniors who are signing up for classes — free training, in many cases — taught right in their own communities.

You'll learn to surf the Web more efficiently, keep track of your finances, do your taxes, research your family tree, and more. Start with these suggestions to find what's available in your town.

Check out the library. Books and magazines are just a small part of what libraries offer these days. Many now provide free use of online computers. And chances are good you can get free computer training there, too. Call the branch nearest you to see what they offer.

Go back to school. Most colleges and universities have continuing education departments that offer low-cost classes. But if you're ready to graduate beyond the beginner level, ask about computer classes in the regular curriculum. Many schools let senior citizens enroll in academic classes at reduced rates or even for free. In most cases you can only audit these sessions, but some let you earn college credits.

Sign in at a learning center. The nonprofit organization SeniorNet provides folks over 50 with low-cost computer training in more than170 learning centers in the United States and Japan. To find the one nearest you, go to **www.seniornet.org** or call 415-495-4990.

Check out other senior centers, recreation departments, and YMCA or YWCA programs as well. The odds are good they, too, offer computer lessons that are discounted or even free to seniors.

Shop for training. Some computer stores offer classes. So if you are looking to buy a new computer, ask if you can get free training as part of the package.

If you already have a computer, you can probably enroll by paying a fee. Gateway Country Stores, for example, offer a wide variety of computer classes, no matter what kind of computer you have. And they give a 10 percent discount to AARP members. Learn more at the AARP Web site at **www.aarp.org**, call 1-800-588-3893, or visit a Gateway Country Store.

Log on to learn more. If you prefer the convenience of learning at home, the Internet is a virtual treasure trove of free instruction. You can fine-tune your basic computer skills or take advantage of more advanced courses. For example, Third Age, at **www.thirdage.com**, has a class on creating your own Web site. SeniorNet and AARP are other good sources.

As you investigate these classes, you are sure to run across other resources as well. And not only will you improve your computer skills, you are likely to make some new friends — in person or online — along the way.

Index

Processor. *See* CPU
Program. *See* Software

R

RAM (random access memory) 2
   upgrading 20
Reading e-mail 276
RealAudio 355
Recycle bin 184-187
Reference 362-365
Refurbished computers 13
Remailers 304
Renaming folders 178
Repairs 34
Replying to e-mail 276
Resizing windows 54
Restarting 167
Restocking fees 15
Restoring
   deleted files 186, 200
   lost files 193
   windows 54
Right-clicking 46

S

Saving 103, 200
Scams 306, 353, 370
ScanDisk 195
Scanner 17
Screen
   elements 224
   magnifiers 18
   savers 77
Scroll bar 51
Search engines 239-246
Secure server 368
Sending e-mail 275
Senior Web sites 365
Serial ports 24
Setting up computers 21-25
Shareware 248
Shopping
   for a computer 9-15
   online 367-376

Shortcut keys
   for dialog boxes 66
   for managing files 188
   for menus 62
   for spreadsheets 157
   for windows 56
   for word processing 141
Shortcut menus 61
Shortcuts 85-88
Shutting down 30
Signatures 278
Sleep mode 30, 200
Software 97-167
   anti-virus 256
   bundles 12, 98
   buying 98-100
   content-filtering 266
   crashes 165-167
   financial 351
   installing 101
   pirated 166
   prerelease 166
Sound card 4
Spam 298-302
Speakers 4
Specifications, computer 88-91
Speeding up your computer 198
Spelling and grammar 124
Spinner 64
Spreadsheets 97, 142-158
Spyware 259
Stamp collecting 375
Standby mode 30, 200
Start menu 57
Startup disk 194
Status bar 51, 225
Status indicator 224
Stream 355
Surfing 203
Surge protector 25
S-video output jack 24

T

Tables 137
Taskbar 41